New Directions in Book

Series Editors

Shafquat Towheed
Faculty of Arts
Open University
Milton Keynes, United Kingdom

Jonathan Rose
Department of History
Drew University
Madison, USA

Aims of the Series
As a vital field of scholarship, book history has now reached a stage of maturity where its early work can be reassessed and built upon. That is the goal of New Directions in Book History. This series will publish monographs in English that employ advanced methods and open up new frontiers in research, written by younger, mid-career, and senior scholars. Its scope is global, extending to the Western and non-Western worlds and to all historical periods from antiquity to the 21st century, including studies of script, print, and post-print cultures. New Directions in Book History, then, will be broadly inclusive but always in the vanguard. It will experiment with inventive methodologies, explore unexplored archives, debate overlooked issues, challenge prevailing theories, study neglected subjects, and demonstrate the relevance of book history to other academic fields. Every title in this series will address the evolution of the historiography of the book, and every one will point to new directions in book scholarship. New Directions in Book History will be published in three formats: single-author monographs; edited collections of essays in single or multiple volumes; and shorter works produced through Palgrave's e-book (EPUB2) 'Pivot' stream. Book proposals should emphasize the innovative aspects of the work, and should be sent to either of the two series editors. Series editors: Prof Jonathan Rose (Drew University, USA) and Dr Shafquat Towheed (The Open University, UK). Editorial board: Marcia Abreu, University of Campinas, Brazil; Cynthia Brokaw, Brown University, USA; Matt Cohen, University of Texas at Austin, USA; Archie Dick, University of Pretoria, South Africa; Martyn Lyons, University of New South Wales, Australia.

More information about this series at
http://www.springer.com/series/14749

Paul Raphael Rooney • Anna Gasperini
Editors

Media and Print Culture Consumption in Nineteenth-Century Britain

The Victorian Reading Experience

palgrave
macmillan

Editors
Paul Raphael Rooney
School of English
Trinity College Dublin
Dublin 2, Ireland

Anna Gasperini
Department of English
National University of Ireland, Galway
Galway, Ireland

New Directions in Book History
ISBN 978-1-349-95459-9   ISBN 978-1-137-58761-9 (eBook)
DOI 10.1057/978-1-137-58761-9

© The Editor(s) (if applicable) and The Author(s) 2016
Softcover reprint of the hardcover 1st edition 2016
The author(s) has/have asserted their right(s) to be identified as the author(s) of this work in accordance with the Copyright, Designs and Patents Act 1988.
This work is subject to copyright. All rights are solely and exclusively licensed by the Publisher, whether the whole or part of the material is concerned, specifically the rights of translation, reprinting, reuse of illustrations, recitation, broadcasting, reproduction on microfilms or in any other physical way, and transmission or information storage and retrieval, electronic adaptation, computer software, or by similar or dissimilar methodology now known or hereafter developed.
The use of general descriptive names, registered names, trademarks, service marks, etc. in this publication does not imply, even in the absence of a specific statement, that such names are exempt from the relevant protective laws and regulations and therefore free for general use.
The publisher, the authors and the editors are safe to assume that the advice and information in this book are believed to be true and accurate at the date of publication. Neither the publisher nor the authors or the editors give a warranty, express or implied, with respect to the material contained herein or for any errors or omissions that may have been made.

Cover image © The National Trust photolibrary / Alamy Stock Photo
Cover design by JennyVong

Printed on acid-free paper

This Palgrave Macmillan imprint is published by Springer Nature
The registered company is Macmillan Publishers Ltd. London

Acknowledgements

The editors are indebted to the many people who contributed to the publication of this book.

A number of the chapters originate in papers presented at a 2014 conference on the history of nineteenth-century reading held in the Moore Institute at the National University of Ireland, Galway. Professor Daniel Carey, Dr Niall Ó Ciosáin, Dr Justin Tonra, Dr Muireann O'Cinneide, the administrative and support staff at the Moore, and the Society for the History of Authorship, Reading, and Publishing (SHARP) were all extremely generous in their support of that event. Dr Stephen Colclough was amongst the plenary speakers at the conference. Dr Colclough sadly passed away in the intervening time since that 2014 conference and the publication of this collection. His work is and will remain an inspiration to scholars of reading and his particular contribution to that gathering proved invaluable in ensuring the event's success.

Work on the collection was made possible owing to the assistance from various quarters. Dr Paul Raphael Rooney was a Government of Ireland Irish Research Council postdoctoral fellow in the School of English, Trinity College Dublin as well as a Trinity Long Room Hub Institute resident researcher during his work on the collection. He would like to express his gratitude to the Council for its crucial support and the Long Room Hub Institute for providing such a stimulating and convivial scholarly environment.

Advice, assistance, and encouragement were forthcoming from a number of more distinguished scholars throughout the editorial process. Special thanks are due to Professor Eve Patten, Dr Elizabeth Tilley, Professor

John Spiers, Dr Simon Frost, Professor David Finkelstein, and Dr Katie Halsey who all contributed to our work in this capacity.

The editors of Palgrave Macmillan's New Directions in Book History series, Dr Shafquat Towheed and Professor Jonathan Rose, have been most generous in their support of the collection. The contributions of the Palgrave reader also proved critical in planning and shaping the volume. Finally, collaborating with Palgrave on this book has been a wonderful experience; the editorial input of Ben Doyle and Tomas René has been all-important and both are very much deserving of our thanks.

Contents

1 Introduction   1
   Paul Raphael Rooney and Anna Gasperini

2 Reader-Help: How to Read Samuel Smiles's
   Self-Help   15
   Barbara Leckie

3 More than a 'Book for Boys'? Sir Thomas
   Malory's *Le Morte Darthur* and the Victorian
   Girl Reader   33
   Katie Garner

4 The Manuscript Magazines of the Wellpark
   Free Church Young Men's Literary Society   53
   Lauren Weiss

5 Black Victorians and *Anti-Caste*: Mapping
   the Geographies of 'Missing' Readers   75
   Caroline Bressey

6	John Dicks's Cheap Reprint Series, 1850s–1890s: Reading Advertisements *Anne Humpherys*	93
7	Serialization and Story-Telling Illustrations: R.L. Stevenson Window-Shopping for Penny Dreadfuls *Marie Léger-St-Jean*	111
8	Sensation and Song: Street Ballad Consumption in Nineteenth-Century England *Isabel Corfe*	131
9	Reading Reynolds: *The Mysteries of London* as 'Microscopic Survey' *Ruth Doherty*	147
10	Cross-Media Cultural Consumption and Oscillating Reader Experiences of Late-Victorian Dramatizations of the Novel: The Case of Fergus Hume's *Madame Midas* (1888) *Paul Raphael Rooney*	165
11	Reading Theatre Writing: T.H. Lacy and the Sensation Drama *Kate Mattacks*	183
Bibliography		199
Index		219

Notes on Contributors

Caroline Bressey is a Reader in the Department of Geography UCL. Her research focuses upon the historical geographies of the black presence in London, alongside Victorian theories of race and anti-racism and the links between contemporary identities and the diverse histories of London as represented in heritage sites in Britain. Her work on the black presence has mainly focused upon black women and their experiences in four arenas of life: institutions, imperial elite society, work and anti-racist politics. Her monograph, *Empire, Race and the Politics of Anti-Caste* (Bloomsbury Academic, 2013) won the 2014 Women's History Network Book Prize and the 2015 Colby Scholarly Book Prize.

Isabel Corfe completed an MA in Culture and Colonialism at the National University of Ireland, Galway in 2012 before gaining Irish Research Council funding to undertake research into nineteenth-century, English-printed broadside ballads. Isabel began a structured PhD programme in October 2013 in the Discipline of English at the National University of Ireland, Galway. She is seeking to apply a multi-disciplinary approach to her work, using historical, sociological, and musical approaches, as well as literary theory, to explore her research area.

Ruth Doherty recently completed her PhD thesis 'Representations of Overpopulation in Nineteenth-Century British Fiction', which was supervised by Professor Darryl Jones, Trinity College Dublin, and funded by the Irish Research Council. Ruth has taught on a variety of modules in Trinity College Dublin, University College Dublin, and the Saor Ollscoil. She has published articles in Trinity College's *Journal of Postgraduate Research* and in *Leeds Working Papers*.

Katie Garner is a Teaching Fellow in English Literature at the University of St Andrews. She has published articles on women's use of the Arthurian legend in *Studies in Medievalism* and *Romantic Textualities: Literature and Print Culture, 1780–1840*.

Anna Gasperini is a final year PhD candidate at the National University of Ireland, Galway, where she is completing a thesis on discourses of ethics, monstrosity, and medicine in the Victorian penny blood. She is the current Membership Secretary of the Victorian Popular Fiction Association (VPFA). Her first article, 'Anatomy of the Demons: The Demoniac Body Dealers of the Penny Bloods', appeared in the 2015 Spring-Summer issue of the *Journal of Supernatural Studies*.

Anne Humpherys is a Professor Emerita of English at Lehman College and the Graduate Center, City University of New York. She is the author of *Travels in the Poor Man's Country: The Work of Henry Mayhew* and co-editor of *G.W.M. Reynolds: Fiction, Politics, and the Press* as well as articles and chapters on Victorian fiction, poetry, popular literature, and the press. She is currently working on the impact of the divorce laws on the nineteenth-century British literature and a second project on the penny libraries published by John Dicks and the way high culture is disseminated to the working classes through construction of a hybrid canon of established works (such as those of Shakespeare) and popular works that are now largely unknown.

Marie Léger-St Jean During her doctoral research at the University of Cambridge, book historian Marie Léger-St-Jean created the online bibliography *Price One Penny: A Database of Cheap Literature, 1837–1860*. In addition to recording all penny bloods published in London, it includes an electronic edition of *The Mysteries of the Inquisition* (1845) which presents the original French novel alongside two competing translations. Now a professional translator, she still travels worldwide to visit rare book libraries and collect information about readers through ownership marks. Her research interests include popular fiction, adaptation, translation, and the transatlantic circulation of texts.

Barbara Leckie is an Associate Professor cross-appointed in the English Department and the Institute for the Comparative Study of Literature, Art, and Culture at Carleton University. She has published *Culture and Adultery: The Novel, the Newspaper, and the Law, 1857–1914* and *Sanitary Reform in Victorian Britain: End of Century Assessments and New Directions* (an edited collection of primary documents on sanitary reform forthcoming with Pickering & Chatto). She has just completed 'Open Houses: The Architectural Idea, Poverty, and Victorian Print Culture, 1842–92' and is beginning a new project now on procrastination and unfinishedness in the nineteenth century.

NOTES ON CONTRIBUTORS   xi

Kate Mattacks is a Senior Lecturer in Drama at the University of the West of England, Bristol. She has worked on *The Victorian Plays Project* and the *'Buried Treasures' Project* at Royal Holloway/British Library and published numerous articles on M.E. Braddon, dramatic copyright and T.H. Lacy. She is currently working on a monograph entitled *Awkward Silences: Changing Representations of Speech Disability in the Long Nineteenth Century*.

Paul Raphael Rooney is an Irish Research Council Postdoctoral Fellow in the School of English in Trinity College Dublin where he is working on a project examining the circulation of books in series via railway bookstalls in late-nineteenth-century Ireland and England. His doctoral studies completed at the National University of Ireland, Galway reflect his research interests in the areas of book history and Victorian popular fiction. He has published in *Victorian Periodicals Review*, *Women's Writing*, and *Publishing History* and is currently completing a monograph entitled, *Railway Reading and Late-Victorian Literary Series*, to be published by Routledge in 2017.

Lauren Weiss graduated from the University of North Carolina at Wilmington with a BA (cum laude) in 1997 majoring in Anthropology with a minor in Classical Studies. In 1999, she completed her MPhil in Celtic Archaeology at the University of Glasgow, and in 2002 she graduated from the University of Southampton with an MA in Osteoarchaeology. Having recently completed her MLitt in Victorian Literature at the University of Glasgow in 2014, she is currently a doctoral student in English Studies in the Literature and Languages department at the University of Stirling. Her research investigates nineteenth-century literary clubs and societies in Glasgow, their impact on education and literacy in the city, and their contribution to the history of reading over the course of the century.

List of Figures

Fig. 4.1	Age range of the Wellpark Free Church Young Men's Literary Society	57
Fig. 6.1	John Dicks's Standard Plays List	102
Fig. 7.1	Google Ngram chronicling historical patterns of use of the term 'Penny Dreadful'.	115
Fig. 9.1	'Microcosm, dedicated to the London Water Companies "Monster soup commonly called Thames Water, being a correct representation of that precious stuff doled out to us"' (1828)	150
Fig. 10.1	*Madame Midas* Cover Illustration (1888) (London: Hansom Cab Publishing Company). Image reproduced courtesy of © The British Library Board, DRT lsidyv3ad542cb	169

CHAPTER 1

Introduction

Paul Raphael Rooney and Anna Gasperini

In opening a study of the history of nineteenth-century reading, a useful point of departure is perhaps the cartographical metaphor that Richard D. Altick employed in introducing his field-defining scholarly enterprise, *The English Common Reader*.[1] Such a concept, like much in that foundational study, remains a vital and apposite way of approaching research on this topic. Accordingly, where once the map of the nineteenth-century reading landscape charted by book historians constituted little more than an incomplete sketch that delineated some of the area's principal landmarks, the accumulation of a critical mass of scholarship on this subfield within the past two decades has contributed to a decidedly clearer (but still by no means complete) sense of the breadth and variety of the Victorian reading experience. Thus, this collection has the advantage of emerging at a moment when it is feasible to examine this period's readers and their reading from the kinds of standpoints that would not have been possible for the initial wave of scholars piloting this recovery endeavour. Accordingly,

P.R. Rooney
Trinity College, Dublin, Ireland

A. Gasperini
National University of Ireland, Galway, Ireland

© The Author(s) 2016
P.R. Rooney, A. Gasperini (Eds.), *Media and Print Culture Consumption in Nineteenth-Century Britain*, New Directions in Book History, DOI 10.1057/978-1-137-58761-9_1

framing our enterprise within the parameters sketched by Robert Darnton in his seminal 1986 examination of the history of reading, it is questions of why and how that will concern the essays featured in this collection.[2] First, we wish to probe the reasons why nineteenth-century audiences consumed reading matter. Additionally, the macro- and micro-analysis case studies that essayists present look to juxtapose their reconstructions of these motivations with the actual dividends that consumers likely realized from their temporal, monetary, and mental investments in these acts of reading. A parallel and ancillary objective also informs this dimension of proceedings. While it has absolutely been our editorial intention in determining the composition of the volume to reflect the plurality and diversity of the period's reading landscape, achieving comprehensiveness was not one of our objectives and arguably would be foolhardy even to attempt. Rather, we have particularly looked to illuminate areas of the period's reading not yet comprehensively explored. Correspondingly, the collection's second core concern looks to spotlight the heretofore little-examined question of how nineteenth-century readers conducted their reading when such consumption of print culture texts was framed by kindred contemporaneous encounters with content emanating from other media. In foregrounding this latter strand of enquiry, it is our wish to explore the viability of studying nineteenth-century reading in conjunction with affiliated activities like listening and viewing so as to acquire a more complete sense of cultural consumption during this time.

The 2011 three-volume collection of essays, *The History of Reading*, edited by Shafquat Towheed, Katie Halsey, and W.R. Owens, in many respects represented the culmination of the vision that Darnton had charted in his 1986 meditation on the viability of documenting historical readers' activities. Commendably ambitious in its scope and coverage, this monumental piece of scholarship casts a wide geographical and chronological net in its exploration of audiences' consumption of reading matter. The reflections on the methods one can adopt in studying reading and in the accumulation and interpretation of evidence of this activity, which the editors advance in opening each of the trio of volumes, along with the strategies modelled by the prodigious body of contributors offer a blueprint (and indeed a veritable smorgasbord of approaches) for future work on the subject. In our exploration of Victorian reading, this collection also subscribes to the idea of methodological eclecticism and making use of a multifarious body of evidence that Towheed and Owens espouse in opening the first volume.[3] Moreover, one of the key points of departure of the contribution to the field that we as editors wish to register originates in an observation offered by Towheed in his introduction to volume three that emphasizes that 'reading does not (and has not) ever existed in isolation from a variety of other different forms of communication'.[4]

In zeroing in on the Victorian period, this collection follows in the footsteps of two other recent edited volumes of note. Matthew Bradley and Juliet John beautifully capture the joys and challenges of this kind of scholarly enterprise in the wonderfully self-reflexive evaluation offered in the introduction to their 2015 volume, *Reading and the Victorians*, which frames this kind of research as an exercise in 'reading the Victorians reading'.[5] Granted, a certain proportion of the volume's coverage does orbit somewhat conventional territory in the kind of subjects foregrounded. However, the Bradley and John collection also pursues some pioneering avenues of enquiry featuring scholarship like Simon Eliot's illuminating essay on the impact of lighting on readers' experiences, Stephen Colclough's revisionist take on Mudie's role in furnishing Victorian readers with their reading matter, and Rosalind Crone's social network analysis of data harvested from that magnificent boon to the historian of reading, *The Reading Experience Database*. It is our particular intention to expand further the horizons of the field with this collection with the kinds of topics and questions we spotlight. Beth Palmer and Adelene Buckland's 2011 *A Return to the Common Reader: Print Culture and the Novel 1850–1900* frames itself as 'fruitfully complicating'[6] or engaging in a disaggregation of the portrait of the Victorian reader that emerged from Richard Altick's magisterial and trailblazing 1957 *The English Common Reader*. This is an enterprise in which the collection admirably succeeds. While a relatively compelling case is articulated for the key premise and resulting subject emphasis of the Palmer & Buckland collection, which contends that the 'novel [is] the form that can reveal most to us about the conditions and concepts of reading that operated in the Victorian period',[7] *The Victorian Reading Experience* aims to reflect the eclecticism of nineteenth-century audiences' reading matter by also considering the consumption of factual writing, drama, and song alongside the novel.

THE FRUITS OF READING: THE RATIONALE DRIVING VICTORIAN AUDIENCES' PRINT CONSUMPTION

But suppose we first ask, quite simply and candidly, What is the object of our reading?—to answer which simple-looking question would perhaps to some people be a puzzle indeed. Reading, to some people, is a mere pass-time, a mere kill-time, we might call it. [Haultain offers a lengthy anecdote about 'a portly matron' he supposedly encountered on a train who confessed to a particular fondness for reading love stories—an appetite he deems entirely legitimate and harmless in a person of her maturity] Youth should read— What for? Surely to settle a creed, or at least to discover grounds for believing few things credible, to form ideas, or to give reasons for lacking them, about the constitution of the world and its relation to its Maker, to gain estimates of philosophy, and science, history and art; to learn something of man, of nature, and of human life; to obtain relief from care or recreation from toil; to quicken our perceptions of beauty; to make keen our conceptions of truth; to give clarity to thought, and learn expression of emotion; to plumb the deeps of friendship and take altitude of love; to study character as depicted by those who could read it; to watch how great lives have wrestled with problems of life; to set us standards and samples of nobility; to 'cheer us with books of rich and believing men'; to seek solution for those doubts which come when intellects of different calibre and conviction clash; to find assuagement for the pangs which pierce sundered hearts; 'to maintain around us the "infinite illusion" which makes action easier'; to 'stir in us the primal sources of feeling which keep human nature sweet'; to 'familiarize ourselves with beautiful idealisms of moral excellence'.

Arnold Haultain, 'How to Read', *Blackwood's Edinburgh Magazine* (February 1896), pp. 249–50.

Arnold Haultain's wide-ranging inventory of the prospective gains that he perceived as arising from youthful Victorian audiences' engagement with reading matter points towards the myriad of motivations that could conceivably lead readers of any age, gender, or class to acquire and consume print culture objects. Haultain paints a tremendously rich tableau and the essays featured in this collection will spotlight a number of the principal advantages that particular audiences were likely to hold up as the desired outcomes of their reading. To that end, a number of common themes run through our contributors' reconstructions of these experiences.

Firstly, the belief that reading could stimulate one to become a better person intellectually or morally and perhaps in turn even serve as a catalyst for professional or socio-economic advancement is a principle that Barbara Leckie and Lauren Weiss examine. Leckie's chapter considers the readership of what was perhaps the archetypal and still most widely-known work of Victorian improving reading, *Self-Help* by Samuel Smiles. Leckie focuses on the kinds of reading strategy Smiles's book sought to foster across audiences' wider navigation of the reading environment and also profiles the historical readers likely to have engaged with this work upon its original publication but who have yet to be the subject of sustained examination in scholarship on Smiles. By contrast, Weiss's chapter is an enterprise in recovery that sets out to retrieve the consumption history of an important but now less widely considered class of nineteenth-century edifying reading matter: the manuscript magazine created and consumed by mutual improvement societies. Focusing upon a Glaswegian example of this kind of group, Weiss tracks how reading was undertaken within this kind of communal context and highlights the stimuli that lead such coterie audiences to consume these varieties of text.

Secondly, the sense that investing in the consumption of reading matter would furnish a lens through which one might interpret, frame, or indeed 'read' one's everyday experiences within various different spheres is an idea that Katie Garner, Anne Humpherys, Ruth Doherty, and Caroline Bressey, all explore in the context of a diverse array of print culture texts. Garner's revisionist take on the nineteenth-century readership of Sir Thomas Malory's *Le Morte Darthur* presents a challenge to the conventional conception of this medieval literature text as a work intended for a predominantly male audience. This essay spotlights a noteworthy and substantial female Victorian readership of the tale for whom it furnished a worldview and model of behaviour to which they could aspire. Humpherys's examination of the cheap reprint series publishing ventures of John Dicks also sets out to reframe received thinking about historical audiences' consumption of content repackaged in new and affordable formats. This Dicks chapter underlines how the paratextual material and series configuration of titles in the firm's collection furnished consumers of the series with a decidedly eclectic conception of what constituted legitimate culture. Such heterogeneity had the potential to affirm the tastes and preferences of audiences who sought a more varied diet of reading that comprised both the usual class of 'standard' works alongside more obviously 'popular' content. History of reading scholarship routinely foregrounds the target readership demographic of a particular category of reading matter. Caroline Bressey's chapter treating the late nineteenth-century British anti-racist periodical, *Anti-Caste*, offers an excellent counterpoint to this by exploring why many black British readers of the time did not engage with the kind of publication that featured content that had potential to speak to their experiences of racial discrimination. Doherty's chapter takes as its focus a cultural phenomenon, which was arguably one of the bestselling and most widely-read titles of nineteenth-century fiction, *The Mysteries of London* by G.W.M. Reynolds, and spotlights one particular keystone of the works. Doherty demonstrates that in addition to the entertainment a work of this kind might ostensibly furnish, Reynolds's expansive narrative offered the implied audience of *The Mysteries* a template that they could utilize to interpret and conceive of their everyday experiences of living amidst the urban environment.

Thirdly, the practice of reading for pleasure, diversion, or literally as a pastime (as touched on by Haultain in the context of the mature lady fond of reading love stories whom he apparently encountered during a train journey) will of course figure in any examination of the Victorian reading experience. Chapters by Paul Rooney, Kate Mattacks, Isabel Corfe, and Marie Léger-St Jean all engage with various permutations of print culture encounters that were rooted in audiences' use of reading as a recreational or leisure activity. Focusing on the particular example of the late-Victorian sensation novel, Rooney explores specific intra-media consumption strategies that audiences enlisted to augment the pleasure derived from their readership of ephemeral varieties of light fiction. Similarly, Mattacks's essay on Victorian theatre writing examines the allure of the playtexts of works of contemporary drama circulated in the T.H. Lacy Acting Editions series. These volumes granted readers who were not theatre practitioners access within the medium of print to entertaining cultural matter otherwise only to be encountered within the playhouse. Thus, audiences had the potential to enjoy in their own time and space a genre of writing that would not only amuse but also as Mattacks shows, had the potential to precipitate a process of reflection on the reading process itself. Corfe's examination of Victorian street ballad literature tackles a similar kind of domestic readership. This chapter's discussion seeks to reconceptualize the locus of the appeal of this print culture genre for its historical audience by demonstrating that its allure was significantly more multifaceted than merely satisfying a supposedly debased appetite for tawdry tales of violence. The gratification that a print culture artefact could yield obviously did not manifest in a uniform way for all readers. Léger-St-Jean's chapter on penny dreadfuls and their visual co-texts engages with this sense of diversity from the standpoints of socio-economic difference and reading ability by juxtaposing the consumption of reading matter from this stratum of the reading environment by the young Robert Louis Stevenson and two less advantaged East London boys.

As editors, we are of the view that the sorts of case studies and questions our contributors explore no doubt merit consideration in themselves and have the potential to advance scholarly discourse about the individual topics examined and the larger issue of the intended outcomes of Victorian readers' consumption of print. Additionally, it is our aspiration that the research featured will potentially offer a methodological model for future work on the history of reading within a nineteenth-century context and across the field more broadly. Thus, in curating the scholarship featured in the volume, we have looked to emphasize the merits of pursuing a hybrid or blended approach that draws on and appropriates strategies from both the theoretical and the empirical sides of the methodological divide that Bonnie Gunzenhauser cites as one of the defining factors of this discipline.[8] While we have not opted to structure the collection's ten chapters in quite so formal a manner as the tripartite methodological toolbox, comprising artefactual, paratextual, and institutional approaches, that Gunzenhauser's collection showcases, there are a number of distinct commonalities and strands in the strategies that our contributors bring to bear on the topics they examine. First and foremost, each essay is defined by its use of a composite approach. For instance, Leckie, Garner, Corfe, Rooney, Bressey, Doherty, Humpherys, and Léger-St-Jean all mine extant historical or anecdotal sources such as journalism, criticism, life writing, and literature that attest to the motivations underpinning audiences' consumption of reading matter and then fuse this brand of analysis with discussion of the artefactual or material remnants of this reading. A number of contributors including Garner, Rooney, and Doherty enlist fictional representations of reading often extracted from literary sources that they consider alongside authentic or factual accounts. Given that this is one class of evidence that *The Reading Experience Database* precludes, it is important to weigh up our usage of this kind of data. The insights one can procure here no doubt rank below those combed from historical sources. However, as the chapters in question demonstrate, the sorts of avenues that literary sources open up can prove quite fruitful to study the larger question of why audiences read. A related issue is the thorny question of theory. While few if any scholars of reading would advocate a return to the ahistorical obtuseness of reception study, we wish to suggest it would be foolhardy to dismiss entirely the potential for theory that is deployed judiciously and in a historicized way to advance our understanding of this activity. Therefore, Weiss, Mattacks, Rooney, and Doherty all adopt a framework that combines systems such as folk stylistics, thing theory, and ideas of the cross-media with discussion that is attentive to the bibliographical coding and sociocultural context of the particular reading matter spotlighted.

Frames of Reading: Consumption of Print amidst the Wider Media Environment

This volume's second thematic current or strand of enquiry originates in the editors' wish to delineate new potential avenues in which the field of readership studies might proceed. In keeping with our previous discussion of the place of theory, this should not be read as an effort to swim counter to the largely post-theoretical current of present-day waters but rather an effort to mine and repurpose the past so as to plot future new directions. Thus, building in part upon the concept of the horizon of expectations as formulated by Hans Robert Jauss that offered a theorization of how audiences make meaning when undertaking acts of reading, five of the volume's essays look at an aspect of Victorian reading that we might broadly conceive of as the frame of reference. Understandably, given the philological origins of Jauss's reception scholarship, criteria like genre, forms and themes, and register of language were the pivots of the model of enquiry his work prescribed.[9] Conversely, this project's efforts to illuminate the interpretative fabric of Victorian reading experiences approach this idea from a different perspective that is informed by more recent work on the cross-media. Specifically, our contributors turn their attention to the wider nineteenth-century media climate in order to shed light on the ways in which Victorian readers' exploits in the print media environment were conditioned by contemporaneous contact with cultural content encountered in other media. Accordingly, this is an enterprise first and foremost concerned with reconstructing the convergences that surrounded particular acts of reading when encounters with print intersected with other modes of entertainment or knowledge transfer like viewing or listening. While the case studies featured focus in the main upon literary works, we would suggest that there is wider relevance to this examination of pan-media 'reading'. Thus, in larger terms, it is also an effort to probe how the figurative conceptual spaces delineated by Victorian reading were mediated or conditioned by the period's cultural and commercial milieux. The volume's discussion zeroes in on three major domains.

Firstly, the rich cross-fertilization between the Victorian novel and theatre of the period is an issue that has elicited increasing attention from scholars of Victorianism in recent times.[10] For the most part, questions of cultural production have been to the forefront of this research. In an effort to counter this comparative marginalization of the consumer, chapters by Paul Rooney and Kate Mattacks approach this topic from the perspective of Victorian audiences whose reading was conditioned by the two cultural spheres. The particular lens that each essay employs reflects the distinct disciplinary backgrounds of the two scholars. Mining both conventional theories of adaptation and repurposed ideas of the cross-media originally articulated with reference to the present-day media environment, Rooney considers the representative example of the late-Victorian popular fiction of Fergus Hume. Historical readers' encounters with this novelist's output was conditioned in a distinctly intra-media mode of consumption that encompassed both the print media incarnation of Hume's writing and the adaptations of his work dramatized for the stage. Consequently, the sort of cultural experience furnished was one where the frame encircling the act of reading this sensational literature could owe much to visuals, dialogue, and orchestral music encountered within a performance medium of stage melodrama. Addressing the subject from the standpoint of theatre and performance studies, Mattacks explores the circulation and readership of print media renderings of playtexts in the Victorian period so as to illuminate some of the potential crossovers between the act of reading and the experience of taking in a stage performance. This chapter focuses in the main on the genre of sensation drama and the circulation of this kind of content in Lacy's 'Acting Editions' series. Mattacks demonstrates the potential for such reading matter to precipitate a process of meta or self-conscious reflection in the reader about the defining characteristics of the printed medium through which this literature was accessed and the impact occasioned by cultural matter encountered in interconnected media.

Secondly, Isabel Corfe foregrounds a related medium in her chapter looking at mid-nineteenth-century consumption of street ballad literature. Corfe spotlights the experiences of less privileged readers capable only of expending a modest outlay on their reading matter whose engagement with the textual content diffused in this genre of cheap printed matter intersected with and was framed by oral culture and song. Corfe argues that the inherent scope for amateur musical entertainment, which was often mounted in communal settings that existed at the frontier between the domestic and public, was amongst the principal criteria that led consumers of street ballads to acquire these items of reading matter. Challenging the prevalent impression of these objects that emphasizes their propensity for dealing in grisly and violent subject matter and partial resemblance to the modern tabloid press, this chapter contends that judgements on the perceived singable properties of these sheets was paramount in shaping consumer choices in this sector of the print marketplace. The ways in which these print culture exploits were framed by oral and/or aural stimuli that played upon audiences' musical awareness and appreciation of popular song is at the heart of Corfe's discussion. Her chapter profiles the strategies that ballad sellers employed to disseminate this material, the circumstances of consumers' acquisition of the artefacts in public spaces such as town centres, and the subsequent consumption of this content in communal or familial settings.

Thirdly, the potential for visual media that were exhibited in public spaces (and particularly within the urban environment) to frame audiences' reading is an analogous issue that both Ruth Doherty and Marie Léger-St-Jean examine. Doherty positions G.W.M. Reynolds's *The Mysteries of London* within the context of contemporaneous public entertainments that exhibited advancements in urban mapping and microscopy. This Reynolds-focused chapter spotlights this juxtaposition to demonstrate the affinity between the experience of reading the verbal text of a prodigious print culture phenomenon like *The Mysteries of London*, which sought to document contemporary city life, and encounters with kindred visual-based content. Doherty illustrates how the Ordnance Survey mapmaking initiatives and Polytechnic displays of the magnifying potential of the microscope also yielded an illuminating representation of the topography and hidden depths and layers of the metropolis. Much the same as Corfe, Doherty also sets about recovering the performative dimension associated with the consumption of this print culture content and posits that the representation of the urban that emerges with Reynolds's capitalization on these convergences had the potential to stimulate both the private solitary reader and the auditor exposed to this material as it was read aloud. There was an inclusivity to the latter class of cultural experience, which meant it could involve in the reading process individuals whose literacy was not particularly advanced or those who had missed out entirely on the opportunity to learn to read. Léger-St-Jean takes as her focus this specific nineteenth-century constituency. Concentrating on a similarly inexpensive variety of print culture, the penny dreadful serial, this chapter zeroes in on an anecdote of juvenile London East-End readership. Documented by James Greenwood in *Saint Paul's Magazine*, this particular reading experience was set in motion by the act of decoding or 'reading' the woodcut cover visuals that the local area's newsvendors exhibited in their shop windows with a view to drumming up interest in the latest numbers of the weekly penny narrative. Gazing upon the illustrations stirred the two young boys (one illiterate and the other semi-literate) to acquire the verbal content of the instalments to satiate their appetite to clarify their conjectures about the highwayman's adventures, which reputedly drove the impoverished youths to theft to muster sufficient funds to purchase a copy of the printed matter. Léger-St-Jean juxtaposes these boys' experience of reading illustrated advertising matter with the reminiscences that Robert Louis Stevenson shared of his youthful forays into similar window-shopping territory, in order to attest to the distinct classes of visual-verbal convergences that existed in this period.

In tackling questions about reading that revolve around issues of the sort examined by Rooney, Mattacks, and Doherty, which are not necessarily as simple as who read what book during which particular moment in time, it is not always possible to root all of one's inferences in evidence that is entirely anecdotal, historical, or empirical. Thus, we would suggest that a comparatively more speculative brand of enquiry, which naturally uses as its point of departure the extant, accessible evidence of reading, but also has recourse to perspectives and frameworks derived from more theoretically inclined branches of scholarship is often a necessary first step in beginning to recover experiences where consumption of print culture converged with other media. On the other hand, even when seemingly abundant quantities of evidence on a particular kind of reading matter lie at the scholar's disposal, it may not necessarily be the case that unmediated access to these readers' histories emerges as a result. Corfe's essay on street ballad literature is an excellent example of this methodological and evidentiary dilemma. It offers an examination of a genre of print culture defined by its veritable ephemerality where scholars' present-day sense of readership of the form owes much to factors beyond our control. While there is little doubt that the revisionist objective that underpins the chapter is capably and convincingly achieved, Corfe is also attentive to the fact that the conclusions presented emerge from *extant* data whose precise composition is a product of the principles and ideals of the individuals responsible for compiling these collections. Reflections of this kind that weigh up the kinds of evidence that we as scholars of print culture and historians of the book can legitimately employ in turn also calls forth the question of the relationship between the study of reading within book history and the treatment of this topic in the wider field of literary studies. Chapters by Doherty, Rooney, and Mattacks all grapple with assorted permutations of this issue. Unsurprisingly, given the literature background of many scholars who work in this field, the rich vein of material culture scholarship in Victorian studies, along with the prevalence of research on the readership of literary texts in the wider history of reading domain, we wish to suggest that there are reasonable grounds to query the scope for (and indeed wisdom of) imposing a hard and fast distinction between the two areas. It is interesting to note that two of the more significant works of scholarship that one might conceive of as bookending the study of Victorian reading to date—Amy Cruse's *The Victorians and their Books* (1935) and Leah Price's *How to do Things with Books in Victorian Britain* (2012)—were each replete (arguably in very different ways) with material that spoke to both communities of scholars. It is our hope that the essays featured in *The Victorian Reading Experience* will achieve a similar bilingualism.

CONCLUSION

In the spirit of that philosophy, there is perhaps merit in concluding these opening remarks and ushering in our assembled contributors' chapters by reminding our readers of two notable moments that occur in George Gissing's 1894 novel, *In the Year of Jubilee*—a work where individuals are quite literally defined by the reading matter that they consume. We would suggest that these particular episodes illuminate a great deal about the practice and politics of reading in Victorian times and specifically in the context of the two questions that this collection explores. First, the inadvertent meeting between the novel's heroine, Nancy Lord, and Lionel Tarrant, the young gentleman to whom she is drawn, at the circulating library of the seaside town where she is vacationing prompts the young woman to alter her initial intentions to acquire a novel for light reading in favour of borrowing a volume of lectures on scientific subjects. Her choice elicits incredulity and bemusement on Tarrant's part. As Nancy is conducting her business at the library, two of her fellow female customers seek the aid of the library attendant in their quest for 'a pretty book',[11] which serves as a source of amusement to Nancy and Lionel. Thus, Nancy's change of mind, Tarrant's bemused reaction at her choice of book, the other women's enquiry, the couple's derision at what they witness, along with Tarrant's subsequent claims to have abjured any interest in reading matter like the volume of lectures (articulated when he and Nancy have left the library), all reveal a great deal about what audiences then and now seek to derive from the act of reading. The second episode of note also involves Nancy but this time the young woman is in conversation with another possible suitor, the less genteel advertising agent, Luckworth Crewe. Over the course of the pair's first sustained encounter at the titular Jubilee celebrations, Crewe offers Nancy an extended explication on the remit, reach, and significant societal influence of the advertising hoardings that are the cornerstone of his line of work. The thrust of his discourse underscores how visual and/or verbal matter disseminated in media aside from the book, the periodical, the broadside, or the penny serial number had the potential to constitute a comparatively potent and impactful presence in consumers' wider diet of reading. Therefore, the figure of Crewe and the type of culture he embodies emphasize the importance of casting a wide net when looking to reconstruct Victorian audiences' horizons or fabric of signification given the considerable evidence that attests to the weight of a potential pan-media context framing audiences' reading activities during this period.

Notes

1. R.D. Altick, *The English Common Reader* (Chicago: University of Chicago Press, 1957), p. 9.
2. R. Darnton, *The Kiss of Lamourette: Reflections in Cultural History* (New York: Norton, 1990), p. 157. Originally published in *The Australian Journal of French Studies* 23 (1986), 5–30.
3. S. Towheed and W.R. Owens, 'Introduction', in S. Towheed and W.R. Owens, eds., *The History of Reading. Volume 1: International Perspectives c. 1550–1990* (Basingstoke: Palgrave Macmillan, 2011), p. 2.
4. S. Towheed, 'Introduction', in S. Towheed, ed., *The History of Reading. Volume 3: Methods, Strategies, and Tactics* (Basingstoke: Palgrave Macmillan, 2011), p. 2.
5. M. Bradley and J. John, 'Introduction', in M. Bradley and J. John, eds., *Reading and the Victorians* (Farnham and Burlington: Ashgate, 2015), p. 4.
6. B. Palmer and A. Buckland, 'Introduction', in B. Palmer and A. Buckland, eds., *A Return to the English Common Reader: Print Culture and the Novel 1850–1900* (Farnham and Burlington: Ashgate, 2011), p. 5.
7. Palmer and Buckland, pp. 4–5.
8. B. Gunzenhauser, 'Introduction', in B. Gunzenhauser, ed., *Reading in History: New Methodologies from the Anglo-American Tradition* (London: Pickering & Chatto, 2010), p. 2.
9. H.R. Jauss, *Toward an Aesthetic of Reception*, translated by Timothy Bahti (Minneapolis: University of Minnesota Press, 1982), p. 22.
10. See for example R. Pearson, *Victorian Writers and the Stage: The Plays of Dickens, Browning, Collins and Tennyson* (Basingstoke: Palgrave Macmillan, 2015).
11. George Gissing (1894) *In the Year of Jubilee* (London: The Hogarth Press, 1987), p. 120.

CHAPTER 2

Reader-Help: How to Read Samuel Smiles's *Self-Help*

Barbara Leckie

In an early review of Samuel Smiles's *Self-Help*, *Fraser's Magazine* singles out the canal-builder, James Brindley, for discussion. Impressed by Brindley, the reviewer elaborates on his endurance, enterprise, and courage. I want to focus here, though, on one of Brindley's more unsettling experiences. Unable to read and write proficiently, Brindley compensated for the lack of these skills through stamina-bending feats of memory. Since he was unable to read an operating manual, for example, Brindley would simply study the machine and commit to memory its workings. One evening he went to the theatre, however, and found his impressive abilities 'were so much disturbed that … it rendered him unfit for business'. '[H]umiliated and distressed', Brindley swore off all future theatre-going.[1] If going to the theatre were to compromise his ability to work, Brindley reasoned, then he would cease attending. The reviewer concludes the anecdote as follows: 'The noble quality of self-help which is so finely illustrated in Brindley's career has long been, and still remains the distinguishing characteristic of Englishmen'.[2] We move seamlessly here from the individual experience of one figure discussed by Smiles to a generalization that embraces all Englishmen. How does the production of

B. Leckie (✉)
Carleton University, Ottawa, ON, Canada

this tension, or toggling, between the singular self and 'all Englishmen' relate to *Self-Help*'s production of the self *as* a reader, the specific readers to whom it is directed, and its readership history?

Self-Help is a rich text for readership studies. With its publication in the same year as Mill's *On Liberty* and Darwin's *Origin of the Species*, its rapid rise as a bestseller that neatly outpaced both Mill's and Darwin's books, its appeal to a vast spectrum of readers ranging from working people to the Queen, its translation into over twenty foreign languages, its semi-official and its pirated American editions, and its complicated relationship to the rise of the self-help genre itself (now the fastest growing and best-selling book genre), it repays any numbers of questions that scholars of reading history may seek to pose. How are specific readers (singular selves) and their experiences delineated? How does this best-selling book—with its quotations, summarizing examples, and extracts—relate to the extracts and quotations that one finds in book reviews? And how are both, in turn, related to the intersection of industrial modernity and print proliferation that *Self-Help* embodies? *Self-Help* raises questions about the working-class readers to whom it was, in part, directed. These readers' experiences are all but silent in the typical resources to which critics tend to turn (book reviews, letters, marginalia, and autobiographies). This chapter offers preliminary groundwork for these questions as well as a prolegomenon for future work in the history of the reader.

I am interested at once in Engelsing's idea of the reading revolution (that kept pace with the Industrial Revolution); Roger Chartier's sensitivity to the history of the categories—like reader—that we use to interpret this reading revolution and, indeed, all previous periods[3]; and Janice Radway's call for a shift from the text itself to the 'complex social event' of reading.[4] My turn to reading history is further supported by the fact that critics of *Self-Help* focused on—one could even say they were obsessed with—the book's origins to the exclusion of its reception.[5] This chapter, then, also begins to fill a gap in Smiles's studies while also addressing larger questions of the history of readers, print culture studies, and book history.

Professional Readers: A Preliminary Reading History of *Self-Help*

Smiles wrote *Self-Help* in his leisure time. He makes this point clear in the Introduction to the first edition of the book, references it in defence of plagiarism accusations, repeats it in the Preface to the second edition, and returns to it once again in his *Autobiography*. In this latter work, he explains that because he was working full-time he could only write in the small blocks of time available to him in the evenings when his business as a railway administrator was done.[6] These comments on his writing practice relate both to the form of *Self-Help* and to the reader for whom it was intended.[7] The book, what one reviewer calls the 'biographical miscellany',[8] is composed of 13 chapters further subdivided into sections ranging from a paragraph to a few pages. It is not linear. In most ways, indeed, it resists the typical teleological momentum of a biography despite (and because of) the many—he refers to over 750 names—micro-biographies it contains.[9] Composed of fragments and examples collected by Smiles over 15 years and knitted together in a relatively loose and repetitive manner, *Self-Help* was meant to be read in the way it was written: in the small parcels of time available to the full-time worker seeking to get ahead in his work, career, or profession.

Self-Help was published in 1859 and was immediately a success; as Peter Sinnema notes, it was 'one of most popular works of non-fiction published in England in the second half of the nineteenth century'.[10] It sold 20,000 copies in its first year and more than a quarter of million by the time of Smiles's death. These sales 'far exceeded' the sales of the great nineteenth-century novels.[11] Its biographies, often of working men, highlight figures who exhibit the self-help traits—independence, thrift, temperance, character, duty, perseverance—that Smiles admired. The book promoted the idea, key to liberal ideology, that with a little stamina, character development, and dedication, anyone could succeed. It was a message, then as now, that was appealing. Sinnema stresses, rightly, that Smiles was not an apologist for capitalism. His ideas emerge out of 1830s and '40s radicalism and his efforts to improve the lives—by education primarily—of the working classes. Still, he does retreat from his radical roots and by the time of *Self-Help* he advocates 'better habits, rather than … greater rights'[12]; his goal, in other words, is not to advocate for systemic change but rather for personal change. Most critics are quick to link the success of *Self-Help* with industrial modernity.[13] Indeed, one of the most interesting things about this book is the way that it chimes with changing comprehensions of time, work, and the 'self'. In other words, *Self-Help* has been recognized by many critics as both responsive to the demands of industrial modernity and as shaping a new sense of the self for whom those demands could be more readily calibrated.

Self-Help *and Reading*

Smiles values reading in *Self-Help*. Indeed, to succeed in one's work (and, needless to say, to read *Self-Help*) one needed a certain level of literacy.[14] But he does not value all forms of reading. His comments on reading can be divided into two polarized categories: good reading (a 'habit of well-directed reading'[15]) and bad reading (reading that is like 'dram drinking'[16]). Good reading bolsters individual development and national progress and is to be applauded; bad reading weakens self-identity and dulls one's desire for self-advancement. Those with well-directed habits of reading are described as follows: Sir Walter Scott dedicated his evenings to 'reading and study'[17]; John Britton 'devoted his leisure principally to perambulating the bookstalls, where he read books by snatches which he could not buy'[18]; Dr Pye Smith made 'copious memoranda of all the books he read, with extracts and criticisms'[19]; and many other figures learned foreign languages in their leisure time. Dr Livingstone worked as a child in a cotton factory:

> With part of his first week's wages he bought a Latin grammar, and began to learn that language, pursuing the study for years at night school. He would sit up conning his lessons till twelve or later, when not sent to bed by his mother, for he had to be up and at work in the factory every morning by six. In this way he plodded trough Virgil and Horace, also reading extensively all books, excepting novels, that came in his way, but more especially scientific works and books of travels. ... He even carried on his reading amidst the roar of the factory machinery, so placing the book upon the spinning jenny which he worked that he could catch sentence after sentence as he passed it.[20]

Livingstone is a model for good reading: he teaches himself, spends his hard-won money on books, reads extensively, chooses the classics and scorns novels, and integrates reading into his factory work. His reading discipline ends happily: he becomes a doctor to fulfil his desire to be a missionary and later writes *Missionary Travels*.

But what of the novels that Livingstone avoids? '[P]opular literature' encourages 'a mania for frivolity and excitement.' 'To meet the public taste,' Smiles continues, 'our books and periodicals must now be highly spiced, amusing, and comic, not disdaining slang, and illustrative of breaches of all laws, human and divine'.[21] He cites, approvingly, John Sterling, who derides contemporary periodicals and novels as 'a new and more effectual substitute for the plagues of Egypt, vermin that corrupt the wholesome waters and infest our chambers'.[22] If reading material generates certain modes of reading—the disciplined habit, on the one hand, and the excited mania, on the other—what sort of reading practice does *Self-Help* encourage?

Smiles is not Horace or Virgil. *Self-Help* does not require the study of any foreign language to comprehend, it is not demanding, and it is not difficult. On the contrary. With its short sections, fragmented, anecdotal style, and inspiring biographies, it is designed for easy consumption. This type of popular self-improvement book, which had been on the rise since the mid-eighteenth-century and was much admired by Smiles, is not referenced at all in *Self-Help*.[23] What sort of reader, then, does Smiles seek, and at the same time, shape, for his book? It is here that some contradictions emerge: thematically his book encourages continual, unflagging application in all activities; formally, he writes a book that does not require this sort of application and that indeed resists it. Smiles criticizes interruptions to attention and yet industrial life is full of such interruptions and his book demands to be read in a manner that capitalizes on them. I want to turn now to how *Self-Help* was read and the 'social area of reception' it produced.[24]

Reading Self-Help

Of the many critical disputes generated by the publication of *Self-Help*, one of the most interesting is the focus on plagiarism. In an *Athenaeum* article entitled 'Literary Adoption' Samuel Bailey places a section from his book, *Essays on the Formation of Opinions* (1831), side-by-side with a passage from *Self-Help*. In a later article, *The Westmoreland Gazette* published 'Plagiarisms in *Self-Help*' with three passages from three different authors, alongside their unattributed parallels in *Self-Help*.[25] What interests me about these accusations is Smiles's nonplussed response and his rationale. In a letter published a few weeks after the initial *Athenaeum* article, he attributes the 'accidental omission' to 'the circumstances under which the book was written'.[26] He recalls his comments from the 1859 Introduction in which he outlines the book's origins in his lecture, 'The Education of the Working Classes', delivered to working men at the Leeds Mutual Improvement Society in 1845.[27] The lecture itself emerged out of a growing discourse on individual self-development with which Smiles was familiar as well as his political experience in the 1840s and his work with mutual improvement societies. At the time, he had not the 'remotest view' of publication; further, the unattributed passage embodied 'no new truth'.[28] What is of 'more general interest' than the plagiarism, Smiles insists, is that the audience to whom he delivered the initial lecture was composed of 'apprentices, young mechanics, and factory operatives' who had, in the intervening years, gone on to do 'good work' as the East Ward Mechanics Institute.

What should we make of this connection between plagiarism and audience? The audience's response to the book and the good work that it generates is clearly more important to Smiles than what he perceives as the minor and accidental omissions related to its composition. Indeed, whenever Smiles had the opportunity, he sought to remind readers of his book's origins; this point is most evident in the Introduction to the first edition of *Self-Help*, referenced by Smiles above, that powerfully binds the book to its original working-class audience as follows:

> Several years after the incidents referred to [the delivery of the lecture and its warm reception], the subject was unexpectedly recalled to the author's recollection by an evening visit from a young man—apparently fresh from the work of a foundry—who explained that he was now an employer of labour and a thriving man; and he was pleased to remember with gratitude the words spoken in all honesty to him and to his fellow-pupils years before, and even to attribute some measure of his success in life to the endeavours which he had made to work up to their spirit.[29]

Inspired by the lecture's impact on this foundry worker, Smiles returns to it in his 'leisure evening moments' to jot down notes derived from his 'reading, observation, and experience of life' that had a bearing on the topic.[30]

These comments, positioned as they are as an introduction to reading, cannot help but shape how the book will be read. Indeed, even the shortest reviews tend to note the book's origins in the 1845 lecture. In a typical response one reviewer writes, 'It is a book that ought to be in the hands of every young man. It was originally written, in the shape of lectures, to be delivered before a society of young men, formed for mutual improvement, in one of the manufacturing districts of the north of England'.[31] Many reviews cite from Smiles's Introduction and one review *only* cites from the Introduction.[32] Several critics have tried to recover Smiles's radical commitments, all too easily lost sight of in the scramble to fold his philosophy into the mainstream middle-class norms that it partially served to constitute. It is tempting indeed to be distracted by *Self-Help*'s phenomenal success and to forget what a hybrid marketing venture it was. Nevertheless, despite Smiles's repeated appeals to the working-class audience's response that had both shaped his book and served as its catalyst, it is the working-class reader's experience that is effaced in the reviews.

It was not only his early working-class audience, however, that was highlighted in Smiles's Introduction, it was also the book's form: the notes that he casually jotted down in his leisure time. Smiles returns to this mode of composition in his second 1866 Preface, remarking on the book's 'fragmentary character' 'put together principally from jottings during many years' and not intended for publication.[33] If the failures of attribution following from this composition method could be corrected in subsequent volumes, the disjointedness and randomness of his book's structure—it sense of arbitrariness—could not. This critique has plagued *Self-Help* since its first publication.[34] This sense of fragmentation, however, can be seen to parallel the intended readership for Smiles's book. Written in spare moments because Smiles himself had to attend to his full-time job it was meant also to be read in the spare moments available to those individuals who sought to hone their skills, succeed in their work, and, importantly, shape the nation. And yet, this is a mode of reading not captured in either the 'good reading' or the 'bad reading' modes discussed by Smiles above. We have, then, a double erasure: working-class readers are not referenced in the book reviews; and the form of the book that is arguably tailored for these readers is not referenced in Smiles's, admittedly simplistic, categorization of readers.

If, as Donald Hall puts it, 'interpretive, ideological, and material contexts govern [...] forms of reader activity [...] for specific historical audiences',[35] what category of reader is, in fact, legible in the response to *Self-Help*? Book reviewers, needless to say, approach *Self-Help* from specific ideological and class positions. There are, moreover, implicit and explicit conventions that dictate how reviews are written.[36] Almost all of the reviews I address put their emphasis not on the working-class readers for whom the book was in good part intended but on the readers of the periodical for which they were writing. This emphasis makes sense of course. Nevertheless, it is worth noting because we often inherit these readers' responses as normative. Just as the *Fraser's* reviewer moves from Brindley to all Englishmen, so reviewers and critics often move from their response to all responses. Later critics, for example, read the reviews and summarize the early critical reception; these summaries elide differences between reviews and they also do not tend to address the fact that the journals in which we might find working-class responses are not as readily available. This point is especially important, however, for a book like *Self-Help* that is pitched for the very audience that does not fall under the typical periodical's umbrella.[37] It is instructive, moreover, that this tension is written into the reviews themselves: the introduction and intended audience is acknowledged and, usually, applauded, and then the reviews continue with a focus on artists, writers, and professionals.

There was, however, one exception. Joseph Brotherton, an MP, is mentioned in no fewer than four of the reviews I consulted.[38] Given that Smiles refers to over 750 names in his book and to 350 in some detail and that reviewers usually refer to only a handful of names, this overlap demands some explanation. As it happens, Brotherton offers the reviewers a stirring affirmation of the possibility of upward mobility in the British class system; most of these reviewers reference Brotherton by way of self or national congratulation. Further, where Smiles combines the working-class biographies with other classes, sometimes in a single paragraph, to the extent that reviewers reference the working-class biographies, they tend to divide them and to reinstall a division between working-class and middle-class readers that *Self-Help* is at pains to diminish. The typical review, in short, if it acknowledges the working-class biographies at all, does so at the beginning of the review and then settles in, by way of lengthy extracts of the middle- and upper-class biographies, to the main body of the review.

These extracts are also interesting *as* extracts. That is, they illustrate one of the dominant mid-century conventions of book reviewing. Reviews were often, as Hazlitt concisely put it, 'mere summary decisions and a list of quotations'.[39] The emphasis on quotation is especially significant for a book that is itself comprised of quotations and follows no particular narrative line. To be sure the definition of self-help could be defined (and it was, repeatedly) and Smiles's goals could be stated (to advance self-help). But the definition of self-help as application/diligence/perseverance was in tension, as we have seen above, with the interrupted, dispersed, and random reading encouraged by the strings of quotations and anecdotes and extracts. Smiles's reviewers, whether positive or negative, do not consider the book as a carefully constructed whole, but as a rich (or thin depending on the view) compendium of varied biographical anecdotes. In some ways, then, the book review was consonant with, and formally replicated, the form of *Self-Help*. Smiles's 1859 Introduction and 1866 Preface, his book itself, and its reviews, taken together, function as guides for the reader: a how-to for reading *Self-Help*.

Everyday Readers: A Prolegomenon for Further Reading Histories of *Self-Help*

I now turn to a prolegomenon for further histories of reading prompted by the rich complexity of Smiles's text. My section above focuses on the professional readers—the reviewers—who responded so energetically to *Self-Help* and defined many of the terms by which we still understand it today. But what about the everyday readers—the readers whose responses are not documented in the standard archives to which scholars turn, the readers who confide in a friend about a book's impact and then carry on with their work, the readers who copy out passages from the text and keep them in their wallets, the readers who fall outside our established scholarly frameworks? These readers' responses are more difficult to access. Because *Self-Help* enjoyed such a wide readership, however, it may also help us to define new categories of readers and new avenues of readership study.

Smiles's book, for example, did not remain confined within national boundaries. The North American reading public took up Smiles's book itself with great enthusiasm.[40] Indeed, the idea of self-help, several critics have convincingly demonstrated, derives, in part, from Ralph Waldo Emerson and William Ellery Channing (Tyrell and Travers).[41] It was quickly adopted for school curriculums, extracted in American periodicals, and issued in many other pirated editions. These forms of "reading"—as a pedagogical tool, as an extract, and as a pirated (and sometimes altered) work—all invite different approaches. How did school-children respond to the work? How did teachers teach it? How did a magazine editor decide which passages to include and which to exclude? How often did their readers seek out the full text? What editions were they working with?

Further, Smiles's idea of self-help bears very little similarity to contemporary versions of self-help that have largely taken hold in a North American context. Nevertheless, these works are indebted to, and often cite, *Self-Help* and they testify to the text's remarkable endurance. It would be worth tracing this history from its early incarnations. As Briggs writes: 'There is a line of descent from *Self-Help* through books like J.C. Ransom's *The Successful Man in his Manifold Relations with Life* (1887) to A.E. Lyons's *The Self-Starter* (1924), Dale Carnegie's *How to Win Friends and Influence People* (1936), C.E. Popplestone's *Every Man a Winner* (1936) and Norman Vincent Peale's *The Power of Positive Thinking* (1955).'[42] Many critics note the misappropriation of Smiles in subsequent interpretations of self-help but a history of this misappropriation—the investments in misreading—would also help us to understand its mutation from a manual for social advancement and character moulding to psychological self-fashioning.[43]

If *Self-Help* can be defined and understood in a transatlantic context, it can also be understood in a transnational context. It was translated into French, Russian, German, Italian, Swedish, Dutch, Spanish, Czech, Croatian, Turkish, Egyptian, Tamil, Murati, Gujarati, Hindustani, Canares, Magyar, Siamese, Armenian, Pali, Albanian, and Arabic among other languages. These translations raise interesting questions about the relationship between self-help and industrial modernity in countries in which modernization developed unevenly. The difficulty that many languages had translating 'self-help' also tells us something about the mobility of Smiles's ideas.[44] Several critics reference Smiles's comments that his book was interwoven with passages from the Koran at the Khedive's palace in Egypt. This sort of appropriation invites a different sort of reading history. In addition, it would be valuable to consider the countries—notably Italy and Japan—in which *Self-Help* was especially popular.

It is readers' letters, however, that perhaps offer the most abundant record of the impact of *Self-Help* on everyday readers. To date, all of our information on this correspondence comes almost entirely from Smiles himself. 'It would be considered absurdly eulogistic', he writes in his *Autobiography*, 'were I to detail the many marks of sympathy and gratitude which I have received from all classes of the community, at home and abroad.'[45] Nevertheless, the absurdly eulogistic is fascinating. Over the course of his *Autobiography* Smiles records 19 reader's responses to his book from a working man in Exeter to a surgeon in Blackheath and a Count in Rome.[46] One gentleman named his son after Smiles, another his store. A 'curate in a country church' only read his Bible more than *Self-Help*, an Indian in Bombay notes that he has read the book over a dozen times, another young man excised quotations from the text and pasted them on his bedroom walls for easy reference.[47] A would-be sculptor 'sat up nearly all night to read' *Self-Help*[48]; another young man read the book 'constantly, in the morning and at night'.[49] Almost all of these letter writers offer success stories made possible by their reading of *Self-Help*: it provokes an 'entire alteration' in the life of one young man in New Zealand, another moves from factory boy to chemist to surgeon thanks to Smiles,[50] and many others describe becoming partners in their firms after following Smiles's advice. Of the 19 letters, only two are from women, a percentage that may or may not reflect the book's actual readership. It would certainly be interesting to have more copious information on this material. Given the sales that capped over a quarter of a million by his death, there are presumably many more letters to be mined for similar, as well as divergent, responses. Smiles's book also invites a consideration of collective reading. To what extent was *Self-Help* read collectively, either with others at home (in forms of family reading) or in Mechanics Institutes and Mutual Improvement Societies (which continued to be vital despite their diminished political urgency)? To what extent was it read aloud? Seeking out the answers to these questions would provide a better appreciation of working-class responses to the text as well as capturing an interactive dimension of Victorian print culture—shaped by reader feedback and response[51]—that is often overlooked today.

Finally, we might consider those female readers whose responses are often difficult to trace in extant records. *Self-Help* was first delivered as a lecture to working men, it is primarily composed of biographies of men, and it constructs an implied reader that is male. *Self-Help*'s relative exclusion of examples of exemplary women has been much remarked in the criticism. That said, when we turn to the book's reception it seems reasonable to assume that it was read with great interest by girls and women. The first book to follow it with 'self-help' in the title, for example, was Jesse Boucherette's *Hints on Self-Help: A Book for Young Women* (1863). While *Self-Help* is often compared to Isabella Beeton's *Book of Household Management* (1861), it seems that women responded to the idea of self-help, an idea that is borne out by the disproportionate number of women drawn to the genre of self-help as it developed in the intervening century and a half.

Smiles's *Self-Help* offers an unusual diversity of approaches because its reach was so far and so unusual; as a result, it was rewriting the range and reach of reading histories themselves. Jonathan Rose observes that while critics are interested in how people read, they have not 'explored mass intellectual responses to reading'.[52] He suggests that one of the questions Altick himself had asked much earlier in *The English Common Reader*— 'How do texts change the minds and lives of common (i.e. nonprofessional readers?)'—remains unanswered.[53] *Self-Help*, with its many biographies of personal transformation that have inspired its readers to relate similar stories, its resonance with Altick's chapter on 'The Self-Made Reader', and its multi-faceted readership, offers fertile ground for this sort of inquiry.

Conclusion: Reader-Help

I want to return now to James Brindley. The comments to which the reviewer refers in my introduction do not, in fact, occur in *Self-Help* but rather in a book that Smiles published two years later, *Lives of the Engineers*.[54] Brindley's story, relayed over many pages (Smiles would later write a full biography on him), is compelling, and it amplifies the comments from *Fraser's* in a manner that is important to me here. The theatre is not to blame for the dissolution of Brindley's self-help efforts, Smiles suggests; rather, his lack of sympathy with the theatre was caused by the absence of books in his life. 'Shut out from the humanizing influence of books', Smiles writes, 'and without any taste for the politer arts his mind went on painfully grinding in the mill of mechanics.'[55] And yet, how is a worker like Brindley to gain access to this humanizing influence? Smiles's answer of perseverance and continuous application is hardly satisfying. *Self-Help* repeatedly humanizes industrial modernity by drawing on biographies of men like Brindley to demonstrate how success is within the grasp of all men who are willing to work hard. But, as Brindley's case demonstrates, and, of course, as *Self-Help* demands, reader-help is a precondition of self-help. The reading experiences related in *Self-Help*, as well as the discontinuous reading practice encouraged by its form, sit uneasily with its repeated paean to continuous application. One could imagine, however, a reading practice that highlighted episodic reading for the self-made man and, in turn, enabled at once the rise of literacy rates and the legibility of men like Brindley in the historical record. It is this reading practice that *Self-Help* begins to formulate.

Self-Help was written by Smiles; he arranged his anecdotes, determined which to include and which to set aside, which to elaborate on and which to limit, and, in his 1859 Introduction and 1866 Preface made suggestions about how the book might be read. Nevertheless, the book that was read, and the book we now read, is also a production of its readers. Readers read. They imagine, interpret, fabricate, and get confused. They sometimes even assign stories, like Brindley's, to texts in which these stories are not in fact told. *Self-Help* sought to reach in book form that early working-class audience to which it was first directed; it sought an audience of readers rather than only an audience of listeners.[56] Its episodic, anecdotal, and straightforward writing was designed to reach such readers, but it is also precisely that audience about which we now have so few details. While Smiles amended the citation oversights from his first edition, most of the accounts of industrial workers like Brindley rely on unattributed anecdotes. It does seem clear, however, that *Self-Help* shapes a reading practice of discontinuous reading perfectly attuned to the demands of industrial modernity. Much has been written on the ways in which new technological innovations and shifts in modes of production generate new written forms; these forms, in turn, produce new categories of readers, and these categories, in the case of books like *Self-Help*, are only just beginning to be delineated.[57]

NOTES

1. *Fraser's Magazine*, *Self-Help* by S. Smiles reviewed, June 1860, 778–86, 779.
2. *Fraser's*, 779.
3. R. Chartier, *On the Edge of the Cliff: History, Language, Practices*, translated by L. Cochrane (Baltimore: Johns Hopkins University Press, 1997), p. 4.
4. J. Radway, *Reading the Romance: Women, Patriarchy, and Popular Literature* (Chapel Hill: University of North Carolina Press, 1984), p. 8.
5. See V. Trendafilov, 'The Origins of *Self-Help*: Samuel Smiles and the Formative Influences on an Ex-Seminal Work', *The Victorian* 3.1 (2015); R.J. Morris, 'Samuel Smiles and the Genesis of *Self-Help*: The Retreat to a Petit Bourgeois Utopia', *The Historical Journal* 24.1 (1981), 89–109; T. Travers, 'Samuel Smiles and the Origins of "Self-Help": Reform and the New Enlightenment', *Albion: A Quarterly Journal Concerned with British Studies* 9.2 (1977), 161–87; A. Tyrrell, 'The Origins of a Victorian Bestseller—An Unacknowledged Debt', *Notes and Queries* 17.9 (1970), 347–49, all of which have origins or genesis in their titles. A host of other articles trace the prehistory without the titular emphasis.
6. S. Smiles, *The Autobiography of Samuel Smiles* (New York: Dutton, 1905), pp. 209–11.
7. In S. Arata, 'On Not Paying Attention', *Victorian Studies* 46.2 (2004), 193–205, Arata notes that by the 1880s reading itself comes to be understood as work. It would be interesting to trace the lineaments of this shift in more detail. I suspect we would be able to draw a clear line from Smiles to this later sense of reading as work. In relation to books like *So Many Books! So Little Time! What to Do?* (1891) Arata writes, 'It is the scheduling that interests me here, the way that the project of self-improvement comes to be placed in the context of time-management systems', 'On Not Paying', 201.
8. *Macmillan's Magazine*, *Self-Help* by S. Smiles reviewed, 1 November 1859, 402–06, 402.

9. P. Sinnema, 'Introduction', in S. Smiles, ed., *Self-Help: With Illustrations of Character, Conduct, and Perseverance* (Oxford: University Press, 2002), p. xxi.
10. P. Sinnema, 'Introduction', vii.
11. A. Briggs, 'Samuel Smiles and the Gospel of Work', in *Victorian People: A Reassessment of Persons and Themes, 1851–67* (Middlesex: Penguin, 1955), p. 126.
12. S. Smiles, *Self-Help: With Illustrations of Character, Conduct, and Perseverance* (Oxford: Oxford University Press, 2002), p. 17.
13. See C. Clausen, 'How to Join the Middle Classes: With the Help of Dr. Smiles and Mrs. Beeton', *American Scholar* 62.3 (1993), 403–18, 405; R.J. Morris, 'Samuel Smiles and the Genesis of *Self-Help*: The Retreat to a Petit Bourgeois Utopia', *The Historical Journal* 24.1 (1981), 89–109; A. Briggs, 'A Centenary Introduction', in S. Smiles *Self-Help* (London: John Murray, 1958), p. 23; A. Briggs, 'Samuel Smiles and the Gospel of Work', in *Victorian People: A Reassessment of Persons and Themes, 1851–67* (Middlesex: Penguin, 1955), p. 126.
14. It should be noted, however, that Smiles always privileges action over inaction (often interpreted as reading). Many comments in his book support this emphasis: 'It is also to be borne in mind that the experience gathered from books, though often valuable, is but of the nature of *learning*; whereas the experience gained from actual life is of the nature of *wisdom*', *Self-Help*, 271; 'We must ourselves *be* and *do*, and not rest satisfied merely with reading and meditating over what other men have been and done', *Self-Help*, 271; and 'wisdom and understanding' 'are reached through a higher kind of discipline than that of reading,—which is often but a mere passive reception of other men's thoughts', *Self-Help*, 271.
15. S. Smiles, *Self-Help*, 274.
16. S. Smiles, *Self-Help*, 271.
17. S. Smiles, *Self-Help*, 99.
18. S. Smiles, *Self-Help*, 101.
19. S. Smiles, *Self-Help*, 120.
20. S. Smiles, *Self-Help*, 205.
21. S. Smiles, *Self-Help*, 275–76.
22. S. Smiles, *Self-Help*, 276.
23. See T. Travers, 'Samuel Smiles and the Origins', 234–44, for an excellent summary of *Self-Help*'s antecedents in early self-help literature as well as etiquette books. G.L. Craik, *Pursuit of Knowledge Under Difficulties* (London: C. Knight, 1831), a book of biographies of artists, writers, and philosophers, is probably the most relevant influence here. Smiles knew many of its passages by heart.

24. R. Chartier, *The Order of Books: Readers, Authors, and Libraries in Europe Between the Fourteenth and Eighteenth Centuries*, translated by L. Cochrane (Stanford: Stanford University Press, 1994), p. 14.
25. See also *Fraser's Magazine*, 784–86.
26. Smiles's letter is quoted in *Athenaeum*, 'Our Weekly Gossip', 15 December 1960, 832–33, 832.
27. In K. Fielden, 'Samuel Smiles and Self-Help', *Victorian Studies* 12.2 (1968), 155–76, 176, he notes that Smiles's audience was always aimed at youth and his books were often given as school prizes. In addition to the areas noted below, it would be interesting to track young readers' experience with *Self-Help*.
28. *Athenaeum* (1960), 832. In his 1859 Introduction Smiles acknowledges that there 'was nothing in the slightest degree new or original' in his advice (S. Smiles, *Self-Help*, 7) and many of his reviewers were quick to agree (see *Tait's Edinburgh Magazine*, *Self-Help* by S. Smiles reviewed 27 (1860), 552–55, 554; *The Christian Examiner*, *Self-Help* by S. Smiles reviewed, Vols. 69–70, 5th series (1860), 147–48, 147; and *British Controversialist and Literary Magazinei*, *Self-Help* by S. Smiles reviewed 3 (1860), 44–49, 44).
29. S. Smiles, *Self-Help*, 7.
30. S. Smiles, *Self-Help*, 8. In his *Autobiography*, he describes his writing practice as follows: 'I proceeded at home to work up the subject [of *Self-Help*] from my old notes. I wrote in the evenings, mostly after six; sometimes alternating my occupation with a walk on Blackheath, preparing a sentence or laying out a subject, and returning home to commit the results to paper. I had no library then, but used to write with my children playing about me; I had no difficulty in concentrating my attention upon the subject in hand. While I had been a newspaper editor, I used to write with the clang of the steam-engine and printing-press in my ears; and afterwards, at the railway office, I worked amidst constant interruptions and inquiries which I was always ready to answer', *Autobiography*, 216. This passage nicely captures the relationship between writing and industrial modernity that also informs new readership practices.
31. *Peterson's Magazine*, 'Review of New Books', March 1860, 251–52, 252.
32. *British Controversialist*, 44.
33. S. Smiles, *Self-Help*, 3.
34. Interestingly, Smiles, as critics often note, plagiarized himself repeatedly in subsequent books and *Self-Help* itself was also heavily plagiarized by others. It was also expanded; Smiles marvels that the Japanese edition is a whopping 2,000 words. There was no equivalent in Japanese for self-help and its Japanese title translated as the *European Decision of Character Book*, as noted in S. Smiles, *Autobiography*, p. 230.

35. D.D. Hall, *Cultures of Print: Essays in the History of the Book* (Amherst: University of Massachusetts Press, 1996), p. 180.
36. See L. Price, *The Anthology and the Rise of the Novel: From Richardson to George Eliot* (Cambridge: Cambridge University Press, 2000), pp. 138–40, for an excellent overview of the convention of summary and excerpt.
37. It is worth noting that working-class and occasional periodicals remain the most difficult to access; they are often not digitized and are not as easily available to scholars.
38. See *The Devizes and Wiltshire Gazette, Self-Help* by S. Smiles reviewed, 29 December 1859, 1–2, 1; *Athenaeum, Self-Help* by S. Smiles reviewed, 31 December 1859, 883–85, 883; *Tait's Edinburgh Magazine*, 552; and *British Controversialist*, 46.
39. Cited in L. Price, *The Anthology*, 138.
40. The first publisher, Tickner & Fields, paid a nominal fee for publishing the book to which Smiles agreed since otherwise, given the loose copyright laws of the period, he would have received nothing.
41. Tyrell argues that the concept of self-help comes from Emerson and Channing whereas Travers argues that they 'merely reinforced Smiles' earlier beliefs', 'Samuel Smiles and the Origins', 177.
42. A. Briggs, 'A Centenary', 19.
43. For critiques, see Briggs, 'A Centenary', 19; P. Sinnema, 'Introduction', xxvi; A. Jarvis, *Samuel Smiles and the Construction of Victorian Values* (Stroud, Glos: Sutton Publishing, 1997), p. 72; and C. Clausen, 'How to Join', 404. Clausen notes that the Penguin Business Library referenced *Self-Help* as a 'Management Classic', 'How to Join', 404.
44. As A. Smiles, *Samuel Smiles and His Surroundings* (London: Robert Hale, 1956), p. 89, notes in Hungary, it was called *Smiles' Pearls*; in Italy, *To Will and To Be Able*. In Buenos Aires, it was published later with *Duty, Thrift and Character* in four volumes, the set being called *The Social Gospel*. *Revue des Deux Mondes* complained that the title was untranslatable, noted in A. Briggs, 'Samuel Smiles and the Gospel', 126.
45. S. Smiles, *Autobiography*, 224.
46. Aileen Smiles records many of these letters in her biography of her grandfather but her source is clearly the *Autobiography*. Briggs also cites from many of the letters drawing again on the *Autobiography*. He also writes: 'It would be interesting to collect a twentieth-century anthology of such testimonials, when they have become a familiar feature of the stock in trade of popular psychologists, radio speakers, and correspondence colleges. Smiles was one of the first secular writers to create a public of this kind' (Briggs, 'A Centenary', 19).
47. p. 389.
48. p. 331.

49. p. 389.
50. p. 227.
51. J. Rose 'Rereading the English Common Reader: A Preface to a History of Audiences', *Journal of the History of Ideas*, 53.1 (1992), 47–70, 54.
52. J. Rose, 'Rereading', 48.
53. J. Rose, 'Rereading', 48.
54. Smiles worked on this book for many subsequent years and it came out in several editions.
55. S. Smiles, *Lives of the Engineers*, 1st vol. (London: Murray, 1862), p. 472.
56. After *Self-Help* Smiles focuses more and more on industrial figures. He is not as interested in the artist, writer, etc.
57. The one book I have not yet discussed in relation to *Self-Help* is perhaps the book that it most clearly resembles in terms of its form: the Bible. The references to the 'gospel of self-help' are surely relevant and a study of the relationship between Bible reading and the reading of *Self-Help* demands more space than I have here. It is interesting to note, however, that the Bible is absent in the pages of *Self-Help*.

CHAPTER 3

More than a 'Book for Boys'? Sir Thomas Malory's *Le Morte Darthur* and the Victorian Girl Reader

Katie Garner

In 1817 Robert Southey speculated that if Sir Thomas Malory's *Le Morte Darthur* were to be 'modernised' and 'published as a book for boys, it could hardly fail of regaining its popularity'.¹ Writing in the introduction to one of three new editions of Malory's romance to appear between 1816 and 1817, Southey nostalgically recalled reading a 'wretchedly imperfect copy' of *Le Morte Darthur* as a 'schoolboy'.² '[T]here was no book', he wrote, 'except the Faery Queen, which I perused so often, or with such deep contentment.'³ But no appropriately modernized edition for children appeared for over 40 years. Southey's call was eventually taken up by the architect and editor James Knowles, who produced what is generally regarded as the first edition of Malory for children, *The Story of King Arthur and his Knights of the Round Table* (1862).⁴ Repeating Southey's earlier predictions, Knowles surmised in his preface that, if 'modernised or adapted for general circulation', 'boys … would probably become the

K. Garner (✉)
University of St. Andrews, St. Andrews, Scotland

© The Author(s) 2016
P.R. Rooney, A. Gasperini (eds.), *Media and Print Culture Consumption in Nineteenth-Century Britain*, New Directions in Book History, DOI 10.1057/978-1-137-58761-9_3

principal readers of the Arthur legends in a popular form'.[5] Cultivating knowledge of the Arthurian legend is now firmly a masculine responsibility and a form of patriarchal inheritance: 'The story of King Arthur will never die', writes Knowles, 'while there are English men to study and English boys to devour its tales of adventure and daring and magic and conquest.'[6] The volume was dedicated to Tennyson, whom upon receiving a copy told Knowles that his 'boys of 9 and 7 could think of little else but King Arthur and his Knights', and that he had no doubt that the book would be 'hailed with delight by numbers [of] men no less than boys'.[7]

Knowles's juvenile Malory inspired a host of similar projects, and soon Victorian boys needed to look no further than publishers' lists to see that *Le Morte Darthur* was a book for them. Sidney Lanier's earnestly titled *Boy's King Arthur: Being Sir Thomas Malory's History of King Arthur and his Knights of the Round Table. Edited for boys* (1880) was dedicated, echoing Caxton, to 'many noble and divers boys both of England and America', and his edition has proved popular ever since (it was last reproduced in a new edition in 2006).[8] Charles Henry Hanson also addressed his 1882 collection of Arthurian romances to the modern enlightened 'schoolboy', selecting, he claimed, from the 'great mass of legends' concerning Arthur those that would particularly 'captivate the imagination or excite the attention of the boy-readers of this generation'.[9] And although the 1868 modernized Globe edition of Malory claimed to provide 'an edition for ordinary readers', in the eyes of its editor, Sir Edward Strachey, the book remained 'especially for boys, from whom the chief demand for this book will always come'.[10]

Knowles, Lanier, Hanson, and Strachey all imagined their texts in the eager hands of swathes of Britain's middle- and upper-class boys, and their assumptions about the romance's juvenile readership have passed into modern criticism largely unquestioned. Writing in 1894 in the first critical study of the Arthurian legend's modern reception, M.W. MacCallum located Malory's appeal in his 'quaint and stately charm that school boy and critic can feel and respect',[11] while more recently Debra N. Mancoff has evocatively described how a Victorian 'boy who read about Galahad's first appearance in court, or Gareth's rise from kitchen boy to Round Table knight, or Lancelot's fight with a dragon could imagine himself in the role and spark his desire to emulate these figures as men when he himself attained manhood'.[12] But in 1888 Frederick Ryland, a lecturer at University College, London, offered a somewhat different assessment of Malory's reception in boys' circles:

Sir Thomas Malory's *Morte d'Arthur* is one of the many books whose fate is to be more talked about than read. Most educated men would be ashamed to own they knew nothing of it, but very few could give any account of what took place at the Chapel Perilous and in the Castle of Damsels or indicate the exact relationship between Sir Ector de Maris and Sir Galahad. The work is accessible in a cheap and readable form; but boys fight shy of it, preferring apparently the quasi-scientific romance of Jules Verne and his imitators, while girls are given over to the seductive delights of the love story. Mr Montgomerie Ranking and Mr Ernest Rhys have done something to popularise it by their volumes of selections, but the fact remains that the original is not a book with a large audience of young people.[13]

Rhys and Montgomerie Ranking were two of the latest writers to follow Knowles in preparing abridged versions of Malory suitable for a younger market, but their efforts are enlisted here only to denote their limited appeal.[14] Careful to avoid any criticism of boys' enthusiasm for adventure, Ryland nevertheless casts doubt on the existence of a large-scale interest in Malory among both boys and men; rather, it is the text of *Le Morte Darthur* that they fight against. Girls, on the other hand, are styled as altogether more selective consumers of Malory's 'love story', paradoxically both passively and passionately drawn to its 'seductive delights'. While Ryland offers little in the way of hard evidence, his assessment of readers' responses raises the intriguing suggestion that Victorian girls may have been more in love with Malory's romance than their adventure-loving brothers.

My aim is not to deny the existence of an enthusiasm for Malory among boys, but rather to emphasize the ways in which boys have demanded our attention to the exclusion of a historical corpus of girl readers whose passion for *Le Morte Darthur*, if acknowledged, was often mocked and dismissed as romantic or sentimental. Here Malory intersects with broader debates about women's reading. As Jacqueline Pearson has shown, the 'fantasy of romance' was typically gendered feminine; positioned in opposition to the masculine realism of the novel, romance-reading was denounced for its potential to 'encourage foolish idealism and unjustified paranoia' in women.[15] Pearson is referring to romance in its broadest sense as fiction involving fantastical events, but the same anxieties surround Malory's medieval romance in particular and continue into the nineteenth century. The concurrent rise of the discipline of English studies in the academy and schools also meant that, paradoxically, reading Malory, as Kate Flint remarks of women's reading more generally, could be a sign of '"inappropriate" educational ambition'.[16] Yet from the 1850s onwards, the pages of girls' magazines show young women developing an intellectual curiosity for the Arthurian myth that extends well beyond an infatuation with Tennyson's *Idylls* or the legend's female characters, such as Guinevere, Iseult, or Elaine of Astolat. Rather, it is the grail knight Sir Galahad who emerges as a suitable model for girls.

The editorial comments of Knowles and his fellow adaptors demonstrate how, as Judith L. Kellogg has put it, the 'Arthurian legend became tailored to provide privileged British schoolboys [with] the lessons they needed to become proper chivalric gentlemen', but little research has been conducted to support or deny claims for how widely and successfully Malory was received by child audiences in the Victorian period.[17] Previous studies of children's Arthuriana have tended to concentrate on the moral choices of Malory's nineteenth-century editors, intent on purging the romance of its notorious instances of incest and most of its sex and violence, or on the role of Arthurian principles and chivalric codes in the establishment of children's societies—most famously Baden-Powell's scouting and guiding organizations.[18] As Matthew Grenby has emphasized, '[g]enuine accounts of historical children's actual activities and attitudes are notoriously difficult to come by', and so a simple lack of evidence may account for the relative invisibility of Malory's juvenile readers.[19] Yet the full extent of children's engagement with Malory has for a long time been kept out of view by a methodological preference for book-length editions of his romance over versions that have appeared in other forms of print media. The succession of Victorian adaptations of Malory for children by male editors offer a ready foundation of material upon which to plot the development and increasing popularity of *Le Morte Darthur* as a children's text, but this narrative alters when we consider the more scattered but no less influential presence of Arthurian and Malorian content in periodicals aimed at younger readers, in which the interest of girls as well as boys in the legend is registered and recognized. Using a range of evidence from readers' queries, essay competitions, and book club reading recommendations in the pages of girls' magazines, as well as examples from fiction, letters, and diaries, this chapter uncovers a small portion of Malory's girl readers to suggest that, despite the persistent marketing of male editors, *Le Morte Darthur* in the nineteenth century was not just for boys.

Malory's Juvenile Readers

By 1900, Knowles's *The Story of King Arthur and his Knights* had passed into eight editions, a fact that seems to offer firm proof of the popularity of his text among juvenile readers. Contemporary surveys of juvenile reading habits, however, can help to set such success in context. In the preface to his adaptation, Knowles expressed his ambition that Malory would now find a place in 'boys' libraries anywhere beside "Robinson Crusoe" and "The Arabian Nights"'.[20] Edward Salmon's 1886 survey of children's reading preferences suggests that, by the 1880s at least, Knowles's wish for his volume was still a fantasy. Knowles was right about which other books boys liked best; on the basis of responses from 'just over two thousand' boys and girls between 11 and 19, Salmon revealed that *Robinson Crusoe* topped the list of boys' favourite prose works, and *The Arabian Nights* also made the top ten.[21] Malory, however, failed to enter Salmon's lists. On this evidence, Ryland's assessment that Malory was 'not a book with a large audience of young people' would seem accurate.

Le Morte Darthur did not feature in Salmon's list of girls' favourite prose works either, but their list of favourite poetry included an Arthurian work in the form of Tennyson's *Idylls of the King* (ranked eighth), while only 'The Charge of the Light Brigade' made it onto the equivalent list for boys.[22] Again Ryland's comments are suggestive in pointing towards a genuine and widespread appreciation for Tennyson's Arthurian poetry in girls' circles. A passion for Tennyson's Arthurian poetry does not automatically equate to an interest in Malory, of course, but could function as a stepping stone to the medieval romance. In Dinah Mulock Craik's 1884 travelogue, *An Unsentimental Journey Through Cornwall*, the narrator and her two young female companions, 'one just entered upon her teens, the other in her twenties', take two books with them for their holiday in 'King Arthur's Land' to occupy them on rainy days: 'a one-volume Tennyson, all complete, and a 'Morte d'Arthur'—Sir Thomas Malory's'.[23] A similar pairing is also reflected in fictional portraits of young women readers: 18-year-old Christabel Courtenay, the Cornish protagonist of Mary Elizabeth Braddon's *Mount Royal* (1882), knows 'just enough of Sir Thomas Mallory's [sic] prose to give substance to the Laureate's poetic shadows'.[24] Contrary to Knowles's vision of a Malory passed from boys to men, it was often mothers who first introduced their children to his romance. Tennyson may have conveyed his sons' enjoyment of Malory to Knowles, but it was Emily Tennyson who read 'Mr Knowles's Arthurian stories' to

Hallam and Lionel in October 1861; earlier that year she also read them some of 'Sir Gareth', apparently from Malory's original.[25] Dinah Mulock Craik's adopted daughter Dorothy was 11 when her mother recorded reading her 'endless tales out of Morte D'Arthur—Elaine—& Arthur—& Launcelot'.[26] Malory also made it onto girls' reading lists. 'Ten Books' (1886), a short article published in Charlotte Yonge's *Monthly Packet of Evening Readings for Members of the English Church*, offered an instructive list of books that might constitute a girl's 'life friends'. These included Ruskin's *Modern Painters*, Carlyle's *The French Revolution*, Eliot's *The Mill on the Floss*, Brontë's *Shirley*, and *Le Morte Darthur*, valued because it 'contains the noblest of allegories': 'the "Quest of the Sangrael"—told with great beauty and touching simplicity'.[27] And in 1893 Una De Grey, a young débutante, described a visit to Edward Burne-Jones's latest exhibition where her enjoyment of his Arthurian paintings was only tempered by her regret at 'having left dear Malory's *Morte d'Arthur* in the country': 'it is so difficult to make a good choice of one's pet books to bring to London', she complained.[28] By the close of the century, female educationalists were recommending that 'a copy of Malory's "King Arthur" should find a place in every school library' for 'there will always be found one or two girls by whom the loveliness of the story and language will be recognised'.[29]

Boys' and girls' magazines in circulation from the middle of the nineteenth century also confirm that the juvenile readership for Malory's text was not as uniform as Knowles and his successors thought. From the 1860s onwards Arthurian material featured regularly in boys' magazines such as *Boys of England* and the *Boy's Own Magazine*, often commanding front page prominence.[30] But the legend also had a strong presence in *Young Folks*, in which Arthurian stories were marketed more democratically as formative reading 'for boys and girls'.[31] One *Young Folks* article promoting *Le Morte Darthur* as 'a good story-book' begins by describing it in familiar terms as 'one of the most beautiful story-books for boys ever written', but ends by acknowledging its attractions for a wider audience of 'young people':

> As a book for young people it is admirable. The adventures of Sir Tor, of Sir Tristram, of Sir Lancelot, these afford narratives which a boy who is fond of reading can absolutely revel in. Then the feminine characters of the book, Queen Guenevere, Elaine, Lynette, the beautiful Isolt, and the wicked Morgan la Fay, what girl can read of them without interest?[32]

Gendered assumptions about what kind of content would most appeal to boys and girls still prevail, but the magazine's full list of Malory's female characters demonstrates a commitment to drawing its girl readers to his romance. Leading magazines for girls also ran a regular assortment of Arthurian articles. *The Girl's Own Paper* (1880–1956), which Sally Mitchell notes attracted a wide readership from servant girls to the educated daughters of academics, offered miscellaneous Arthurian articles from its inception, ranging from travel pieces recording 'A Visit to King Arthur's Castle', to literary criticism profiling 'The Women of the "Idylls of the King"'.[33] Contributions also ventured beyond Tennyson and Arthurian tourism to more particular engagements with Malory in the magazine's fiction. In the Hampshire writer Sarah Doudney's 'A Long Lane with a Turning', serialized in the *Girl's Own Paper* between April and September 1883, the heroine, Mary, is a keen reader of Malory's *Morte Darthur*. The book becomes a point of connection between Mary and her lover, Arthur, who observes her copy of the romance lying open at King Arthur's dying speech to Bedivere, famously beginning with his instruction to 'Comfort thyself'.[34] A wild flower Mary has collected from the garden marks the passage, and when Mary and Arthur are united at the climax of the story, Malory's book reappears between them, the same 'little dried flower ... between its pages'.[35] Doudney's story rather straight-forwardly aligns her modern-day Arthur with the medieval king of romance, but the addition of the flower signals that Malory's book belongs firmly to Mary. Through a variety of content, from essays to romantic fiction, the *Girl's Own Paper* accepted that Malory and the Arthurian legend might be a possible topic of interest for its readers.

With a circulation of 250,000 at its peak, readers of *The Girl's Own Paper* responded enthusiastically to the magazine's Arthurian offerings and took the opportunity to ask questions about the legend in the regular correspondence columns.[36] Letters were received from 'Pomona' and 'A Highland Lassie' requesting information about Sir Galahad, while 'Rose England' received answers to enquiries about 'The Lady of Shalott', Elaine, and Guinevere. A curious 'Yorkshire Lass' was provided with the dates of Arthur's supposed reign.[37] 'Moss Rose' and 'Laura' wrote with questions about the 'San Grail', and the editor recommended consulting Chrétien de Troyes's 'Percival'.[38] All levels of enquiry were encouraged: when 'Ruby' asked for help with the pronunciation of Arthurian names, the magazine provided phonetic renderings of Guinevere, Caerleon, Ettare, and Gawain.[39] Yet as Stephen Colclough reminds us, we should be wary of taking such activity as representative of all readers, and as Beth Rodgers has demonstrated, despite its inclusive marketing, the competitions and opportunities for readerly engagement in the *Girl's Own Paper* could result in the exclusion of some girls through race or class.[40] The class of readers whose letters were printed in the magazine is difficult to ascertain, but their identification with a variety of geographical locations, ranging from the Highlands to Yorkshire and Cornwall, suggests that the Arthurian legend entranced a wide compass of British girls.

A similar level of interest can be seen in *Atalanta* (1887–98), a new incarnation of *Every Girl's Magazine* (1877–88), and the main competitor to *The Girl's Own Paper*. In 1897 the magazine ran a version of 'The Tale of Balin and Balan, from Sir Thomas Malory's *Le Morte D'Arthur*', abridged and modernized by Maud Venables Vernon and lavishly illustrated by Amor Fenn.[41] Edited by the popular children's author L.T. Meade, *Atalanta* placed a strong emphasis on literary knowledge for self-improvement: a regular feature of the magazine was the 'Atalanta Scholarship and Reading Union', which set essay competitions and literary quizzes each month. In April 1889, the essay competition asked readers to 'give an outline of the Arthurian legend as found in Tennyson's *Idylls of the King*'.[42] Monthly 'Search Questions in English Literature' challenged readers to identify the source of quoted passages of prose and verse or identify literary characters; these frequently included extracts from Tennyson's *Idylls of the King*, but also asked readers detailed questions about the Arthurian myth, and assumed a knowledge of Malory. One asked readers to identify Hector's famous eulogy on Lancelot's death from 'The Death of Arthur', which celebrates Lancelot as the 'head of all Christian knights', while another asked 'Who was the unknown knight of the Black Shield?' (The two possible answers were revealed the following month: Sir Tristram from Malory's *Morte Darthur*, or Richard I from *Ivanhoe*.)[43] Demanding knowledge of Malory as well as Jane Austen, Byron, Keats, Shakespeare and Spenser, the selection of competition questions in *Atalanta* reveal an expectation that any girl serious about studying English literature would be familiar with *Le Morte Darthur*.

GIRLS, GALAHAD, AND THE *MONTHLY PACKET*

Both *Atalanta* and the *Girl's Own Paper* demonstrate how Arthurian matters had become a firm fixture in girls' realms by the 1880s, but another, much older periodical for girls had already been promoting

Arthurian material for some time. Releasing its first issue in 1851, the *Monthly Packet of Evening Readings for the Younger Members of Church of England* (1851–99) was the creation of Charlotte Yonge, whose interest in Arthurian romance is evident in her immensely popular novel *The Heir of Redclyffe* (1853) and her Arthurian-orientated adaptation of the popular fairy tale of Tom Thumb, *The History of Sir Thomas Thumb* (1855). In *The Heir of Redclyffe*, a parlour game requiring the participants to set down 'his or her favourite character in history and fiction' gives rise to a debate about the merits of *Le Morte Darthur* led by Yonge's hero, Guy Morville, after he chooses 'Sir Galahad'. At first shocked that his cousin Charles has not heard of the book, Guy then staunchly defends Malory's text against sceptical attacks from his older and more conservative cousin, Philip:

> "Sir how much?" exclaimed Charles.
> "Don't you know him?" said Guy. "Sir Galahad—the Knight of the Siege Perilous—who won the Saint Greal."
> "What language is that?" said Charles.
> "What! Don't you know the Morte D'Arthur? I thought everyone did! Don't you, Philip?"
> "I once looked into it. It is very curious, in classical English; but it is a book that no one could read through."
> "Oh!" cried Guy, indignantly; then, "but you only looked into it. If you had lived with its two fat volumes, you could not help delighting in it. It was my boating-book for at least three summers."
> "That accounts for it," said Philip; "a book so studied in boyhood acquires a charm apart from its actual merits."[44]

Guy and Philip debate the merits of Malory in the company of Charles's sisters and other female visitors, but the girls play no part in the conversation, and Philip's reference to Malory as 'a book so studied in boyhood' seems to align Yonge with the promotion of his romance for masculine improvement in a manner akin to Knowles and his followers.

Yet at the same time that she was writing *The Heir of Redclyffe*, Yonge was promoting Malory and particularly the legend of Sir Galahad in *The Monthly Packet*, her magazine aimed at 'girls' between the ages of 15 and 25. From the beginning Yonge contributed much of the magazine's content, including a regular feature entitled 'Conversations on the Catechism' which opened the magazine for the first ten years of its long run. Consisting of a series of didactic dialogues between two girls, Audrey and Helena, and their godmother, the rather prim if deeply pious Miss Ormesden, Yonge soon took the opportunity to introduce Malory into the conversation. As part of a larger discussion of the temptations of the flesh and the importance of practising self-restraint, Miss Ormesden directs the girls' attention to Lancelot's experience on the Grail quest, and describes his partial vision of the grail in a dream. Modelling an allegorical interpretation of the episode for the reader, Miss Ormesden tells Audrey and Helena that Lancelot's state signifies the 'dull heavy sleepy trance, that indulgence of the body brings over us, obscuring our soul so as to make it unable to discern or profit by the holy things around us'.[45] When Audrey asks if any knight achieved the San Grail, Miss Ormesden gives a brief summary of Galahad's success. All this took place in Yonge's magazine two years before the publication of *The Heir of Redclyffe*. The conversation between Miss Ormesden and her goddaughters indicates Yonge's firm belief in *Le Morte Darthur* as a suitable spiritual instruction book for Anglican young ladies, as well as an entertaining romance fit to interest the fictional Audrey and the *Packet*'s real-life readers.

Miss Ormesden's praise for Galahad as the 'most pure and blameless of all the Knights of the Round Table' anticipated the subject of the magazine's first Arthurian serialization, a ten-part version of 'The Legend of Sir Galahad' (July 1852–July 1853), which began the following year.[46] In the magazine's preface to the story Sir Galahad is lauded as a model for good behaviour:

> You shall hear of the deeds of Sir Galahad, the best knight and the most virtuous of all of the fellowship of the knights of the great King Arthur. Sir Launcelot was not so brave as he; Sir Percival not so holy. He was the pattern of all true knights in all times; and if in these ages we do not wear armour, nor ride in search of noble chances, there are always enemies within us and without, who would fain spoil our purity, and harm our holy Church, and these foes we must be always ready to fight and overthrow, after the example of Sir Galahad.[47]

In the *Monthly Packet* the appeal of Malory's text is not limited to his queenly women; rather, girls are invited to identify with the knights and quests at its centre. It is Galahad's spiritual qualities, and above all his purity, that the young lady readers of the *Packet* are invited to model in their own lives, following a 'pattern' neither retiring nor domestic:

Yonge's extended metaphor of knightly adventure places the modern girl firmly in the centre of the 'fight'. The *Monthly Packet*'s religious agenda is seldom far from view, and in contextualizing Galahad's adventures among the moral and religious challenges posed to the modern girl, the magazine offered young women an unusually active example to emulate. Similar sentiments were expressed towards the end of the century in a fictional epistolary exchange in the *Girl's Own Paper* between an older, advisory woman, Mrs. Winterbourne, and Mona Smith, a young girl looking for a purpose in life. After recommending that Mona apply herself to helping the poor and improving her skills in 'music, painting, literature, art of any kind', Mrs. Winterbourne adds:

> Side by side with this self-culture do strive, my dear girl, to do the homely tasks of every day as in God's sight. Remember that no character can be great or noble that cannot efface self in some degree for the sake of others. We must all "lose ourselves to save ourselves" like Sir Galahad. I think girls in the present day are a little bit apt to forget this.[48]

Like Miss Ormesden, Mrs. Winterbourne evokes Galahad to promote humility and selflessness alongside self-improvement. Galahad's spiritual quest for the grail and Christ-like sacrifice grant him a place in didactic literature for girls, while, according to Mancoff, for boys, his attractiveness as a model hero lay in more secular qualities: 'the unlimited scope of adolescent potential, and his boundless and unquestioning determination— motivated by youthful energy and sheer naiveté'.[49] Galahad's chastity also lent him a certain degree of androgyny, and his conduct could therefore be more easily aligned with the expectations for girls in society than the careers of Sir Lancelot or Sir Tristram, both renowned for their illicit love affairs as well as their martial prowess.

Creating a stand-alone serialization of Galahad's quest for the *Monthly Packet* required some careful handling of the behaviour of other knights involved in his story. 'The Legend of Sir Galahad' in the *Monthly Packet* is a composite of selections from Malory's 'The Tale of Sir Tristram' and 'The Noble Tale of the Sangreal', rendered into modern English. 'Alas!' becomes 'Woe is me!'; 'anon', 'by-and-by'; 'wit you well', 'understand'; and any expressions considered blasphemous (such as 'Ah, Jesu!') are omitted. Other changes are more subtle. Knights and ladies are given manners thought to be more appropriate for the girl reader. Sir Bors, rather than bluntly telling King Pelles he will stay overnight at his castle, as he does in Malory ('I woll lye in thys castell thys nyght'), more politely assures the king he will only stay as his guest 'if you please'.[50] Similarly, Elaine of Corbenic, in love with Lancelot and the mother of Galahad, 'weeps' compassionately when Sir Bors tells her that Lancelot is imprisoned by Morgan le Fay, whereas in Malory she displays no similar sentimental reaction to the news.[51]

There is also some censorship, especially surrounding the portrayal of sexual relations and adultery that would become increasingly problematic for Malory's Victorian adaptors and editors.[52] As Sir Edward Strachey would do in his popular Globe edition of the following decade, the *Monthly Packet* omits the full description of how Lancelot was tricked into sleeping with Elaine by an enchantment arranged by Dame Brisen, in which she is made to take Guinevere's form.[53] This makes for some decreased causality in Malory's careful plotting: in Yonge's magazine, the subsequent onset of Lancelot's madness seems baffling rather than a logical—if extreme—reaction to being tricked into sleeping with Elaine a second time.[54] This represents only a light deletion, however, in comparison to Knowles' omission of Lancelot's relationship with Elaine of Corbenic altogether in his version for boys of 1862, so that Galahad appears in the text for the first time when he gains the Siege Perilous.[55] As Yuri Fura has shown, Strachey in his later edition tended to cut 'episodes not to the credit of the "noble" Lancelot', and in this he was following Knowles's earlier example.[56] Cleaning up Malory's text became common practice: according to Marylyn Parins, between 1858 and 1889 'every edition published was either abridged or expurgated or both'.[57] The girl readers of the Monthly Packet received an account only lightly retouched in comparison; as they had already been told that the knight to take as their model was Galahad, not 'Sir Lancelot', who 'was not so brave as [Galahad]', Lancelot's less honourable activities had an important comparative role to play in bringing Galahad's superiority to the fore.[58] Lancelot's shortcomings had also been impressed on readers of the *Packet* via the earlier discussion of his failure to see the grail in 'Conversations on the Catechism'. The *Monthly Packet's* consistent promotion of what Kristine Moruzi calls an 'ideal of religious girlhood' meant that the magazine offered a relatively accurate rendering of Malory's treatment of the Grail quest in which Lancelot's love affair with Elaine was permitted to remain, even if the exact details were eclipsed. In the *Monthly Packet's* allegorical interpretation of Malory's 'half-romantic, half-religious' tale, no matter how noble Lancelot might be it was the virtuous and sacrificial Galahad who would always claim the title of 'best knight'.[59]

After seven instalments the series ended abruptly without notice in July 1853, only a few pages into Malory's 'Tale of the Sangreal' and leaving Galahad tantalizingly poised for greatness after gaining the Siege Perilous. Answering a query from a particularly keen reader, Yonge explained that 'Sir Galahad has not been forgotten, but other vocations have prevented his compiler from continuing his adventures'.[60] This was not an editorial front: although a likely candidate for authorship, Yonge does not seem to have been behind the Galahad series. 'The chapters in the Packet were offered me as a way of putting before people the good part without that which is objectionable', she told her friend Elizabeth Roberts (adding that in her opinion 'they ought to have been more condensed').[61] But as Yonge's contributors were 'almost invariably women', 'The Legend of Sir Galahad' nevertheless likely represents the earliest adaptation of Malory by a female hand, and predates Knowles's adaptation for younger readers by over a decade.[62] The interest it generated among readers, both in the public pages of the magazine and in Yonge's private correspondence, shows that her audience enjoyed the Malorian serial, and were eager for more.

Owing to the strong presence of informative Arthurian articles and extracts in the *Monthly Packet* from its beginning, the queries it received from readers about the legend tended to be more advanced than those seeking advice on Arthurian matters from the *Girl's Own Paper*. Already equipped with a cursory knowledge of the legend, readers of the *Packet* are less fixated on the legend's particular characters and more concerned with how to get hold of a complete copy of Malory. Despite the appearance of Thomas Wright's edition in 1858 and Strachey's Globe edition ten years later, practical advice about how to access Arthurian texts and scholarship remains a frequent topic of enquiry, an anxiety that seems to have arisen from the fact that girls had been overlooked in the marketing of so many of the modernized editions of Malory. Children's and young people's reading habits are often largely structured by their parents, and with reviews of Lanier's, Knowles's, Hanson's and Strachey's texts reinforcing the romance as ideal reading for boys, girls were far less likely to have a copy gifted to them by an educating relative. As a result, girls take up a more proactive role in magazines, looking to track down Arthurian texts and scholarship on their own accounts. In December 1862, Yonge told a correspondent with the appropriately chivalric pseudonym of 'Una' that 'Southey's Morte D'Arthur is the most easily accessible of the old English Romances', and recommended she start with the French medievalist Theodore Claude Henri Hersert de la Villermarqué's scholarship on the legend.[63] Again in May 1865, Yonge explained to 'K. L.' that 'the *Morte D'arthur* is an old book by Sir Thomas Mallory, who wrote in the fifteenth century'.[64] Almost 20 years later, readers were still writing in about Malory, but Yonge was no longer recommending Southey, by now 'out of print', but suggesting readers contact second-hand booksellers.[65] By the 1890s, the magazine was able to confidently recommend Strachey's Globe edition, priced at an affordable 3s 6d, but as this was first published in 1868, there seems to have been a considerable lag-time during which even Yonge was reluctant to recommend any of the more recent new editions.[66] Part of this reluctance may have stemmed from the magazine's desire to present its own version of Malory, in the form of 'a prose edition, taken verbatim from that "well of English" and "undefiled" in matter as well as in choice of language', and more suitable for her young female readers than Thomas Wright's 1858 edition of Malory.[67] True to its promise, in March 1859 the magazine introduced another long-running series entitled 'King Arthur and His Knights, with the Quest of the Sancgrael', by Ellen J. Millington, which mixed extracts from Malory with plot summaries taken from a wide range of medieval writers and chroniclers, including Geoffrey of Monmouth, Chrétien de Troyes, and William of Malmesbury.[68]

Active for almost 50 years, the *Monthly Packet* offered a platform for the development of women's interests in Arthur—from girlhood to womanhood—throughout the second half of the nineteenth century. Though the magazine began with an explicit audience of 'young girls, or maidens, or young ladies', as Moruzi has pointed out, the removal of 'Younger' from the magazine's title in 1866 suggests that Yonge soon realized she was attracting a much broader readership.[69] Arthurian articles continued to feature in the *Packet*'s pages right up to its final years, by which time many of its readers were accomplished medievalists. In 1896, with Christabel Coleridge now acting as editor, the magazine announced its 'Variety Subject' for the month: short essays were invited on the topic of 'The Grail Legend: Its Origin and Treatment in Literature'.[70] When the results were published in July, the winner was revealed as one 'Miss Weston' of Landsdowne Road, Bournemouth. This was none other than

Jessie Weston, folklorist and Arthurian enthusiast, and the future author of *From Ritual to Romance* (1920). When she won the *Packet* competition, Weston had already published a translation of Wolfram von Eschenbach's *Parzival* (1894), and, at 46, was far from being one of the magazine's girl readers, but her appearance in the *Packet* nevertheless signals the important role the magazine played in fostering a new generation of Arthuriennes.

At the same time, the assumption that girls were only interested in Tennyson's Arthurian poetry and not serious consumers of Malory's story proved remarkably pervasive. Almost 30 years after Ryland's comments on girls' infatuation with the legend's 'love story' alone, a report by William Barry for *The Bookman* divided young people's Arthurian interest along similar and by now familiar lines. 'Our brave English boys have dipped into Sir Thomas Malory's fighting epic of the "Morte Darthur"', wrote Barry, while 'many young women, sentimentally disposed—the Elaines of our modern school-training—have taken to themselves passages learnt by heart from Tennyson's "Idylls"'.[71] Boys, it was still assumed, could cope with the *Morte*'s violent content and what Charles Henry Hanson termed his 'quaint' prose style, but girls would always prefer the more refined rhythms of contemporary Arthurian poetry.[72] The presiding attitude towards young women interested in Arthur remains one of mockery as their love for the text is easily dismissed as sentimental fanaticism. Throughout the nineteenth century and beyond there remained an insidious and continued sense that women were not supposed to have a serious interest in the legend or in Malory. In 1912 T.S. Eliot expressed his dislike for Tennyson's *Idylls of the King*, complaining that Tennyson had 'adapted this great epic material—in Malory's handling hearty, outspoken and magnificent—to suitable reading for a girls' school.'[73] Eliot's expression of his distaste hinges on the assumption that Malory's *Morte Darthur* in its original middle English has no place in all-female environments, for in his opinion its magnificence far outstrips the confines of girls' smaller, and less magnificent, worlds. Yet the remains of readerly evidence preserved in periodicals and magazines would suggest that many Victorian girls took as keen an interest in Malory's work as their brothers, attracted by his combination of fantasy and spirituality and by the grail quest in particular. While Lanier's *The Boy's King Arthur* remains in print, however, the post-medieval reception of Malory continues to be a story of patriarchal inheritance. Now, as in the nineteenth century, many of Malory's girl readers remain in the shadows.

Notes

1. Robert Southey, 'Preface' to Sir Thomas Malory, *The Byrth, Lyf, and Actes of Kyng Arthur; of his noble knyghtes of the rounde table, theyr merveyllous enquestes and adventures [...] With an Introduction and Notes by Robert Southey, Esq.*, [edited by William Upcott], 2 vols. (London: Longman, Hurst, Rees, Orme, and Brown, 1817), Vol. 1, pp. i–lxiii (p. xxviii).
2. Southey, 'Preface', p. xxviii.
3. Southey, 'Preface', p. xxviii.
4. See Andrew Lynch, '*Le Morte Darthur* for Children: Malory's Third Tradition', in Barbara Tepa Lupack, ed., *Adapting the Arthurian Legends for Children: Essays on Arthurian Juvenilia* (Basingstoke: Palgrave Macmillan, 2004), pp. 1–34 (p. 3).
5. James Knowles [as J.T.K.], 'Preface' to *The Story of King Arthur and His Knights of the Round Table* (London: Griffith and Farran, 1862), pp. i–iii (pp. i–ii).
6. Knowles, 'Preface', p. i.
7. Alfred Tennyson to James Thomas Knowles, 10 December 1861 in *The Letters of Alfred Lord Tennyson*, edited by Cecil Y. Lang and Edgar F. Shannon, Jr., 3 vols. (Cambridge, MA: University of Harvard Press, 1987), Vol. 2, p. 288.
8. Sidney Lanier, 'Introduction' to *The Boy's King Arthur: Being Sir Thomas Malory's History of King Arthur and His Knights of the Round Table, Edited for Boys with an Introduction by Sidney Lanier* (New York: Charles Scrivener's Sons, 1881), pp. iii–xxiii (p. xx).
9. Charles Henry Hanson, 'Preface' to *Stories of the Days of King Arthur*, ill. Gustave Doré (London: T. Nelson and Sons, 1882), pp. v–vi (pp. vi, v).
10. Sir Edward Strachey, 'Preface' to Sir Thomas Malory, *Morte Darthur. Sir Thomas Malory's Book of King Arthur and his Noble Knights of the Round Table. The Original Edition of Caxton Revised for Modern Use* (London: Macmillan and Co., 1868), pp. vii–xxxvii (p. xvii).
11. M.W. MacCallum, *Tennyson's Idylls of the King and Arthurian Story from the XVIth Century* (Glasgow: James Maclehose and Sons, 1894), p. 90.
12. Debra N. Mancoff, *The Return of King Arthur: The Legend through Victorian Eyes* (London: Pavilion, 1995), p. 111.
13. Frederick Ryland, 'The Morte D'arthur', *The English Illustrated Magazine* 61 (October 1888), 55–64 (55).
14. Ernest Rhys, *Malory's History of King Arthur and the Quest of the Holy Grail* (London: Walter Scott, 1886); Boyd Montgomerie Ranking, *La Mort D'Arthur: The Old Prose Stories whence the "Idylls of the King" have been taken by Alfred Tennyson* (London: J. C. Hotten, 1870).

15. Jacqueline Pearson, *Women's Reading in Britain, 1750–1835: A Dangerous Recreation* (Cambridge: Cambridge University Press, 1999), p. 199.
16. Kate Flint, *The Woman Reader, 1837–1914* (Cambridge: Cambridge University Press, 1993), p. 11.
17. Judith L. Kellogg, 'Introduction', *Arthuriana*, Special issue: Essays on the Arthurian Tradition in Children's Literature 13.2 (2003), 1–8 (3).
18. See Jane L. Curry, 'Children's Reading and the Arthurian Tales', in Valerie M. Lagorio and Mildred Leake Day, eds., *King Arthur Through the Ages* (New York and London: Garland, 1990), Vol. 2, pp. 149–64; Lynch, '*Le Morte Darthur* for Children'; Anna Caughey, 'Once and Future Arthurs: Arthurian Literature for Children', in Carolyne Larrington and Diane Purkiss, eds., *Magical Tales: Myth, Legend and Enchantment in Children's Books* (Oxford: Bodleian Library, 2013), pp. 113–51; Velma Bourgeois Richmond, 'King Arthur and His Knights for Edwardian Children', *Arthuriana* 23.3 (2013), 55–78.
19. M.O. Grenby, *The Child Reader, 1700–1814* (Cambridge: Cambridge University Press, 2000), p. 11.
20. Knowles, 'Preface', p. iii.
21. Edward Salmon, *Juvenile Literature As It Is* (London: Henry J. Drane, 1888). *Robinson Crusoe* received 43 votes; *The Arabian Nights* ranked eighth with 10 votes. The results of Salmon's survey were first published in two earlier articles: 'What Boys Read', *Fortnightly Review* NS 39 (1886), 248–59; 'What Girls Read', *Nineteenth Century* 20 (1886), 515–29.
22. Salmon, *Juvenile Literature As It Is*, pp. 16, 24.
23. Dinah Mulock Craik, *An Unsentimental Journey Through Cornwall* (London: Macmillan and Co., 1884), pp. 2, 54.
24. Mary Elizabeth Braddon, *Mount Royal: A Novel*, 3 vols. (London: John and Robert Maxwell, 1882), Vol. 1, p. 81.
25. Emily Tennyson, entry for 28 October 1861, *Lady Tennyson's Journal*, edited by James O. Hoge (Charlottesville: University Press of Virginia, 1981), p. 164; entry for 19 February 1861, p. 154.
26. Dinah Mulock Craik, diary entry for 20 April 1880, handwritten manuscript. Dinah Mulock Craik Collection; container 3.4. Harry Ransom Center, University of Texas.
27. 'Ten Books', *Monthly Packet* 66 (1 June 1886), 594–95.
28. Una De Grey, 'Impressions of a Débutante', *Atalanta* 67 (1 April 1893), 526–27.
29. Frances H. Low, 'Books for Schoolgirls', *Hearth and Home* 221 (8 August 1895), 464.
30. See the front page of *The Boy's Standard* 580 (18 June 1892), which depicts Merlin announcing Arthur as king.

31. M.K. Dallas, 'The Story of Excalibar', *Young Folks* 565 (1 October 1881), 114.
32. 'A Good Story-Book', *Young Folks' Paper* 774 (3 October 1885), 214–15.
33. Sally Mitchell, 'Girls' Culture: At Work', in Claudia Nelson and Lynne Vallone, eds., *The Girl's Own: Cultural Histories of the Anglo-American Girl (1830–1915)* (Athens: University of Georgia Press, 1994), pp. 243–58 (p. 246). Edith Orsmond Payne, 'The Women of the "Idylls of the King"', *Girl's Own Paper* 674 (26 November 1892), 143–44; 'A Cornish Sister' (aged 16), 'A Visit to King Arthur's Castle', *Girl's Own Paper* 70 (30 April 1881), 496; J.M.B., 'The Legend of the Grail', *Girl's Own Paper* 653 (2 July 1892), 638–89.
34. See Sir Thomas Malory, *Le Morte Darthur*, edited by Stephen H.A. Shepherd (New York and London: W. W. Norton, 2004), p. 668.
35. Sarah Doudney, 'A Long Lane with a Turning', *Girl's Own Paper* 193 (8 September 1883), 769–70 (770).
36. Terri Doughty, '*Girl's Own Paper*', *Dictionary of Nineteenth-Century Journalism in Great Britain and Ireland*, Gen. eds. Laurel Brake and Marysa Demoor (London: Academic Press, 2009), p. 249.
37. 'Answers to Correspondents', *Girl's Own Paper* 181 (16 June 1883), 591; 'Answers to Correspondents', 259 (13 December 1884), 174.
38. 'Answers to Correspondents', *Girl's Own Paper* 19 (8 May 1880), 304; 'Answers to Correspondents', 732 (6 January 1894), 224.
39. 'Answers to Correspondents', *Girl's Own Paper* 69 (23 April 1881), 479.
40. Stephen Colclough, *Consuming Texts: Readers and Reading Communities, 1675–1870* (Basingstoke: Palgrave, 2007), p. 166. Beth Rodgers, 'Competing Girlhoods: Competition, Community and Reader Contribution in *The Girl's Own Paper* and *The Girl's Realm*', *Victorian Periodicals Review* 45.3 (2012), 277–300.
41. Maud Venables Vernon, 'The Tale of Balin and Balan, from Sir Thomas Malory's *Morte D'Arthur*', *Atalanta* (1 March 1897), 343–48.
42. '*Atalanta* Scholarship and Reading Union: Scholarship Competition Questions', *Atalanta* 7 (1 April 1889), 493.
43. 'Search Passages in English Literature', *Atalanta* 9 (1 June 1888), 532. 'Search Questions in English Literature', *Atalanta* 29 (1 February 1890), 334. 'Answers to Search Questions (February)', *Atalanta* 30 (1 March 1890), 396.
44. Charlotte Mary Yonge, *The Heir of Redclyffe*, 2 vols. (Leipzig: Bernhard Tauchnitz, 1855), Vol. 1, pp. 169–70.
45. [Yonge], 'Conversations on the Catechism: The Flesh', *Monthly Packet* 5 (1 May 1851), 328–43 (339–40).
46. 'Conversations on the Catechism', 340.
47. 'The Legend of Sir Galahad' [Part 1], *Monthly Packet* 19 (1 July 1852), 49–53 (49).

48. Lily Watson, 'A Modern Mistake' [Chapter 2], *Girl's Own Paper* 767 (8 September 1894), 778–79 (779).
49. Mancoff, *The Return of King Arthur*, p. 123.
50. 'The Legend of Sir Galahad' [Part 1], *Monthly Packet* 19 (1 July 1852), 49–53 (52); *Le Morte Darthur*, edited by Shepherd, p. 467.
51. 'The Legend of Sir Galahad' [Part 1], 51; *Le Morte Darthur*, edited by Shepherd, p. 467.
52. For accounts of censorship in later nineteenth-century adaptations of Malory, see Lynch, '*Le Morte Darthur* for Children', pp. 16–17, and Yuri Fuwa, 'The Globe Edition of Malory as Bowdlerised Text in the Victorian Age', Studies in English Literature (Japan), English Language No. (1984), 3–17.
53. For Strachey's editorial methods see Fuwa, 'The Globe Edition of Malory', 12–13.
54. See 'The Legend of Sir Galahad' [Part 2], *Monthly Packet* 24 (1 December 1852), 457–62 (p. 458).
55. See Knowles, *The Story of King Arthur and His Knights*, p. 238.
56. Fuwa, 'The Globe Edition of Malory', 13.
57. Marylyn Parins, 'Introduction' to *Sir Thomas Malory: The Critical Heritage*, edited by Parins (London: Routledge, 1987), p. 16.
58. 'The Legend of Sir Galahad' [Part 1], 49.
59. Kristine Moruzi, '"Never Read Anything that Can at All Unsettle Your Religious Faith": Reading and Writing in the *Monthly Packet*', *Women's Writing* 17.2 (2010), 288–304 (288). 'The Legend of Sir Galahad' [Part 2], 462.
60. 'Notices to Correspondents', *Monthly Packet* 97 (1 January 1859), 112.
61. Yonge to Elizabeth Roberts, 17 March 1853. *The Letters of Charlotte Mary Yonge (1823–1901)*, eds. Charlotte Mitchell, Ellen Jordan, and Helen Schinske, http://www.yongeletters.com/3008/to-elizabeth-roberts-25
62. June Sturrock, 'Establishing Identity: Editorial Correspondence from the Early Years of *The Monthly Packet*', *Victorian Periodicals Review* 39.3 (2006), 266–79 (268).
63. 'Notices to Correspondents', *Monthly Packet* 144 (1 December 1862), 668.
64. 'Notices to Correspondents', *Monthly Packet* 173 (1 May 1865), 559.
65. 'Notices to Correspondents', *Monthly Packet* 45 (Second Series) (1 September 1884), 298.
66. 'Third Shelf. Odds and Ends. Queries', *Monthly Packet* 534 (1 August 1895), 242. See a similar request by Miss Norah Powys, who is looking for an account of the Holy Grail ('Third Shelf. Notes and Queries', *Monthly Packet* 549 [1 November 1896], 589–90).
67. 'Hints on Reading', *Monthly Packet* 92 (1 August 1858), 233–34 (234).

68. Ellen J. Millington, 'King Arthur and his Knights, with the Legend of the Sancgrael', *Monthly Packet* 99 (1 March 1859)–159 (1 March 1864).
69. Kristine Moruzi, '*The Monthly Packet*', *Dictionary of Nineteenth-Century Journalism* (2009), p. 424.
70. Further Arthurian essays in the *Monthly Packet* include Yonge's 'Cameos of English History: Arthur of Brittany', 41 (1 May 1854); [Anon.], 'Thoughts on Mr. Tennyson's Poem of "The Holy Grail"', 65 (1 May 1871); Eva Knatchbull-Hugessen, 'Papers on English Literature: 600–1400 A.D.', 91 (1 July 1888); Christabel Coleridge, 'Arthur as an English Ideal' [4 parts], 14–15 (1 February–1 March 1892); Helen Shipton, 'A Romance of Chivalry', 528 (1 February 1895); Roma White, 'Elves, Knights and the Great King' [6 parts], 551–56 (January–June 1897).
71. William Barry, 'New Books: Not Lancelot, but Galahad' [review of Arthur E. Waite, *The Hidden Church of the Holy Grail, its Legends and Symbolism*], *The Bookman* 35.210 (March 1909), 271–73 (271). See Salmon, *Juvenile Literature As It Is*, pp. 16, 24.
72. Hanson, *Stories of the Days of King Arthur*, p. v.
73. From *The Listener* (12 February 1942). Cited in Andrew Lynch, '"…If Indeed I Go": Arthur's Uncertain End in Malory and Tennyson', *Arthurian Literature* 27 (2010), 19–32 (25).

CHAPTER 4

The Manuscript Magazines of the Wellpark Free Church Young Men's Literary Society

Lauren Weiss

This case study examines the three extant manuscript magazines produced by the Wellpark Free Church Young Men's Literary Society, one of many similar types of clubs and societies in Glasgow throughout the nineteenth century formed for the purpose of 'mutual improvement'. The society's magazines provide useful tools to book historians and historians of reading. They gave members a chance to practise and develop their style, penmanship, and skills in writing essays and poetry, and an opportunity to display their artwork, offering a platform for their work to be critically assessed by their peers. Members' contributions—along with the peer criticisms that immediately follow—offer a wealth of information on various aspects of late-Victorian life more generally. Importantly, they are also a genre that has not been previously studied.

These magazines are an unexamined source of information on reading in historic communal groups, with first-hand evidence demonstrating 'reception as a collaborative process'.[1] Criticisms in the Wellpark society's magazines are used here to analyse readers' responses employing the 'folk stylistics' methodology.[2] The results differ in significant ways from Halsey's

L. Weiss (✉)
University of Stirling, Stirling, Scotland

© The Author(s) 2016
P.R. Rooney, A. Gasperini (eds.), *Media and Print Culture Consumption in Nineteenth-Century Britain*, New Directions in Book History, DOI 10.1057/978-1-137-58761-9_4

study of readers in the long nineteenth century, which I suggest occur as the result of communal reading practices which were framed by the voluntary associational life of this group.

To date, mutual improvement societies are still greatly understudied. Richard Altick states that due to the (supposed) lack of information available:

> [w]e know little about those mutual-improvement clubs. No statistical society ever collected information about them—*an impossible task, of course* [author's emphasis], since they were deliberately kept informal—and we cannot tell how numerous they were. But from the many allusions found in memoirs of working-class men, it appears that hardly a village was without at least one such group, and usually there were several; for they had various purposes. Some went in for theology, some for radical politics, some simply for general literature. In some the emphasis was on reading and discussion, in others it was on the writing of essays and verse, which were passed among the members for criticism.[3]

Altick was discussing the small, informal groups that were formed in response to perceived deficiencies in mechanics' institutions. However, in light of recent research on these societies more generally, mutual improvement societies should be re-examined and their research expanded. While limited, it is not a foregone conclusion that evidence generally does not exist, and studies over the last 40 years have helped to address this gap in the research.[4] Nevertheless, there are currently only a handful of studies on mutual improvement societies or literary societies in eighteenth- and nineteenth-century Scotland,[5] and only two studies have been published that concentrate on literary societies, specifically in North America.

Elizabeth McHenry's monograph on African American societies and Heather Murray's on societies in Ontario in the nineteenth and early-twentieth centuries are significant for their recognition of and concentration on the role of literature in mutual improvement societies whether or not they specifically addressed themselves as a literary society.[6] Only Murray's work includes literary analysis, largely through the use of societies' minute books, and while she notes the production of literary magazines by some Ontario societies, they are not discussed in detail even while informing and illustrating her analysis.[7]

Recent studies on reading groups in the late twentieth and early twenty-first century have been influential in the analysis of historic reading societies and communal groups.[8] Stephen Colclough's examination of manuscript books produced by non-professional readers in reading societies during the late Romantic Period significantly 'focuses on reception as a collaborative process'.[9] The manuscript books in his study include notes and transcriptions of texts from various print sources that were copied or clipped and pasted into albums. These manuscripts, however, are distinctly different from the magazines produced by literary societies throughout the nineteenth century (and beyond): while also being the product of a collaborative process, the purpose of the magazines was to encourage the production of original essays, poetry and artwork by individual members and to solicit 'criticism' from society members.

Manuscript magazines were produced by literary societies in Scotland, England and North America (at least), but, remarkably, are a genre that has not yet been studied.[10] As Altick notes, the production of original essays and poetry to be shared with fellow society members was one possible objective of societies, and it is precisely in this area that some new insights on nineteenth-century reading and readers can be made. Such sources can illuminate the questions of what materials readers read, and, crucially, what they thought about what they read. Evidence from the manuscript magazines of the Wellpark Young Men's Mutual Improvement Society is important because the 'literary' productions of these readers and the accompanying critics' responses offer new evidence lacking in other sources on mutual improvement societies.

Wellpark Free Church Young Men's Literary Society: 1883–88

Wellpark Free Church was located on Duke Street in Dennistoun, in the east end of Glasgow, and the society met at the church Session House located around the corner on Ark Lane.[11] Evidence for this society consists of five printed brochures and three 'literary' magazines that were produced by the members covering the 1883–84, 1887–88, and 1888 sessions.[12] The brochures offer information on the society's object, organization, order of business in running its meetings, and an overview of the meetings and events in that year's session, which included social and political events.

The object of the society was 'the Religious, Moral, and Intellectual Improvement of its Members, to be promoted by the reading of Essays and by debates, &c.'.[13] Membership was restricted to young men, but they did not necessarily have to be members of Wellpark Free Church.[14] Although formal female affiliation to the society was not permitted, this restriction did not apply to involvement in the production of the society's magazine. In the 1883–84 magazine, there are two poems by the same contributor whom the critics speculate was a woman[15]; in the 1887–88 issue, there is one poem by a woman, and a musical score possibly composed by a second woman[16]; and in the 1888 magazine there are two essays by women.[17]

However, in the absence of any minute books from the society's meetings, it is not possible to know what the discussions surrounding the debates and readings entailed. This is why their magazines are important; these publications offer a multi-level, interacting series of negotiations and dialogues between the editor, contributors, critics and the society as a whole involving reading, rereading and the distribution of texts. For example, members provided contributions of non/fiction essays, poems and artwork, some of which make references to authors or quote their works. Some address or appeal to the critics within the essay or poem. The magazines were then passed between readers. The critics wrote their responses in the blank pages immediately following each work. They offered their opinions regarding the text (or artwork or music), which included a critique on various aspects, offering advice and recommendations, but also recording negative responses in almost equal measure.[18] Occasionally, the author/artist would then add their response to the critics' reviews. These dialogues took place within the framework set out by the editor,[19] who summarily chose which pieces to include (or not) in the issue. In this way, he acted as a gate-keeper to the society's publication. The parameters for what was an acceptable contribution were pre-established under the banner of the society's objects, the improvement of its members, but also by the definitions of what it meant to be literary in this reading community, and, arguably, in the broader context of the socio-cultural environment of the city at the end of the century.[20]

READERS AND CONTRIBUTORS OF THE WELLPARK FREE CHURCH YOUNG MEN'S LITERARY SOCIETY MAGAZINE

Located at the back of the magazines are lists of 'Readers', which give the names, addresses and dates when the magazine was issued to its members and/or readers, which may not have been the same. In total, there are 66 known individual readers of these three magazines, along with one member who was not a reader, for a total of 67 readers and/or members.[21] There are 34 readers in the 1883–84 session, 32 in the 1887–88 session, and 30 listed in the 1888 issue.[22] These numbers, however, may not indicate the total number of the society's members: in the absence of minute books, the lists of readers can only act as a guide. In addition, it is important to acknowledge that the magazine may well have been read by other individuals while it was in the possession of the ascribed reader.

Using the lists of readers and their respective addresses, it is possible to obtain more detailed biographical information on some of the society's members. The Glasgow Post Office directories for the years 1882 through 1888 and census reports for 1881 and 1891 were consulted. For the purposes of this case study, only the readers' ages and occupations will be considered. Approximately one-third of the readers could be positively identified, and another 30 % of readers identified with somewhat less certainty are also included. Thus, the approximate age range of readers could be assessed for 36 readers, or just over half the readers from all three magazines (54 %). The census data for 1881 and/or 1891 were used to determine the age of the reader in the first year that the name appeared in the magazines' lists. The results are shown in Fig. 4.1. The majority of the readers (27 %) were 18, and 77 % were under 30.

Using the directories and census returns, we can consider the social class of the magazine's readers. Social class here follows E.P. Thompson's

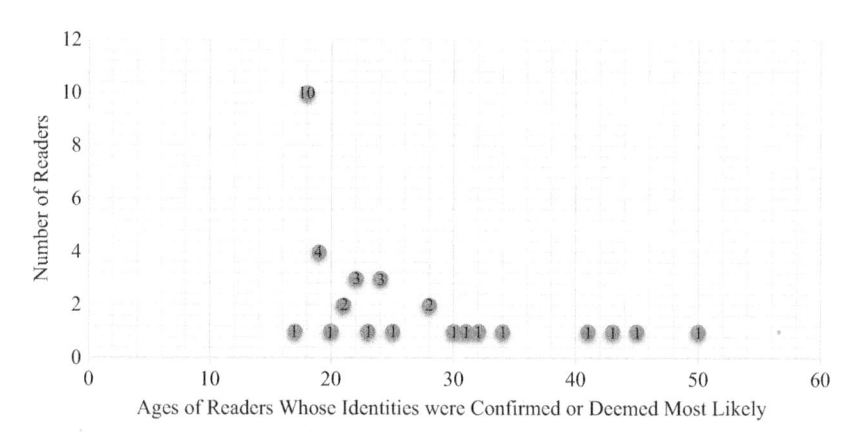

Fig. 4.1 Age range of the Wellpark Free Church Young Men's Literary Society

usage, in that it is an '*historical* [sic] phenomenon', the product of a complex, fluid set of relationships between people which cannot be determined by income or occupation alone.[23] Altick points out that during the nineteenth century, in regards to class, there was in fact 'no uniform system of nomenclature or of consensus classification', and while distinctions were made between working, middle and upper classes, '[t]he greatest disagreement was on the difference between the lower-middle and the lower classes, and especially on the social level to which skilled artisans belonged'.[24] After 1860, growth in the number of retail sales and clerking jobs saw a rise in this lower-middle class category, which allowed an unprecedented opportunity for social advancement.[25] These were precisely the types of jobs that many of the readers of this literary society held at approximately the time of the magazines' issue.

Given the above caveat, a consideration of the types of work in which the readers were employed nonetheless offers an insight into the dynamic socio-cultural environment in which they lived and of the society itself. There were five readers employed as clerks, and five employed in the retail trade either as salesmen or as the manager of a shop. There were three warehousemen, a joiner, a mason, a bootmaker, a hatter, a dyer and two apprentices. In addition, there were four reverends or ministers, an accountant, a surgeon, a head-master and a teacher, a chemist, and a merchant. It is of note that the three women readers of the magazines were not able to be identified as their names were recorded in the lists under their pen-names with no addresses. 'Pedra Zorrica', if a woman and using her real name, would be the exception. From this small sample of the readers, it appears that the Wellpark society was made up of working-class, lower-middle and middle-class men, with a small number of women who read and contributed to the society's magazines. The range of occupations might be seen to reflect the amenable nature of the society in its offering a platform for aspirational men (and women, in the case of magazines) from different personal and social backgrounds (and gender) to engage in 'literary' discussions through the medium of the meetings and magazines which allowed for the mutual improvement of its readers and its members.

There are 20 contributions in the 1883–84 magazine, which were the creative output of 17 of the society's members or listed readers, or in the cases of John Thomson and James Walker who were neither.[26] In the 1887–88 magazine, there are 20 contributions provided by 15 contributors, and in the 1888 magazine, 13 contributors provided 16 contributions, or 14 contributors and 17 contributions if the essay-cum-criticism by 'Baehead' is included. This means that approximately half of the listed readers submitted work for inclusion in each of the magazines. If we presume that editors rejected at least some of the submissions, this figure is likely to be even higher. Thus, the percentage of readers submitting work to the magazines was overall relatively high, underlining the members' contention that the production of original essays, poems, artwork and music were an important part of the 'improving' process promoted more generally by the society.

With few exceptions, most of the contributors wrote under a *nom-de-plume*, with more contributors writing under their own names or identifiable initials in the later magazines. Contributions ranged from essays and poetry, to artwork in various media, to a musical score of a song for two voices and piano accompaniment. As these different types of submissions were thought suitable to be included in a 'literary' magazine, all of these types should be considered. Critics were in effect 'reading' the essay, poem, artwork or piece of music and were responding to them as 'literary' readers: the underlying presumption of the critical remarks is that the critic had the education and/or developed cultural acumen to offer an informed response in the assessment of grammar, compositional style, theories regarding facets of non/fiction, poetry, and works of art and music.

READERS' RESPONSES: THE 'FOLK STYLISTICS' OF THE WELLPARK LITERARY SOCIETY

The critics' responses help to answer an important question for historians of reading: what did readers think about the materials that they read? The 'criticisms' may represent readers' immediate, first responses: the strictly enforced rules listed at the front of the magazines only allowed three days for reading irrespective of the calendar, and its readers would have had to find the time to read—as well as respond—within that time, presumably around their work and personal commitments. The next reader would have read not only the original contributions, but also the responses that the previous readers had recorded and they would add their comments in turn.

However, readers are not choosing from a potentially infinite range of responses when they record their thoughts, but are, in effect, recording the literary and artistic preconceptions, or the 'horizon of expectations' that they held which framed their responses, and inform us about the historically contingent interpretive community/ies in which they lived. These constructs underlie reader-response theory and the basis of work by Wolfgang Iser, Hans Robert Jauss, and Stanley Fish.[27] These largely theoretical concepts in conjunction with Katie Halsey's work on first-hand readers' responses will serve as the foundation for my historicized assessment of critics' responses in the Wellpark magazines. Halsey established that readers in the long nineteenth century had a horizon of expectations regarding works that they read, particularly in regards to style. She outlines a method based on techniques used in stylistics to assess what she terms 'folk stylistics', or the beliefs held by readers regarding conventions or the 'popular beliefs about language' in the assessment of a work's style.[28] She found that there were three main stylistic concerns for readers which included: 'the value placed on works that are suitable for reading aloud'; 'conflations of style and morality; and the frequency with which readers respond to texts viscerally'.[29] As the magazines' critics frequently commented on the style of the contribution (among other aspects), the works from the three magazines are assessed using this method as a starting point. I then move to a more general discussion of readers' expectations regarding the texts (including the art and music) they read.

Across the three magazines, none of the critics remarked about the ease or suitability of the texts for recitation aloud. This could be due to readers' preconceptions that the magazines were primarily for personal 'perusal', a term that was repeatedly used, suggesting private reading. However, the society's printed syllabus for the 1883–84 session lists three meetings whose sole function was the 'Review of [the] Manuscript Magazine'.[30] At these meetings, parts of the magazines may in fact have been read aloud. One possible exception to this exclusion is the response made by the critic, 'P. T. Jr.', in regards to the musical score submitted by Pedra Zorrica in the 1887–88 magazine:

> This contribution is beyond criticism on my part as a musical piece, but, I should like to hear it played and sung. It is very well written [.] I have heard this played over, and I think it really sounds very nice and sweet. The writing of the notes is well executed and can be easily read. The Author is to be congratulated.[31]

While Halsey applied her model to texts, the stylistic concerns she found prevalent could also be applied to music scores, as this reader—and listener—commented on the score's suitability to be read on the page as well as being pleasant to listen to.

There were only two critics' responses in the 1883–84 magazine where readers conflated style with morality. In his response to a light-hearted poem entitled 'Carrick Castle, Loch Goil. A Holiday Reminiscence' by Fred Reid, the critic 'Jabez' initially praised the piece, but took exception to its repeated references to alcohol:

> This composition has some merit. The 9th verse—foot of page 16—is well expressed, and by far the best lines in the piece
> > Wee burns wi'gurly, brawlin din,
> > Gang swirlin doon, noo oot, noo in;
> > If we, like them could loup and rin
> > > We'd shune be doon at Carrick
>
> The poem as a whole is too redundant, and the many references to the "modest sma' refreshment" is in bad taste—although I hold as a refreshment it tasted well.[32]

His reference to 'bad taste' suggests a value judgment of the poem based on its subject matter, but in the last sentence the response is lightened with a pun regarding the poem as being a 'refreshment'.

The second instance of this stylistic concern is found in the response by 'Orion' to a poem on Christian faith by 'M. S.', as well as to a criticism written previously by 'Dugal Darroch':

> I am astonished that "Dugal Darrock" was unable to percure [sic] the beauty—both poetical & spiritual—of the last verse of the second poem. He surely does not mean his last sentence ['It would be very difficult for MS to find the world anywhere else than beneath her feet'] to be accepted by any rational minds [sic] as a criticism! In my opinion the verse in question is one of the finest in the poem. 'M.S.' means that in her hours of pain & trouble she turns the eye of faith to the cross of Christ, and that spectacle of self sacrifice & pain so patiently borne raises her own mind above the cares of the world—in her own words, the world is there "beneath her feet". Very beautiful & very comforting. I thank thee, 'M.S', for the lesson, & all the more heartily if thou be'st a lady.[33]

While 'Dugal Darroch's' comment—along with the rest of his criticism—focuses on the unrealistic elements of 'M. S.'s' poem (i.e. the existence of gravity precluding any poetic notions of floating above the earth's surface), 'Orion's' response is both moral and visceral. He upbraids 'Darroch' for his criticism, particularly for not following an implied set of norms regarding what constituted 'correct' forms of criticism in the magazine which was evident to 'any rational minds'. This might mean that the emphasis of criticism, particularly poetry, was to be on the aesthetics of the work:

for 'Orion', the poem's merits were both 'poetical & spiritual', and lie in its successful relating of the renewal and confirmation of one's faith, which were 'very beautiful & very comforting'. The fact that the poem and its accompanying moral 'lesson' were written by a woman heightened its merit, which might suggest underlying (negative) assumptions about women poets, or in fact on the suitability of poems that married the subjects of religious faith, patience and self-sacrifice with the feminine.

The 1887–88 magazine has five instances where the comments of the readers view the work's style and its morality intermixing. To the poem entitled 'A Renunciation', an eponymous poem on love lost and regained by Alexander Lamont, the critic 'Aliquis' wrote:

> What beautiful poems Mr Lamont has given us! The easy grace of language, the sweet, beautiful sentiments carry one completely out of the earthly habitation to higher and more heavenly regions. It fills one's soul till it is almost bursting into poetry. I'll always read his contributions first after this. It is our honour and his glory *all* his contributions [.][34]

His response clearly demonstrates the equating of the work's style with its morality. The poem called forth a moral, spiritual response in this reader, but one that was also clearly affective, where the language transports him away to 'heavenly regions', and his soul is 'almost bursting into poetry'. Other comments by readers in this issue give some indication of this pairing of style and morality, but are centred on what constituted good taste or, more specifically, a lack thereof. For example, 'Aliquis', in responding to the previous comments of a reader on a pen and ink drawing of Queen Victoria wrote that 'P. T. Jr.'s remarks are in very bad taste and quite uncalled for'.[35] 'Gemini' wrote that the poem submitted by the Editor, Alexander Small, used expressions that were 'scarcely in good taste',[36] while on an essay about a volunteer training exercise with the Clyde Brigade, 'Jacobus' thought that there was a 'slight tinge of vulgarity pervading it', and that the author should have refrained from the use of slang.[37]

Critics in the 1888 magazine responded to what they saw as vulgar language in one essay,[38] but only in one reader's comments might the case be made for equating style with morality. More correctly, the critic was passing judgment on the writer's personal, political and religious beliefs. 'Sardanapalus' recorded his thoughts regarding an essay entitled 'Royalty Considered', by 'Democrat', which soundly denounced the institution of

British royalty. In a lengthy response which filled over two pages in the magazine, 'Sardanapalus' severely upbraids the author for his 'ill-natured ebullition' along with his 'rabbid [sic] republicanism'. In response to a previous critic's comment on the author's vulgar use of slang, 'Sardanapalus' continues:

> Regarding Democrat's "slang" I am not surprised. Men who preach his rabbid [sic] republicanism are not usually of a very high moral tone—Their heterodox political ideas are often (I don't say in his case) the outcome of heterodox theology—hence we find that the morals of the "Champions" of the art—Bradlaugh and his friend Mrs Besant are to say the least "startlingly revolting" [...] The nation with one voice which completely drowns the convulsive squeeking [sic] of Bradlaugh, Besant, Democrat, and his washerwoman declares it [sic] reverence for the throne—and publishes to the world its glorious motto –
> **Dear God! honour the King!!** [sic].[39]

The critic here is claiming that the author of the essay—similarly to other men of questionable moral character who share similar beliefs—doesn't argue for but instead 'preaches' his ill-considered political ideas which are based on an amalgamation of his political and religious beliefs that are not only offensive but 'startlingly revolting'. To the miscreants Bradlaugh and Besant—atheists and advocates for political reform—are added Democrat and the figure of his washerwoman as a metaphor for the views held by the uninformed, even effeminized, working-class people of small social importance who are effectively vermin. Their collective voices, or 'convulsive squeeking', need to be overcome or 'drown[ed]' out, denying a voice to both Democrat and the principle of democracy concurrently, advocating instead the traditional institution of a non-representative, heritable system of government which is sanctioned by God. This extreme reaction by one reader, however, is not representative of the responses from the three magazines as a whole.

The frequency of readers' visceral responses varies between the different issues of the magazine. The 1883–84 magazine has only three examples. One example is a critic's musings on a pencil drawing of a man's face. The response by 'Orion' shows a projection of his own views onto the figure, which may be said to describe the mental exertion involved in the process of writing: 'each contributor may see in it a reflection of himself in the agony of composition'.[40] Similarly, a poem on an excursion to Carrick Castle invokes pleasant memories in the same reader: 'Having spent a delightful week at Carrick last summer, the reading of this poem has afforded me much pleasure, recalling by many graceful touches the beauties of Loch Goil.'[41]

The readers' comments in the 1887–88 magazine had five times more visceral responses than the 1883–84 issue. Of the six readers who responded to the Alexander Lamont's essay, 'The Gloaming of the Year', four readers recorded visceral responses. For example, 'Lexa' wrote that he 'read this article with very great pleasure',[42] while 'P. T. Jr.' wrote that the essay had left him speechless: 'Words fail me, Mr. Lamont, to express my thankfulness at having had the privelege [sic] of reading this splendid article.'[43] The essay inspired 'Jacobus' to conjure up mental images inspired by the text: 'As I read this paper I just imagined I saw the scenes which are so vividly portrayed, the language is so expressive.'[44] The fourth visceral comment to this essay by 'Aliquis' has been considered above, and is one example wherein readers were responding to at least one stylistic conception, in this case the equating of style with morality, and having a visceral response to the text. 'Aliquis' recorded that Alexander Lamont's poem, 'By the Gates of the Sea', 'opened' his mind: 'It opens up one's mind to a most wonderful degree, how narrow, cramped, and small I felt my mind must have been before I read this. It has recalled scenes to my memory, in which I see things now I never saw before.'[45] Very common responses recorded were those of the piece evoking some form of pleasure and/or enjoyment.

Visceral responses in the 1888 were low with only three instances where this was the case. 'Mercury' records that Alexander Lamont's, 'The Stranger's Nook', was a '[v]ery pleasant, and yet sad, poem'.[46] 'Lexa' was initially 'satisfied' with 'Royalty Considered', by 'Democrat', but then changed his mind:

> During the perusal of this article the first feeling experienced is one of satisfaction at finding the nonsensical longsuffering [sic] of the British tax-payer so fearlessly exposed. On concluding its perusal, however, one regrets that Democrat, holding as he does the correct views on the situation should have damaged his own case with language which can only be called coarse, if not vulgar.[47]

The most visceral response was that recorded by 'Democrat' upon reading 'An Awful Tragedy', by 'Temyllut', wherein the author recounts a walk through the woods at night and was scared by a creature in the dark:

Rather too sensational for a magazine of this kind. I don't like my hair to stand on end when reading anything. If you could only have seen me when I was reading this awful Tragedy I am sure you would have been heartily sorry for writting [sic] it. My eyeballs protruded half an inch beyond their sockets, my hair stood up stiff and straight, my knees knocked together with fright, and my hands shook like an aspen leaf in the summer wind. After all this preparation for something astonishing, it was rather a damper to find that, after all, the "brown monster" was only a stag. Don't do it again.[48]

This response, however, should be considered with caution: 'Democrat' is writing this tongue-in-cheek. When considered alongside his other comments, it seems unlikely that a writer of brash, controversial essays and responses should have had such an extreme reaction as the one he described.

In general, the three stylistic concerns that Halsey found to be prevalent in nineteenth-century readers—with the exception of the more frequent recording of a visceral response by the readers of the 1887–88 magazine—were on the whole not shared by the readers of the Wellpark magazines. Instead, there were other responses recorded regarding the style of a text. For example, an essay was thought to be worthy of merit if it was straightforward, pleasant to read, written in the manner of a conversation between the author and reader, and with an appropriate gender-specific style. With regards to poetry, recommendations regarding commendable style were more vague: it was more likely a critic would say it was 'good versification', but qualify it by saying that 'it can't be called poetry',[49] or that the lines 'contain some genuine feeling; although the versification is stilted and the ideas sometimes crudely expressed',[50] or alternatively 'the idea on which the verses turn is good enough ... but AVC's muse is not aspiring'.[51]

Beyond these stylistic concerns, there were two major trends that recurred in the magazines. The trend most frequently noted in both the contributions and criticisms was the tendency to use quotations of and references to authors and/or their poetry, plays, and books, and includes references to periodicals, a comic opera, and two painters. In the 1883–84 magazine, there are quotations or references that can be attributed to: the Bible; Thomas Campbell; Benjamin Franklin; Horace Mann; James Thomson; Norman Macleod; Oliver Goldsmith; Lord Alfred Tennyson; Alexander Wallace, D.D. in *The Christian Leader*; William Congreve; Archibald Alison; Dugald Stewart; Walter Scott; William Black; Thomas Reid; Edmund Burke; and Shakespeare. The 1887–88 magazine includes quotations and references to: Robert Burns; Allan Ramsay; Robert Tannahill; James Hogg; Robert Southey; Jacob Rysdale (possibly Jacob van Ruisdael); Claude Lorrain; William Wordsworth; Henry David Thoreau; Gilbert White; Alexander Pope, Thomas Carlyle; Shakespeare; Percy Bysshe Shelley; *Jeems Kaye: His Adventures and Opinions*; Lord Bacon; Sir Isaac Newton; Revd John Todd; Thomas Chalmers; Lord Byron; and Frederick Marryat. In the 1888 magazine, there were references and quotations to: Shakespeare; Richard Brinsley Sheridan; David Garrick; Charles Kemble; Henry Irving; the Bible; Robert Burns; Shelley; 'Guy Fawkes' (a comic song); the *Daily Mail*; Isaac Watts; Tennyson; Gilbert and Sullivan's 'Ruddigore: or, the Witch's Curse'; John Milton; Cervantes; Dante; the correspondence in *Tit-Bits*; and Artemus Ward. These were most often used to lend weight and authority to the contributor's own text, concurrently intending to inform the reader as to the breadth, and, presumably depth of the author's reading. In addition, the references to books, plays and popular entertainment added colour—local (i.e. Scottish), and aesthetic—to the respective texts.

Readers made reference or quoted most frequently from English then Scottish poems across the three issues. Novels, on the other hand, were the least frequently cited, with Walter Scott's works generally, Black's *A Princess of Thule* (1874), and Marryat's *Poor Jack* (1840) being the only works cited. Philosophic and 'educative' works were the next most frequently referenced in the 1883–84 and 1887–88 issues (e.g. Mann, Alison, Stewart, Reid, Burke, Bacon, Newton, and Todd), but only Milton's *Areopagitica* (1644) was quoted in the 1888 issue. However, the frequency of references to plays and to the theatre more generally increased over the three issues. Shakespeare was quoted in all of the magazines, but in the 1888 issue, eighteenth- and nineteenth- century actors and plays were most frequently discussed and quoted after poetry. References to periodicals were low, with only *The Christian Leader* cited in the 1883–84 issue, and the *Daily Mail* and *Tit-Bits* in the 1888 magazine. While canonical authors were commonly quoted, contemporary works and authors were less so. This trend suggests that the magazines were in effect public statements of the reading of sanctioned works that these readers chose to record. On the other hand, it must be considered that they did not altogether neglect to cite what might be considered 'leisure' activities and materials in the form of 'light' periodicals like *Tit-Bits*, a comic opera that recently opened ('Ruddigore'), a comic song ('Guy Fawkes') and work by a humorous writer (Ward).

One other major trend was the tendency for readers to offer suggestions or corrections to the authors/artists regarding the usage of correct grammar, spelling, punctuation, and language. In addition, the authors' handwriting also came under scrutiny. These comments were in line with a purpose of the magazine: the provision of a forum in which authors/artists could submit their work to an audience of their peers who would offer their 'criticism' for the benefit of what were largely 'amateur', or non-professional, contributors. One contributor even states that his essay, 'Church Music', was his first composition: 'I only wish to add, that I trust the Critical [sic] will not be too severe, seeing this is my first attempt at Essay writing'.[52] Critics' comments, however, did not always live up to the contributors' hopes, as a critic could offer such harsh advice as that offered to 'St Mirren': '[He] would be the better of a course of lessons from a writing master, before he writes another paper for Wellpark M. S. Magazine.'[53] Other critics did not forgo a bit of encouragement along with their criticisms:

> [...] there is little concentration of thought in the working out of "An Old Pupil's" ideas. The style is fitful & rambling & shows a want of experiences [sic] in composition, however the writer may improve by practice.[54]

Conclusion

The results of using Halsey's 'folk stylistics' methodology demonstrate that the prevailing stylistic concerns held by readers in the long nineteenth century were not the same as those in one group of readers in a literary society. I argue that this is the result of the communal reading practices established within the framework of this 'improving' society. The formal meetings of the group—involving debates and discussions governed by a set of rules and regulations—structured this essentially social activity, and the magazines were an extension of the 'improving' process. The production of the magazines redirected the social activities of this community, providing another medium for discussion: while not necessarily reaching a consensus, the magazines did consolidate a diverse set of readers from different social backgrounds into a reading community with a collective identity.

Outwith the contributions and criticisms themselves, it appears that this group read a range of materials. However, in a similar fashion to the texts read and discussed by reading societies in Colclough's study, the quotes and references to authors here—along with the contributions and criticisms—should be seen as a 'public record of those texts that it was legitimate to share in public'.[55] By extension, the non-conformity of these readers' responses to established stylistics conventions could be seen as being due in part to this 'public performance'.

The manuscript magazines produced by this one late nineteenth-century group share other similarities with the albums that were produced in the late Romantic Period. In the same manner as the magazines, most albums were 'a product of the group', 'who shared the communal space of the manuscript book', which in turn 'helped to construct and maintain a network of readers based upon the sociable exchange or creation of texts'.[56] Similarly, Leah Price reminds us that '[b]ooks don't simply mediate a meeting of minds between reader and author. They also broker (or buffer) relationships among the bodies of successive and simultaneous readers.'[57] It was through the mobility of the magazines that the social network between Wellpark's readers was underlined. Its readers were *not* meant to forget or ignore the 'improving' framework which called the magazines into existence, how the magazines were manufactured and their materiality, how these objects reached his/her hands, and that after reading (or not), they were called upon to pass the manuscripts to the next reader on the list. The magazines were then 'association copies' (to use Price's term) in both the literal and figurative sense, but which derived their meaning from their transmission history *in addition* to the text.[58]

NOTES

1. S. Colclough, *Consuming Texts: Readers and Reading Communities, 1695–1870* (Basingstoke: Palgrave Macmillan, 2007), p. 118.
2. K. Halsey, '"Folk Stylistics" and the History of Reading: A Discussion of Method', *Language and Literature* 18 (2009), 231–46.
3. R. Altick, *The English Common Reader: A Social History of the Mass Reading Public, 1800–1900* (Chicago: University of Chicago Press, 1957), p. 205.
4. For example, Michael D. Stephens and Gordon W. Roderick demonstrate English mutual improvement societies' impact on the provision of adult education (M.D. Stephens and G.W. Roderick, 'A Passing Fashion in Nineteenth Century English Adult Education: The Camborne Debating and Mutual Improvement Society', *Paedagogica Historica: International Journal of the History of Education* 10 (1970), 171–80; M.D. Stephens and G.W. Roderick, 'Nineteenth Century Education Finance: The Literary and Philosophical Societies', *Annals of Science* 31 (1974), 335–49).

C.J. Radcliffe, R.J. Morris, and Jonathan Rose offer overviews of how these societies developed on a local level, and how they changed and grew across Britain (C.J. Radcliff, 'Mutual Improvement Societies in the West Riding of Yorkshire, 1835–1900', *Journal of Educational Administration and History* 18 (1986), 1–16; C. Radcliffe, 'Mutual Improvement Societies and the Forging of Working-Class Political Consciousness in Nineteenth-Century England', *International Journal of Lifelong Education* 16 (1997), 141–55; R.J. Morris, 'Clubs, Societies and Associations', in F.M.L. Thompson, ed., *The Cambridge Social History of Britain 1750–1950* (Cambridge: Cambridge University Press, 1990), III, pp. 395–443; J. Rose, *The Intellectual Life of the British Working Classes* (New Haven, CT: Yale University Press, 2001), pp. 58–91).

5. D.D. McElroy investigates literary clubs and societies in the eighteenth century, which includes clubs in Glasgow (D.D. McElroy, 'The Literary Clubs and Societies of Eighteenth Century Scotland, and Their Influence on the Literary Productions of the Period From 1700 to 1800', unpublished doctoral thesis, University of Edinburgh, 1952). Ian R. Carter examines mutual improvement societies in the nineteenth century around Aberdeen, while Christine Lumsden reviews the history of the Bristo Place Mutual Improvement Society in Edinburgh (I.R. Carter, 'The Mutual Improvement Movement in North-East Scotland in the Nineteenth Century', *Aberdeen University Review* 46 (Autumn 1976), 383–92; C. Lumsden, 'Bristo Place Mutual Improvement Society: Victorian Self-help in Action', *The Baptist Quarterly* 45 (2014), 356–68). John C. Crawford includes mutual improvement societies and associational life more generally as part of his larger study of libraries and reading in Paisley in the late-eighteenth to the early-nineteenth century (J.C. Crawford, '"The High State of Culture to Which this Part of the Country has Attained": Libraries, Reading, and Society in Paisley, 1760–1830', *Library & Information History* 30 (2014), 172–94).

6. E. McHenry, *Forgotten Readers: Recovering the Lost History of African-American Literary Societies* (Durham, NC: Duke University Press, 2002); H. Murray, *Come, Bright Improvement! The Literary Societies of Nineteenth-Century Ontario* (Toronto: University of Toronto Press, 2002).

7. Murray, p. 15.

8. For example, Elizabeth Long's work on communal reading practices in contemporary and historic groups in Texas, and Jenny Hartley's research involving a survey of over 300 modern groups have shaped subsequent research (E. Long, *Book Clubs: Women and the Uses of Reading in Everyday Life* (London: University of Chicago Press, 2003); J. Hartley, *Reading Groups* (Oxford: Oxford University Press, 2001)).

9. Colclough (2007), p. 118.

10. Inclusive of the evidence from Murray, to date, I have located magazines produced by societies in the following places: Wick; Dundee; Glasgow; Edinburgh; Melrose; the Scottish Borders; Shrewsbury; Walton, Liverpool; Manchester; London; and Cheshire.
11. *Wellpark Free Church Young Men's Literary Society. Session 1883–84* [1883] (Dennistoun, Glasgow: Robertson), (Wellpark F. C. Literary Society M. S. Magazine, 1883–84, 428697© CSG CIC Glasgow Museums and Libraries Collection: The Mitchell Library, Special Collections, p. 147).
12. Wellpark F. C. Literary Society M. S. Magazine, 1883–84, 1887–88, 1888, 428697-9© CSG CIC Glasgow Museums and Libraries Collection: The Mitchell Library, Special Collections.
13. 'Constitution', *Wellpark Free Church Young Men's Literary Society. Session 1883–84*, Wellpark F. C. Literary Society M. S. Magazine, 1883–84, p. 147.
14. Wellpark F. C. Literary Society M. S. Magazine, 1883–84, p. 147. The society's membership, however, did not exclude older men: exceptions appear to have been made for ministers and for other men of some social standing in the community. For example, Alexander Lamont, listed as a reader of the 1887–88 and 1888 magazines, was 43 in 1887. Lamont was headmaster of one of the local schools, and a published author, whose poetry appeared in *The Argosy* (see, for example: A. Lamont, 'By the Gates of the Sea', *The Argosy* 53 (June 1892), 524; A. Lamont, 'That Evensong of Long Ago', *The Argosy* 54 (August 1892), 170).
15. 'Farewell', as well as 'And they shall spring up as among the grass, as willows by the watercourses. Isa 44, 45', were both by 'M. S.' (Wellpark F. C. Literary Society M. S. Magazine, 1883–84, pp. 39–42).
16. 'A Country Lassie' was the author of 'Hop, Step and Jump' (Wellpark F. C. Literary Society M. S. Magazine, 1887–88, pp. 57–66) and Pedra Zorrica composed 'The Sea Nymphs' (Wellpark F. C. Literary Society M. S. Magazine, 1887–88, pp. 193–96).
17. 'An Old Pupil' wrote 'My Experience of Boarding Schools' (Wellpark F. C. Literary Society M. S. Magazine, 1888, pp. 53–66); 'The Lass o' Gowrie' was the author of 'A Run up the Highlands' (Wellpark F. C. Literary Society M. S. Magazine, 1888, pp. 133–40).
18. The criticisms in these magazines appear to be based on critical strategies that developed over the course of the nineteenth century in local and national newspapers and magazines. Working-class and middle-class journals offered advice and sought to educate their readers in history, politics, and culture, which included literature. For example, *Chambers's Edinburgh Journal*, the Dundee *People's Journal* and Glasgow's *Penny Post* included correspondence columns that offered criticism on readers' submissions (see also Laurel Brake, 'Literary Criticism and the Victorian Periodicals',

The Yearbook of English Studies 16 (1986), 92–116, and K. Blair, '"Let the Nightingales Alone": Correspondence Columns, the Scottish Press, and the Making of the Working Class Poet', *Victorian Periodicals Review* 47 (2014), 188–207). This aspect, however, will not be covered in this study.

19. Hugh Yuill, then Vice-President of the society, was the editor of the 1883–84 magazine, and Alexander Small was the editor of the 1887–88 and the 1888 magazines. Small was listed as a reader in the magazines he edited, and presumably was also a member of the society. It is unclear if editors were elected to their posts.
20. Definitions of the term 'literary' are historically contingent, but for this study will follow Murray (2002) to refer to a range of texts, which could extend to include the liberal arts and/or culture and being 'cultured' (Murray, pp. 10–11).
21. The one person not recorded as a reader in any of the lists was Revd J.T. Ferguson, listed as an Honorary Vice-President in the society's printed brochure for the 1883–84 session (Wellpark F. C. Literary Society M. S. Magazine, 1883–84, p. 146). As he appears to be among the minority, if not the sole exception, the readers and/or members will be referred to simply as 'readers' in this study.
22. As some individuals remained members between 1882 and 1888, there is some repetition in these lists.
23. E.P. Thompson, *The Making of the English Working Class* (London: Victor Gollancz Ltd., 1963). See also R.J. Morris, 'Introduction: Class, Power and Social Structure in British Nineteenth Century Towns' in R.J. Morris, ed., *Class, Power and Social Structure in British Nineteenth-Century Towns* (Leicester: Leicester University Press, 1986), pp. 2–22.
24. Altick, p. 82.
25. S.L. Steinbach, *Understanding the Victorians: Politics, Culture, and Society in Nineteenth-Century Britain* (London and New York: Routledge, 2012), p. 121.
26. John Thomson and James Walker are not listed readers, but both authors included their full names, addresses (South Cobden Street, Alva, and Alloa, Primrose Place, respectively), and, in Thomson's case, his occupation ('letter carrier') at the end of their contributions. Walker identifies himself as a published poet, stating that he is the 'Author of a description of a jaunt of Auld Reekie and other Scotch poems' (Wellpark F. C. Literary Society M. S. Magazine, 1883–1884, pp. 52–53; 56–64).
27. See W. Iser, 'The Reading Process: A Phenomenological Approach', *New Literary History* 3 (1972), 279–99; H.R. Jauss, 'Literary History as a Challenge to Literary Theory', translated by E. Benzinger, *New Literary History* 2 (1970), 7–37; and S. Fish, *Is There a Text in This Class?: The Authority of Interpretive Communities* (Cambridge, MA and London: Harvard University Press, 1980).

28. K. Halsey, '"Folk Stylistics" and the History of Reading: A Discussion of Method', *Language and Literature*, 18 (2009), 231–46.
29. Halsey, 233–34.
30. 'Syllabus 1883–84', Wellpark F. C. Literary Society M. S. Magazine, 1883–84, p. 147.
31. 'P. T. Jr.' (Peter Thamson, Jr.), Wellpark F. C. Literary Society M. S. Magazine, 1883–84, p. 147.
32. 'Jabez', Wellpark F. C. Literary Society M. S. Magazine, 1883–84, p. 21.
33. 'Orion', and 'Dugal Darroch', Wellpark F. C. Literary Society M. S. Magazine, 1883–84, pp. 43–44.
34. 'Aliquis', Wellpark F. C. Literary Society M. S. Magazine, 1887–88, p. 146.
35. 'Aliquis', Wellpark F. C. Literary Society M. S. Magazine, 1887–88, p. 7.
36. 'Gemini', Wellpark F. C. Literary Society M. S. Magazine, 1887–88, [unpaginated, p. 8].
37. 'Jacobus', Wellpark F. C. Literary Society M. S. Magazine, 1887–88, p. 178.
38. 'Lady McPhiny' uses the term to describe the language in an essay denouncing the institution of British royalty. In his comments on the same essay, 'Lexa' shares this view (Wellpark F. C. Literary Society M. S. Magazine, 1888, p. 99).
39. 'Sardanapalus', Wellpark F. C. Literary Society M. S. Magazine, 1888, p. 102.
40. 'Orion', Wellpark F. C. Literary Society M. S. Magazine, 1883–84, [unpaginated preface].
41. Wellpark F. C. Literary Society M. S. Magazine, 1883–84, p. 21.
42. 'Lexa', Wellpark F. C. Literary Society M. S. Magazine, 1887–88, p. 21.
43. 'P. T. Jr.', Wellpark F. C. Literary Society M. S. Magazine, 1887–88, p. 22.
44. 'Jacobus', Wellpark F. C. Literary Society M. S. Magazine, 1887–88, p. 22.
45. 'Aliquis', Wellpark F. C. Literary Society M. S. Magazine, 1887–88, p. 21. It must be noted, however, that this comment was added verbatim after all the comments to the essay by Lamont, and calls into question the extent to which comments recorded by readers were in fact primary, first responses rather than being premeditated.
46. 'Mercury', Wellpark F. C. Literary Society M. S. Magazine, 1888, p. 19.
47. 'Lexa', Wellpark F. C. Literary Society M. S. Magazine, 1888, p. 99.
48. 'Democrat', Wellpark F. C. Literary Society M. S. Magazine, 1888, pp. 187–88.
49. 'Jabez', Wellpark F. C. Literary Society M. S. Magazine, 1883–84, p. 83.
50. 'D. D.', Wellpark F. C. Literary Society M. S. Magazine, 1883–84, p. 55.
51. 'D. D.', Wellpark F. C. Literary Society M. S. Magazine, 1883–84, p. 83.

52. 'mij', Wellpark F. C. Literary Society M. S. Magazine, 1883–84, p. 10.
53. 'R. S.', Wellpark F. C. Literary Society M. S. Magazine, 1883–84, p. 51.
54. 'A Critic', Wellpark F. C. Literary Society M. S. Magazine, 1888, p. 67.
55. Colclough, p. 132.
56. Colclough, pp. 131–32.
57. Leah Price, *How to Do Things with Books in Victorian Britain* (Princeton and Oxford: Princeton University Press, 2012), p. 12.
58. Here I am indebted to Leah Price's discussion of 'Literary Logistics' (p. 31), as well as her definition of 'association copies', which are 'books whose value, like that of a religious relic, derives from the history of their transmission rather than from the text that they contain' (p. 169).

CHAPTER 5

Black Victorians and *Anti-Caste*: Mapping the Geographies of 'Missing' Readers

Caroline Bressey

This chapter focuses upon the known and unknown readers of *Anti-Caste*, an early anti-racist periodical first published in Britain in 1888. Founded, produced and edited by a woman it was not a monthly concerned with 'women's issues', but the forms of racial discrimination women and men faced within countries of the British Empire and the United States in the late nineteenth century. *Anti-Caste's* articles reported on a range of international and local debates, from the increasing speed of European colonization in Africa, to everyday racism at restaurants, on trains and in employment. During my research on *Anti-Caste* I mapped its community of readers; they were a multi-ethnic and international collective, though mostly based in Britain. However, tracing British based readers who were black proved to be particularly difficult. This chapter explores why an anti-racist periodical in Britain might have failed to attract locally based black readers. It also argues that such an absence of real or implied readers can still raise important and productive questions, not only about reading communities and their experiences, but also about the broader communities among whom they lived and worked.

C. Bressey (✉)
University College London, London, UK

© The Author(s) 2016
P.R. Rooney, A. Gasperini (Eds.), *Media and Print Culture Consumption in Nineteenth-Century Britain*, New Directions in Book History, DOI 10.1057/978-1-137-58761-9_5

The Establishment of *Anti-Caste*

Anti-Caste was founded and edited by an English Quaker, Catherine Impey.[1] Born in Street, Somerset in the west of England, Impey owned, distributed, and edited the monthly periodical from this small country town that remained her home from her birth in 1847 until her death in 1923. *Anti-Caste* was a small publication, usually, four printed pages, sold for one penny or one cent, a reflection of Impey's intention that the periodical would be accessible to an international readership from the outset. As outlined in the first issue published in April 1888, *Anti-Caste* dealt with issues of 'colour caste', the political geographies of 'the color/colour line'—the lived realities of racial segregation and the systems of racial prejudice it supported and encouraged. In 1893 Impey passed the editorship of *Anti-Caste* to the West Indian born activist Celestine Edwards and under his tenure the periodical was renamed *Fraternity*. Edwards had settled in Britain during the 1870s, firstly living in Scotland where he developed a lecturing career within the temperance movement. In the 1880s he headed south, moving to Sunderland before settling in London's East End. Here Edwards worked as a casual builder while earning a celebrated reputation as a public speaker in Victoria Park. In addition, following a tour during which he attempted to assess the level of atheism in Britain, he became the editor of *Lux* 'a Christian Evidence Newspaper' in 1892. This position likely made him Britain's first black editor of a periodical.[2] As a popular editor and speaker on subjects from thrift to Darwinism, Edwards drew large crowds and helped form the foundation for the transformation of *Anti-Caste/Fraternity* from an activist readership into a social movement between 1893 and 1894. This collective became known as the Society for the Recognition of the Brotherhood of Man (SRBM). However, working on two periodicals and a heavy public speaking programme took a toll on Edwards's health. Edwards became seriously ill and returned to the Caribbean to stay with his brother hoping to recuperate. Following Edwards's death in July 1894 two periodicals competed for his former readers within the anti-racist movement. Dissatisfied with their editorial focus Impey relaunched *Anti-Caste* in 1895, but this new volume lasted only three issues marking the permanent decline of the *Anti-Caste* movement.[3]

That Edwards had forged a reputation within the temperance community in Britain signals a key reason for *Anti-Caste's* existence. Catherine Impey had been an active member of the temperance movement since making her teenage pledge with the Band of Hope. Like many middle-class women in the movement, Impey gained her first experiences of activism through her temperance work, eventually becoming elected the Templars' Honorary Secretary of the Negro Mission Committee.[4] The temperance movement provided her with opportunities to travel to the United States and Europe, to gain experience of writing essays, reports and letters and to become part of a network of black and white activists that proved crucial for informing and establishing *Anti-Caste*. However, *Anti-Caste* was born from a split within the trans-Atlantic temperance community. As Impey understood the movement, racial equality was a key part of the politics of temperance; she argued that the two deepest principles established by the Templars' international forum at its outset had been the 'Equality and Brotherhood of all mankind, and the moral and physical evil of the use and traffic in Strong Drinks'.[5] These principles of equality were deeply held by Impey but, in 1876 it had been agreed that temperance lodges segregated along the 'color line' in the United States were permissible within the movement. The branch of the community to which Impey aligned argued that by establishing racial inequality along the colour line the original movement had forfeited its legitimacy. In opposition they established an alternative organizational structure with the charismatic Joseph Malins as Secretary and James Yeames, editor of the weekly periodical *Templar*, the Right Worthy Grand Templar of the Right Worthy Grand Lodge of the World.[6]

Impey remained active in the temperance movement until 1887 when she resigned her elected position as Grand Vice-Templar at an annual Grand Lodge meeting in Newport, following confirmation that plans for a unification between Malins and the leadership of the branch of Templary that had established racially segregated Lodges was in place.[7] In November 1887 Impey wrote to her network of temperance activists informing them that she would no longer act as a collector for the Templar Mission among the Freedmen of America. Instead Impey returned to the proposal of establishing an Anti-Caste Society, an idea she had muted as early as 1883.[8] The society Impey envisaged would include an international membership who would publicize the condition of 'coloured races in America, India or elsewhere'.[9] The association Impey proposed would initially take the form of a community of readers through a new periodical to be titled *Anti-Caste*. Impey argued that given only 'occasional access to the ordinary press of the country' the hardships black Americans faced were little known 'except by readers of negro journals. And who reads these journals?' Impey asked,

'Alas! negroes only' with only a very few exceptions.[10] *Anti-Caste* would lay the facts of racial prejudice and the real consequences of agreeing to racist structures such as segregated temperance lodges, as understood by the people who suffered most from those actions, before its readership. However, during seven years of publication, *Anti-Caste's* political concerns broadened beyond the United States to include sites of the British Empire, and occasionally beyond its far-reaching influence.

The Known Readership of *Anti-Caste*

As scholars of Victorian periodicals often experience, it is generally very difficult to trace the readers of nineteenth-century journals, but in the case of *Anti-Caste* Catherine Impey did publish a regular list of subscribers.[11] Initially this list was defined as those who provided financial support for Impey's new venture and appeared in the second issue from May 1888, but from 1890 Impey began to publish annual lists of subscribers. From these enough detail can be gleaned to see that her philanthropic and personal 'kinship networks' of Quakers formed foundational support for the periodical.[12] As she sought to establish *Anti-Caste* in the mid-1880s, Impey saw subscribers to the Aborigines' Protections Society (APS) journal the *Aborigines' Friend* as potential readers for *Anti-Caste*. Impey's letter following up a request for access to their subscription list or for the APS to send out a circular informing their members of *Anti-Caste's* arrival in March 1888, indicates she had not yet heard from the society and was perhaps seen as a rival for readers rather than establishing a complimentary readership.[13] In the end, the subscriber list for *Anti-Caste* probably never reached more than 350 households, but over its lifetime its readers produced a textual community of progressive radicals which included early feminists and socialists, pacifists, vegetarians, and international students based in Britain as well as former and ongoing anti-slavery campaigners. International readers were present from the outset either as subscribers or, like the radical African American journalist and founding editor of the *New York Age* T. Thomas Fortune, were part of the editorial exchange network that provided *Anti-Caste* with its interesting and often provocative content. These international readers were based mostly in the United States, reflecting Impey's trans-Atlantic temperance networks, but *Anti-Caste* also attracted a few subscribers in Africa and the Caribbean.

To reach readers beyond the homes of individual subscribers, the geography of *Anti-Caste's* circulation depended upon the localities of men and women, people Catherine referred to as her 'co-workers', who offered to distribute additional copies of the paper around their towns, places of work or within additional activist networks they belonged to. As Impey explained in an editorial in 1893, these unpaid agents performed their roles at varying scales. Some encouraged readers of free copies to become committed subscribers, others distributed copies amongst their own circle of friends or enclosed a copy in a letter to friends and family abroad while an unnamed man in Yorkshire delivered *Anti-Caste* to 16 public reading rooms.[14] In 1889 Frederic Sessions pledged to circulate *Anti-Caste* amongst the working class in villages around Gloucester. He and his well-networked staff already regularly delivered temperance literature and he estimated they could distribute a hundred copies of *Anti-Caste* a month.[15] His proposal made Sessions one of *Anti-Caste's* most important distributors, and illustrates how Impey and her co-workers made use of pre-existing networks to circulate *Anti-Caste* both at home and abroad.

By the end of 1888, the first year of publication, irrespective of those who received *Anti-Caste* for free distribution, the list of subscribers had reached 189. A year later 137 had renewed their subscription (with a few more late payers to come) and had been joined by 123 new subscribers including Fanny Jackson Coppin, Mary Estlin and W.F. Mackenzie from Demerara. Within these subscribers an international network of 50 individuals at least 13 of whom were women, distributed 1700 to 1900 copies a month. Some like Eliza Clarke in Milverton, Miss Brown in Eversham and Mrs C.A.J. Mann in New Haven, Connecticut took just a few copies each.[16] Impey's 1890 annual editorial address reported 150 copies of *Anti-Caste* were sent monthly to an elder of the AME Church in South Carolina for distribution among leading workers in his District.[17] A year on in Philadelphia Fanny Jackson Coppin and Dr Nathan T. Mossell took 18 copies each, and Dr E.C. Young took nine copies for distribution in Ohio. In the Caribbean half-a-dozen copies were sent to the Bahamas, 15 to two men in Barbados. Nine copies were sent care of R.H. Habgood to West Australia.[18]

Working-class readers are likely to have come mostly through connections with charitable organizations or public institutions. Some, such as a Seaman's Mission in London, requested copies directly from Impey, in this case 100 copies of each issue. The Revd T.R. Couch distributed 100 copies in London, alongside Celestine Edwards who, although not a subscriber at this point, took eight copies for distribution in the capital. Other institutions were brought into the network through successful lobbying by supporters like Peter Mackenzie. In addition to the 50 copies Mackenzie distributed personally, he also persuaded public libraries in Glasgow, Leith, Dundee and Inverness to take regular issues in 1889. A large provincial Sunday school took 100 copies, as did the Headmaster of a school in South Wales. In receipt of free copies and not financially supporting the anti-caste movement Impey never listed these institutions as subscribers though Impey's aim was to provide the widest distribution of *Anti-Caste* to clubs, libraries, sailors' homes and teachers. As such the free distribution of *Anti-Caste* was extended as fast as funds provided by subscriptions allowed.

In 1890 Impey reflected on the possibilities of a largely expanded network of volunteers to support *Anti-Caste's* distribution with each taking 10–50 or more copies to give out monthly. Once printed she calculated it would require little extra work for her or her assistant to send out 20,000 in place of the 2000 they currently distributed, but such expansion involved a considerable outlay in postage and additional printing costs.[19] By Impey's editorial address of January 1893 the subscribers supported the printing of 3500 copies of *Anti-Caste* every month, but the cost of posting these issues and the need to purchase foreign and British journals for content that did not come part of free exchange agreements meant that a deficit lay on the periodical's accounts. But changes in the contexts of production provided new opportunities, including a reduction in the cost of foreign postage that allowed for a record number of free copies to be dispatched abroad in 1892.[20] But any possibilities for further expansion in the distribution of copies continued to rely upon the distribution network and all those who worked to sustain it.

Mapping the Black Readers of *Anti-Caste*

Anti-Caste did not provide the new platform for as broad a range of political writing by African and Indian writers that Impey originally aspired to, but it did help forge an international dialogue on racial prejudice, contributing to an unofficial syndication of news, and images, that helped disrupt the narratives purported by conventional white media. While doing so *Anti-Caste* and *Fraternity* challenged ideas of stable 'white' textual communities that unquestionably supported white supremacy or racial hierarchies. These interventions were seen, particularly by black readers as successes, which makes *Anti-Caste* significant in the making of reading communities and the history of anti-racism and radical politics. Some of Impey's international readers are well known enough to be identified by the brief details given in the subscriber list, among them Orishatukeh Faduma who subscribed in 1889. Previously known as William Stevens Powell, by the time he began subscribing to *Anti-Caste* Powell had changed his name to Orishatukeh Faduma. Born in British Guiana in 1869, his parents returned to Sierra Leone when Faduma was nine. He travelled to England to complete his studies at Queen's College, Taunton and matriculated at the University of London.[21] After graduating in 1885, Faduma returned to Sierra Leone to teach at the Methodist Boys' High School. During this time he rejected his Western name and co-founded the Dress Reform Society, which encouraged the wearing of traditional African robes rather than the fashion for Western Victorian coats.[22] Frederick Douglass, the anti-slavery and civil rights campaigner, then the United States Minister to Haiti, was a life subscriber.

Georgiana Simpson was one of a number of pioneering African American women to read *Anti-Caste*. A subscriber to *Anti-Caste* in 1894 and a close friend of Anna J. Cooper, who would speak at the Pan-African Conference in London in 1900, Simpson would become one of the first of three black American women to be awarded a PhD in 1921. She also undertook a critical edition and translation of a French biography of Toussaint L'Ouverture published in 1924.[23] As noted above Fanny Jackson Coppin took multiple copies for distribution in Philadelphia where she worked as a teacher. Jackson Coppin had been born enslaved in 1837, but was bought out of slavery as a young girl by her aunt Sarah Orr, who, earning $6 a month saved $125 to buy her freedom.[24] After graduating from Oberlin College as a mature student in 1865, she began teaching Latin, Greek, and maths at the Institute for Colored Youth, a Quaker academy in Philadelphia. In 1869 she became principal of the Institute, becoming the first black woman in the United States to hold such a position.[25]

However, within both *Anti-Caste* and *Fraternity* direct mention of black readers is rare. This may be because the labelling of readers in such a way was deemed unimportant or even problematic given the nature of the political project the reading community and its editors were embarked upon. Place and ethnicity are sometimes noted in the subscriber lists, for example on the list of 'Subscribers 1892' are: 'Coppin, Mrs F J, Phila'; 'Moore, Mrs J P. USA' and 'Muthu, Dr C (An Indian in England)', but there are no further comments associated with Edwards, S.J. Celestine, when he is recorded as a new subscriber on the same list.[26] References also came when readers reflected upon their own positionality within the news they shared. In 1890 'A Negro professor of a Southern University' wrote to update *Anti-Caste* readers on the legal aftermath of a brutal lynching fearing they 'may not get it elsewhere'. He regretfully informed them that not one of the lynchers had been brought to trial and lamented that 'People may read of the south and think they know all about it' but really they knew 'nothing of the grievances we have to suffer'.[27] Another reference came during Edwards' editorial tenure of *Fraternity* from a member of the Portsmouth Branch of the movement who reported that Mr Solomon Masse their local agent for *Lux*, the Christian Evidence paper Edwards also edited, had given a short talk about his experiences of black life in the United States at a local meeting for the SRBM.[28] Nothing more about Mr Solomon Masse is published but this reference to him raises many questions, such as when he had moved from the United States, how long he had lived in Portsmouth, how important he was to the *Anti-Caste/Fraternity* network as a speaker/activist and how important it was for him. What his presence in the networks also hints at is that if a reference to working-class African American readers are rarely present, references to a Black British readership are even rarer.

In David Fahey's book *Temperance and Racism*, which as the title suggests is a key text in explaining the important role race played in the temperance movement of which Catherine Impey was a part, he briefly mentions a number of black Templars who lived and worked in British port towns in the 1870s. They were: A man named King who was a member of Divine Providence lodge in South Shields; Jacob Christian, a timber merchant who lived in Toxteth, Liverpool and who had migrated from Africa aged 15, eventually became a member of the Wesleyan Methodists and a 'devoted' member of the IOGT (International Order of Good Templars). He also records that in January 1877 there were at least two black men, one named Brooks, the other named Haig, who were present at a temperance meeting in Glasgow and the Mariner's Friend Lodge based in London that claimed a membership with three dozen black brothers and one black sister.[29] Given that *Anti-Caste* emerged out of the debates about racial inequality within the transatlantic temperance movement there is a legitimate expectation that some of these names might appear on the subscribers' list for *Anti-Caste*. Given the difficulties of finding 'colour' in British archives, where it is rarely recorded as a matter of course, it is possible that one or more of the black brothers and perhaps a black sister of the Mariner's Lodge, Glasgow were subscribers, but there are no clear overlaps with the *Anti-Caste* subscription lists.[30] However, the digitization of newspaper records has enabled Jacob Christian to be traced in a number of archives. It is his presence that forms the focus of the rest of this chapter and allows some more speculative connections to be made between the Black British working class and *Anti-Caste*.

Jacob Christian appears in several newspaper reports published in locally based newspapers. The articles show he was active in local political networks that met to discuss and consider practical challenges to everyday racial prejudice in Liverpool. In August 1880 the *Liverpool Mercury* reported on a well-attended meeting of 'coloured seamen' held in the Trades Hall on Duke Street near the Liverpool docks.[31] They met to discuss the racial prejudice seamen faced in the port city, an issue raised the year before with the Mayor of Liverpool, but with little change in evidence the men decided they must make a determined effort to address the problems themselves. A key issue identified at the meeting was the failure of men to find work, quickly presumably, on an outgoing ship, forcing them to 'tramp' or go into the local workhouse. Mr E.G. Fairchild gave an account of his night visits to the docks where he found 'men of colour sleeping among bales of cotton', unable to find work and starving. A Mr Graham from Belfast proposed a committee be established to investigate the legal avenues for ensuring men were not abandoned by ships coming into port for as Mr Graham said, 'this country sent out missionaries to convert the coloured people, but when any of those people came to Liverpool they were treated like dogs'.[32] It was Mr Jacob Christian 'a coloured man' who seconded Graham's resolution.

Jacob Christian later appears in reports on the Toxteth Aid Society in August 1886, when a group gathered to consider the possibility of establishing the society, begun in January that year, as a permanent collective; the report also states Jacob sat on the Committee of the local Permanent Aid Society.[33] He is one of around a dozen men recorded in attendance, though the colour of his skin, nor that of any other black men who may have been present, was not noted. This was also the case with the *Liverpool Mercury's* report around the sixteenth annual session of the Grand Lodge of England attended by nearly 1200 members, including Joseph Malins, which opened at Manchester's Town Hall in April 1885.[34] Jacob appears among the list of members present at the meeting of the North-western Grand Lodge of the Independent Order of Good Templars, which drew together a membership from Lancashire, Cheshire, and Derbyshire. They met on the opening day of the annual session in the Independent Methodist Free Church in Macclesfield to discuss local

Lodge business and broader aims of the movement, such as the Sunday Closing Bill for pubs in England. Catherine Impey also attended the gathering in Manchester, where she was elected to represent England at the International Right Worthy Grand Lodge that would meet in Stockholm the following July.[35] Although it is not necessarily the case that Catherine Impey and Jacob Christian would have met amongst the 1200 delegates, it seems their interests in battling racial prejudice and advocating for temperance certainly overlapped in the early and mid 1880s. For Jacob Christian, his commitment to the temperance movement remained with him throughout his life. When he died in October 1894, the obituary notice placed by his wife asked foreign papers to 'please copy' and the IOGT to kindly notice his passing.[36]

As suggested by his interest in the plight of seamen Jacob Christian worked aboard ships, but his connections to Liverpool strengthened following his marriage to a local woman in 1861. Jacob married Octavia Caulfield on 25 July at St John's the Baptist Church in Toxteth. At the time of the 1871 census the couple had two young children, Julia aged 8 and Alexander just 8 months old.[37] By the 1881 census Jacob and Octavia were living at 69 Beaufort Street, still in Toxteth Park, where they ran a boarding house. They had six children all of whom were born in Liverpool and were living with them on Beaufort Street along with seven boarders. These boarders were all seamen and it would seem that most, if not all of them were black, coming as they were identified in the census, from America, the British West Indies, South Carolina and Baltimore.[38]

Jacob also appears in a *Liverpool Mercury* report of the eighth annual North-western Grand Lodge of Good Templars meeting in 1884, held in the Templar's Hall on Russell Street, Liverpool. Given that Jacob had now lived in Toxteth for over 20 years, he was presumably connected to the Toxteth Lodge that was congratulated on its success over the previous year. It had quadrupled in size and included 'upwards of 50 coloured members'.[39] At this meeting Jacob was also elected an official of the IOGT, and it is worth noting again that in this report no mention is made of the colour of his skin. By the 1891 census, Jacob had become a Timber Merchant and was living at 79 Mill Street with Octavia and their younger children.[40] When Octavia announced the death of her 'beloved husband' at aged 60 on 22 October 1894, they had moved to 12 Park Road. Her request for the IOGT to take note of Jacob's passing perhaps hints at why he was not a formal subscriber to *Anti-Caste*.

Returning to the reports of Jacob at the 'Seamen's Grievances' meeting in 1886, and given his attendance and willingness to speak out at public meetings, it seems likely that a man such as Jacob Christian would have been interested in the work of *Anti-Caste*. He might also be expected to have been particularly interested in the work of Celestine Edwards, a fellow mariner committed to religious uplift through *Lux*, and to challenging racial prejudice through *Fraternity*, even though he may not have been a formal subscriber to either of Edwards' papers. But newspaper reports which include him clearly indicate that Jacob Christian did not split from the IOGT over the issue of the 'color line' and segregated lodges in the United States. As such perhaps he, and by extension his family, felt unable to publicly support Catherine Impey and thus *Anti-Caste* or later *Fraternity*. For some temperance activists such as Frederic Sessions who arranged for the distribution of *Anti-Caste* in Gloucestershire the split did not deter or prevent them from being involved with both networks; but it is possible that for Jacob the split was more problematic. The *Liverpool Mercury's* report of the successes of the Toxteth Lodge in 1884 suggests that the network of IOGT branches provided an effective space through which black people in Liverpool could come together for support and communion. Perhaps the *Anti-Caste* network of readers was too immaterial—or seemingly uninterested—in the seamen's grievances that Jacob more regularly faced with the men who came in and out of the Liverpool docks, or of the experiences of black working-class people in Britain more generally, to encourage them to join.

During the summer of 1888 Fanny Jackson Coppin stayed with Catherine Impey and her family at their home in Somerset. Jackson Coppin served as President of the Women's Home and Foreign Missionary Society of the AME Church and in her role as president she was elected to represent the society at the international missionary conference in London, prompting her first trip away from the United States.[41] Once in Britain she spent most of her time in London, but found her way to Street where she enjoyed peace and quiet away from the busy capital; she also became an *Anti-Caste* subscriber and distributor. Supporting Jackson Coppin during her visit represented an important strand of *Anti-Caste's* activist work during its first summer of publication. Over the few weeks she was in England Jackson Coppin spoke to audiences in London and other cities in the South, West, and Midlands of England detailing and explaining the racial prejudice faced by thousands of young people in Philadelphia. She told audiences of the hardships black men and women faced and their limited access to employment because they found themselves barred from employment in factories, from serving in shops, and smithing, carpentry and nearly all occupations that were ordinarily open to young white people of a similar age and class.

It is certainly possible that Jacob Christian heard Jackson Coppin speak during her tour. He may have also heard Celestine Edwards speak, who between 1887 and 1894 gave public lectures throughout the country from Bradford, Bristol, London, and Manchester to Sunderland, Sheffield, and Liverpool. In the earlier years of his career the talks were closely connected to the politics of the temperance movement, but as his reputation grew Edwards became a public lecturer on topics from 'Mahomet and the Koran', 'Utility actually a moral guide' to Bible classes.[42] Jacob Christian might well have joined the audiences who came together to discuss the 'demoralisation of native races by the Liquor trade' where Edwards spoke in December 1887 or perhaps he paid 3d for a reserved seat to hear Edwards speak about 'free thinking and free thought' at Hope Hall, Hope Street in Central Liverpool in March 1892, or his thoughts on 'The Negro Race and Darwinism' in April 1892.[43] If he were among these audiences, he would have surely made many connections between the experiences of exclusion and unemployment Jackson Coppin relayed about the United States and the battles with discrimination Celestine Edwards foregrounded, with his own and those of his friends and other seamen around him and perhaps also his own children growing up in Liverpool.

Anti-Caste's geographical imagination was an international one that connected the politics of racial prejudice in the United States with its different formations within the British Empire. This transnationalism is just one of the editorial aims that makes it such an interesting periodical, but why it was so rare that anything about racial prejudice 'at home' was reported upon remains a puzzling question. An exception occurred when *Anti-Caste* reflected upon a speech made by the Prime Minister Lord Salisbury 'in which he sneered at our fellow subjects in India as "Black Men"'.[44] Speaking in November 1888 Salisbury had been referring to the campaign of the Indian nationalist Dadabhai Naoroji who had unsuccessfully stood for election to Parliament in the central London seat of Holborn in 1886. Discussing Naroji's defeat Salisbury argued that however far the British had come in breaking down racial prejudice, he doubted if they had come to the point when any British constituency would elect a black man.[45] His remarks sparked an uproar which likely substantially contributed to Naoroji's successful election for Finsbury Central in London in

1892.[46] The affair entered the public's consciousness with angry letters to the press and satirical songs contributing to the making of Naoroji as the 'Radical hero of the hour'.[47] For *Anti-Caste*, Salisbury's position had provided a rare opportunity to discuss the operation of racial prejudice at home. This was not a claim that racial prejudice was usually absent in Britain but an observation that racial prejudice, 'the prompter of so many a cowardly and bloody act on the part of our rulers' for once could 'be openly seen'.[48]

However, men such as Jacob Christian could have offered Catherine Impey and *Anti-Caste* valuable insight into the way racial prejudice operated 'at home'; it was something they experienced and could clearly see. That the experiences of men like Jacob and those of their families were not drawn upon placed limitations on *Anti-Caste's* editorial framework. Understood as a shortcoming by Catherine Impey herself, the geographical imagination of her periodical was highly dependent upon and formed through Impey-as-editor's direct contact and personal relationships with informants and correspondents. That Jacob Christian, and men and women like him, were not part of Catherine Impey's network meant an important gap in *Anti-Caste's* analysis of racial prejudice persisted throughout its life; their experiences would have challenged and perhaps enabled Catherine Impey and other readers of *Anti-Caste* to better understand and 'see' how racial prejudice operated in Britain.

On the other hand the vast majority of Catherine Impey's correspondence connected to the production of *Anti-Caste* has not survived and perhaps Jacob Christian himself was not overlooked. Or perhaps he did not contribute to *Anti-Caste* because Catherine Impey and *Anti-Caste* just was not for him for a myriad of other reasons; perhaps Jacob just could not afford the cost of a subscription or the time to contribute; perhaps his perceived lack of writing skills, as suggested by the mark on his marriage certificate, eliminated him from the possibility of contributing; perhaps he did regularly read *Anti-Caste* or *Fraternity* as single copies as and when he could afford to, or for free in a Reading Room or café; or he may also have engaged with it through columns in the *Liverpool Daily Post*, which on a number of occasions directly referenced Catherine Impey and reviewed material in *Anti-Caste*.[49] Although drawing Jacob Christian out from the archive does not reveal much more about the diversity of *Anti-Caste's* working-class readers, his non-appearance among them highlights the suggestive and productive possibilities of absence, and that such absence can lead to the uncovering of other kinds of important networks that were in operation. In the case of Jacob Christian this includes networks of family and kinship, but also a network among seamen in the Liverpool docks who knew that, during the 1880s at least, Jacob and Octavia's boarding house was a place where black men would be welcome and perhaps find a space where they could share some of their frustrations and stories, ones that were not usually covered in the pages of *Anti-Caste*.

LIVING TOGETHER: GEOGRAPHIES OF CLASS, ACTIVISM, AND READERSHIP

It is difficult to know how to connect the unnamed and perhaps unknowable individuals in the crowd at talks given by Celestine Edwards to the seamen who joined Jacob Christian at their meeting in Liverpool and the reading networks of *Anti-Caste*. Imaginatively it seems likely that their experiences in Britain interconnected and their personal geographies overlapped in spaces such as lecture halls, reading rooms, and imaginative communities of readers. Being able to know how, when, and where such interactions could have occurred would be an important contribution not only to thinking about the diversity of readership of Victorians and their experiences of reading, but also about the individuals who made up the black presence in Victorian Britain. Men like Solomon Masse, who supported Celestine Edward's work with *Lux* and also worked with and for the Portsmouth branch of the SRBM, remain elusive archival figures in so many ways, and how he was placed with the networks of readers he was clearly closely and actively connected to remains difficult, at present, to reconstruct.

Though examining *Anti-Caste*, a largely unknown periodical, may present a seemingly narrowly focused case study, work involved in researching nineteenth-century periodicals and unpacking the reading experiences of the Victorians can generate and illuminate broader political moments and questions. Uncovering evidence of black lives in the Victorian city beyond the lines of an artists' pen, a witness record in an Old Bailey session paper, a printed note in a newspaper, a photograph in an asylum record or a national census return is not easy. In this instance the productivity of absence creates an opportunity to push a little deeper into the different cultural experiences black men and women encountered and developed within the communities in which they lived and worked. Scholars examining the development of Victorian women's activism have illustrated that reading communities were vital to women who were reflecting upon and developing their political identities, and that for many their participation in the women's movement was primarily a reading experience.[50] It is possible to make a similar argument for the men and women who read *Anti-Caste*. They were seeking to develop their understandings of and create a new political language with which to tackle racial prejudice. But the absence of Jacob Christian and many other potential readers from the Toxteth Lodge suggests that a coming together in physical space to meet and discuss was an essential part of the process for some people's activism, perhaps instead of, but more likely in addition to any reading communities they were a part of.

By placing individuals in the context of overlapping reading networks and their places in or outside them it becomes easier to consider the lives of individuals as part of dynamic processes of identity formations and activism in Britain rather than people fixed in moments of racialized difference. It perhaps also makes it easier to place them within the networks of organizations such as the temperance movement, *Anti-Caste* and *Lux*. As such the stories around them that we have yet to uncover have an important role to play in developing our understandings of social interactions and cultural understandings of the lives of others during the long nineteenth century. Certainly Jacob Christian and the presence of his family in Liverpool suggest that where the historical geography of multi-ethnic and multi-cultural communities in Britain is concerned there is still plenty to be recovered. Examining how and why Jacob and members of his family did or did not become part of particular reading communities is an important tool for us to use in the remapping of their political, cultural and intellectual lives.

Notes

1. Material on *Anti-Caste's* establishment and known readers is taken from and explored in greater depth in C. Bressey, *Empire, Race and the Politics of Anti-Caste* (London: Bloomsbury Academic, 2013).
2. P. Fryer, *Staying Power: The History of Black People in Britain* (London: Pluto Press, 1986).
3. For details of the complexities involved in the relaunch and eventual decline of *Anti-Caste* see C. Bressey, *Empire, Race and the Politics of Anti-Caste*.
4. J. Kneale, 'The Place of Drink: Temperance and the Public, 1856–1914', *Social & Cultural Geography* 2.1 (2001), 43–59.
5. C. Impey, 'Templar Politics', *Village Album*, 29, Alfred Gillett Trust Archive, Street, Somerset.

6. This is, to put it mildly, a simplification of events, for a detailed examination of the split see D. Fahey, *Temperance and Racism: John Bull, Johnny Reb and the Good Templars* (Lexington: University Press of Kentucky, 1996).
7. Impey had first been elected to this post in 1886, see *Liverpool Mercury*, 29 April 1886; Fahey, *Temperance and Racism*.
8. Catherine Impey to Frederick Douglass, 15 February 1883, Frederick Douglass Papers, Library of Congress, Washington.
9. Catherine Impey to Frederick Douglass, 15 February 1883, Frederick Douglass Papers, Library of Congress, Washington.
10. An appeal concerning the treatment of Coloured Races', MSS Brit Emp s. 20 E5/8, The Bodleian Library of Commonwealth and African Studies, University of Oxford.
11. For examples of tracing readers see E. McHenry, '"An Association of Kindred Spirits": Black Readers and their Reading Rooms' in S. Towheed, R. Crone, and K. Halsey, eds., *The History of Reading* (London and New York: Routledge, 2011), pp. 310–22; L. Warren, '"Women in Conference": Reading the Correspondence Columns in *Woman*, 1890–1910', in L. Brake, B. Bell, and D. Finkelstein, eds., *Nineteenth-Century Media and the Construction of Identities* (London: Palgrave, 2000), pp. 122–34.
12. On Quaker kinship networks see S. Holton, 'Kinship and Friendship: Quaker Women's Networks and the Women's Movement', *Women's History Review* 14, no. 3 & 4 (2005), 365–84.
13. Catherine Impey to Frederick Chesson, 1 March 1888, Brit Emp. s. 18 C138/173, The Bodleian Library of Commonwealth and African Studies, University of Oxford.
14. 'Editor's Address to Friends of Anti-Caste', *Anti-Caste*, January 1893.
15. Supplement to *Anti-Caste*, January 1890.
16. 'Promises of Help in Distribution', *Anti-Caste*, March 1889, 4.
17. Supplement to *Anti-Caste*, January 1890.
18. Supplement to *Anti-Caste*, January 1891, 4.
19. Catherine Impey to Albion Tourgée, 16 June 1890, 4785, Albion W. Tourgée Papers, Chautauqua County Historical Society, Westfield, New York.
20. 'Editor's Address to Friends of Anti-Caste', *Anti-Caste*, January 1893, 4.
21. 'Rev. Orishatukeh Faduman, Pastor at Troy, NC and Principal of Peabody Academy', *American Missionary* 63 (1909), 2.
22. William Stevens Powell, *Dictionary of North Carolina Biography*, Vol. 2 (Chapel Hill: University of North Caroline Press, 1986).
23. Simpson received her degree, aged 55, from the University of Chicago for her research on 'Herder's conception of "das Volk"'. See Personal, 'Georgiana R. Simpson', *The Journal of Negro History* 29.2 (1944), 245–47.

24. F. Coppin, *Reminiscences of School Life, and Hints on Teaching* (Philadelphia: A.M.E. Book Concern, 1913).
25. See F. Coppin, *Reminiscences*; Linda M. Perkins, 'Coppin, Fanny Jackson', *American National Biography Online*, February 2000, http://www.anb.org/articles/09/09-00202.html, date accessed 2 November 2015.
26. *Anti-Caste*, List of Subscribers, 1892, January 1893, 8.
27. *Anti-Caste*, July and August 1890.
28. *Fraternity*, December 1893, 6–7.
29. Fahey, *Temperance and Racism*, 79.
30. On examples of the black presence in British archives see C. Bressey, 'Four Women: Black Women Writing in London Between 1880 and 1920', in F. Paisley and K. Reid, eds., *Critical Perspectives on Colonialism: Writing the Empire from Below* (Oxford: Routledge, 2013), pp. 178–98; C. Bressey, 'Geographies of Belonging: White Women and Black History', *Women's History Review* 22.4 (2013), 541–58.
31. *Liverpool Mercury*, 25 August 1880, 'Coloured Seamen and their Grievances', 5.
32. *Liverpool Mercury*, 25 August 1880, 'Coloured Seamen and their Grievances', 5.
33. *Liverpool Mercury*, 5 August 1886, 6; 11 August 1886, 6.
34. *Liverpool Mercury*, 7 April 1885, 'English Good Templary', 3.
35. *Liverpool Mercury*, 11 April 1885, 'Independent Order of Good Templars', 6.
36. *Liverpool Mercury*, 22 October 1894.
37. 1871 England Census, Class: *RG10*; Piece: *3796*; Folio: *8*; Page: *8*; GSU roll: *841901*.
38. Class: *RG11*; Piece: *3637*; Folio: *9*; Page: *15*; GSU roll: *1341871*.
39. *Liverpool Mercury*, 15 April 1884, 6.
40. Jacob's employment here as a Timber Merchant now aligns him with Fahey's findings in *Temperance and Racism*, though Jacob's place of birth is given, not in Africa, but the West Indies in the 1881 census (Class: *RG11*; Piece: *3637*; Folio: *9*; Page: *15*; GSU roll: *1341871*) and the 1891 census returns (Class: *RG12*; Piece: *2924*; Folio: *104*; Page: *3*; GSU roll: *6098034*).
41. F. Jackson Coppin (1913) *Reminiscences*.
42. In London, *Pall Mall Gazette*, 26 February 1887; in Wolverhampton, *Hampshire Advertiser*, 3 September 1887; in Bradford, *Morning Post*, 7 October 1887; *Sunderland Daily Echo and Shipping Gazette*, 28 September 1891; *Liverpool Mercury*, 28 April 1892; 'Mohamet and the Koran', *Lux*, 12 August 1892; 'Moral Guide', 27 August 1892.
43. 'Free Thinking', *Liverpool Mercury*, 31 March 1892, 1; 'Demoralisation of Native Races by the Liquor Trade', *Liverpool Mercury*, 5 December 1887, 6; *Liverpool Mercury*, 28 April 1892, 6.

44. *Anti-Caste*, January 1889, 1.
45. *Pall Mall Gazette*, 1 December 1888, 4.
46. R. Visram, *Asians in Britain: 400 Years of History* (London: Pluto Press, 2002). For examples of the ensuing debate see the *Pall Mall Gazette*, 4 December 1888, 11.
47. *Belfast News-Letter*, 27 December 1888, 5.
48. *Anti-Caste*, January 1889, 1.
49. For example in 'News of the Day', *Liverpool Daily Post*, 2 March 1889.
50. L. Delap and M. Di Cenzo, 'Transatlantic Print Culture: The Anglo-American Feminist Press and Emerging "Modernities"', in A. Ardis and P. Collier, eds., *Transatlantic Print Culture 1880–1940: Emerging Media, Emerging Modernisms* (Basingstoke: Palgrave Macmillan, 2008), pp. 48–65.

CHAPTER 6

John Dicks's Cheap Reprint Series, 1850s–1890s: Reading Advertisements

Anne Humpherys

John Thomas Dicks, though relatively disregarded by modern critics, arguably was the most successful of a new breed of young, savvy, and enterprising nineteenth-century British publishers who successfully catered for the emerging mass market. He is mainly known to most Victorian scholars, if he is known at all, as the business partner of G.W.M. Reynolds and publisher of Reynolds's mammoth 12-volume best seller, *The Mysteries of London* and *The Mysteries of the Court of London* (1844–55), the popular journal *Reynolds' Miscellany* (begun in 1846 and merged with *Bow Bells*,

---

The following essay is a part of a longer project on the dissemination of culture to the working class by the publications of the John Dicks Press. I am indebted to Louis James, not only for his knowledge of G.W.M. Reynolds and John Dicks as well as working-class print culture in general, but for his generosity in suggesting ways to organize the disparate material in this essay.

A. Humpherys (✉)
Lehman College and the Graduate Center, City University of New York, New York, USA

© The Author(s) 2016
P.R. Rooney, A. Gasperini (eds.), *Media and Print Culture Consumption in Nineteenth-Century Britain*, New Directions in Book History, DOI 10.1057/978-1-137-58761-9_6

a major source of popular fiction, in 1869), and the radical working-class weekly *Reynolds Weekly Newspaper* (started in 1850).[1] But in his own time, Dicks was known as much or even more for another series of publishing ventures that bore his own name, that is, Dicks's reprint series, in which he shrewdly combined individual texts—mainly drama and novels—into special numbered and titled series (which encouraged buyers or readers to obtain more of individual entries in the series). These series were aggressively advertised in all of Dicks's publications, a phenomenon that I argue had an impact on what his readers came to think was 'Literature'.

In 1866 Dicks told the firm that published all these works, the John Dicks Press, that he had 'mentally resolved that [the reprint series] should achieve the greatest success in the sphere of cheap literature … and that from 313 Strand, publications were issued which enjoyed the highest circulation ever obtained by any periodicals in this or any other country' (*Reynolds's Weekly Newspaper*, 15 July 1866, p. 5). And he was successful in this resolve. Though circulation figures are hard to come by and potentially unreliable, the individual penny Shakespere (Dicks's spelling) texts were reported in 1868 as having sold 150,000 copies (*Reynolds's Weekly Newspaper*, 15 July 1866, p. 5). Further, William St Clair based his estimate that Dicks's *Frankenstein* (in the reprint series 'Dicks' English Classics' from later in the century) sold in the tens of hundreds or thousands of copies on the known sales of some of Dicks's other reprints.[2]

Dicks's Readers

So who might the readers of these cheap reprints have been? Historians of the period agree that the nineteenth century saw a watershed in English print culture. This came as social and educational developments, in particular the movement to the towns, created mass literacy at a time when revolutions in printing and book distribution made cheap printed matter universally available. Print and reading were no longer the privilege of an educated few, but became central to everyday life.

However, as with all questions of the readership of any periodical or book in the Victorian period, it is difficult if not impossible to say for sure who actually bought any publications, including Dicks's reprint series, and who read them and how. But the price of one penny for the individual plays or sixpence for the novels suggests that these weekly publications, in small type and on inferior paper, were intended for the working classes, as is confirmed by a number of scholars like Jonathan Rose who states that 'autodidacts could afford reprints such as John Dicks' English Classics'.[3]

But while the growth in the reading public is clear, their actual reading experience remains problematic because we have so little record of working-class comments about their reading. We can, in some cases, tally the number of copies printed and sold, but that does not tell us anything about the actual reading experience. Most of the evidence used to determine this has come from working-class autobiographies, largely of autodidacts in quest of 'high' culture, which do not necessarily give an accurate indicator of the general public. Almost all comments about Dicks's reprint series, for example, are about reading Dicks's Shakespere. Thomas Okey, a basket weaver and self-taught Italian scholar, recalled that during his early apprenticeship days at Spitalfields, in order 'to read in secret I encamped to the washhouse' where his grandfather found him 'reading there a copy of Dicks' shilling edition of Shakespeare—the whole marvelous feat of cheap publishing'. Thomas Burt, miner, trade unionist, and politician, wrote that 'the plays [of Shakespeare] published by Dicks cost me one penny each, a sum well suited to my means'.[4] And William Stead, the future editor of the *Pall Mall Gazette*, said he 'formed his taste for literature by reading Dicks' penny-number Shakespeare as an office boy in Newcastle'.[5] In fact Andrew Murphy concludes his chapter on mid-Victorian working-class readers of Shakespeare by saying that 'the real break through came with the efforts of John Dicks who, together with Reynolds, made a real commitment to providing reading material to the poorest members of society at an easily affordable price'.[6]

But while the comments on Dicks's Shakespere series give us a sense of the aspirational elements of working-class autobiographers, there were other works they read which were less—sometimes far less—canonical. As Robert Webb asserts, 'the craze for cheap fiction is the outstanding characteristic of popular literature'.[7] It seems that the working-class autobiographers were less likely to recount their experience of reading popular novels or plays like *Varney the Vampire*, a best-selling serial novel by James Malcolm Rhymer and Thomas Peckett Prest (1845–47) or a melodrama like *The Miller and his Men by* Isaac Pocock (1835), a favourite of Charles Dickens, than of Shakespeare. So how might we locate the other reading experiences of working-class readers, that of reading popular literature? One way is to turn to the advertisements for Dicks's reprint series to see what this shrewd publisher thought his audience might want access to in cheap reprint editions in addition to Shakespeare.

Dicks's reprint series were certainly not the first such publications in nineteenth-century Britain.[8] A number of such reprint series were published in the early part of the century, for instance D. Green's

'Cheap Books', reprints of the classics advertised for the working-class *Northern Star* in 1839 (12 January 1839, p. 1).[9] R.K. Webb notes that novels were published in penny or two-penny volumes or numbers in the early part of the century (Webb, 1954, p. 31), but most of the early fiction reprints were too expensive for individual purchase by members of the working classes. Richard Altick notes that Bohn's 1847 fiction libraries sold for 3s.6d and 5s, and says further that 'these prices remained the standard for at least two decades' (Altick, 1957, p. 309).

Dicks's penny and sixpence prices for his various reprint series were probably not possible until the bigger, faster printing machines became more available and the use of stereotype printing (which meant that the weekly, monthly, and other forms of each work could be printed from the same plate, thus further reducing printing costs) more general.[10] Thus, not until after 1850 was there an explosion of very cheap reprints of English literature, especially fiction. By the 1880s this explosion of cheap material became a deluge, as David Vincent affirms: 'the pioneering efforts of [David] Milner and Dicks in the field of cheap reprints had attracted as many of ninety imitations by the 1890s'.[11]

THE JOHN DICKS PRESS'S REPRINT SERIES

John Thomas Dicks was born in 1818 in London. Not much is known about his early life, but he began in the printing trade around age 14 in the Queens and other printing offices. At age 23, he became the chief assistant of P.P. Thomas, a scholar of Chinese, who was at that time in the business of publishing, printing, and stereotyping in Warwick Square. In 1848 Dicks rescued G.W.M. Reynolds from one of his several bankruptcies and the two formed a connection that lasted until Reynolds's death in 1879. Dicks died two years later. The John Dicks Press survived both.[12] Dicks's business sense saved Reynolds financially and Reynolds's enormous output of popular fiction and periodicals made them both rich. Dicks died in 1881 leaving an estate of £50,000.

In 1852, Dicks, whom Reynolds called his 'managing and confidential clerk', had 'all the details of the business placed under his supervision' (*Reynolds's Weekly Newspaper*, 18 July 1853, p. 2). In 1863 the two formed a formal partnership, and eventually, Dicks purchased the name and copyrights of G.W.M. Reynolds. The firm expanded significantly in the 1860s by reprinting novels and plays in the various Dicks reprint series rather than originating new works, though Reynolds's fiction continued to be printed in several different formats. According to Montague Summers, during the latter half of the century the firm was 'one of the largest and busiest printing and publishing offices in England'.[13]

There were some dozen of Dicks's reprint series beginning in the 1850s and continuing beyond his death. The first, as indicated above, was Dicks's Penny Shakespere that began in the mid-1850s, which the *Bookseller* called 'the most wonderful edition yet published' (18 July 1868, p. 447). Also important was Dicks's massive investment in the printing of other play texts beginning in 1864 (drama was at the centre of Victorian culture in ways we have largely forgotten), the reprint series of which—Dicks's Standard Plays—was second in popularity to that of Shakespeare. Montague Summers later praised this series saying 'It may be sentimental, but is none the less true, that those of us who were brought up on Dicks' Standard Plays will always have a very warm corner of our hearts for these penny scripts, which possess a personality all their own' (Summers, 1942, p. 552). This series began with the publication of two plays a week for a penny. The early numbers were reprints of earlier plays, but eventually the list included contemporary plays, many of which exist in published form only in the Dicks editions. The third literary reprint series was 'Dicks' English Novels' at 6d a volume probably beginning in 1869–70[14] and ultimately numbering 243 titles.[15] The first number was *For a Woman's Sake* by Watts Phillips, originally published serially in Dicks's periodical *Bow Bells* starting 6 July 1870.[16]

All the individual reprints were illustrated with a lively action illustration on the cover, which was repeated on the first page of the text. These illustrations were made from wood engravings and most were, as Brian Maidment says, of similar illustrations in G.W.M. Reynolds's serialized novels, 'often highly finished and tonally complex'.[17] They were rarely signed by the artist. They generally represented a dramatic moment likely to attract a buyer, for as Richard Altick says: 'the popularity of Dicks' books reflected the humble reader's continuing appetite for sensational literature' (Altick, 1957, p. 308). For example, the cover and first page of *Othello*, Dicks's Standard Plays has an illustration showing Othello standing over the sleeping Desdemona. A caption reads 'IT IS THE CAUSE—IT IS THE CAUSE MY SOUL'.

The individual penny texts of the Standard Plays were 4 3/4″ by 7 1/4″ in size and had advertisements for the various Dicks reprint series (and also for the inevitable pharmaceuticals, a mainstay of cheap publications) on the inside and back covers and from one to four pages at the end of the text. The 'English Novels' were in an 8″ by 10″ format. Frequently, when the weekly publications were bound into volume form, the illustrated covers and advertisements were stripped out.[18] What is constant, however, is that the individual weekly numbers were published from the same plates in all formats, though by 1888 these plates were nearly worn out, especially that of the Dicks Penny Shakespere (Guy Dicks, 2015, pp. 95–94).

There was considerable concern in the nineteenth century about working-class reading, the most well-known piece now, perhaps, being Wilkie Collins's 'The Unknown Public' published in *Household Words* in 1858 (21 August, pp. 217–22). Most nineteenth-century commentators were highly critical of the cheap periodicals and novels that the 'lower' classes read, as is Collins in his piece. But later scholars, especially in the last decade or so, have been more circumspect about the Victorian working-class readers, particularly as archives of working-class autobiographies have become available.[19] Jonathan Rose's study of the working-class 'intellectual', perhaps demonstrating the desire to counter the nineteenth-century criticisms of the quality of what was read by working-class readers, emphasizes these readers' desire 'to acquire cultural capital' and their eagerness 'to learn about canonical texts'.[20]

My work in this chapter is part of this later scholarly work, but I have an adjustment to make in the current trend of scholarship on working-class reading. If we look mainly at the totals of how many copies were sold of each of the Dicks reprint series or at the writings of aspirational working-class autobiographers, the evidence definitely supports Rose's and other scholars' conclusions about the desire for 'classics' among working-class readers. As I have previously indicated, the highest selling series of Dicks's reprints was the Penny Shakespere and also very popular was the reprint series of Walter Scott's Waverly Novels (32 novels published priced at 3d apiece.)[21]

But my hypothesis, based not on circulation numbers but rather on the advertisements for Dicks's reprint series, comes to a somewhat different conclusion. A study of the advertisements, with their long lists of sequentially numbered titles paints a different picture of what the readers might have read or at the very least what the canny businessman John Dicks thought they wanted to read. Any final determination of who were the 'real readers' of the advertisements for Dicks's reprint series or what they made of the lists of texts in the advertised lists is probably impossible. But considering the order of the contents in the reprint series lists—that is, the placing of, say, Shakespeare's *King Lear* next to the melodrama *The Gamester* by Edward Moore, and Dickens's *Pickwick* next to *The Doom of the Dancing Master* by C.H. Ross[22] (first serialized in Dicks's popular periodical *Bow Bells* in 1875) in the persistent advertisements of these series—I speculate that the readers of these advertisements might have gained an enlarged and democratic sense of what was 'standard' or even 'classic'[23] literature.[24] That is, the take-away from perusing the heterogeneous ordering of texts in the advertisements for Dicks's reprint series might be that the categories of both 'classic' and 'standard' (and as we'll see later, even 'English') literature were constructed from an apparent equivalency between the 'classics' that later scholars have posited many working-class readers aspired to in Dicks's formats, *and* the popular literature he also published that was actually written for them and that so worried contemporary critics. The fact that the advertisements for 'Dicks' Standard Plays' do not include the authors' names demonstrates this further—a list of only titles suggests an equality among the texts.

However, there are some problems with trying to analyse these series and their advertisements. None of the individual publications or the volumes or the advertisements are dated, another sharp business practice since it allowed the initial numbers to be reprinted frequently in different formats—monthly, collected or in other series, as with the Penny Shakespere. Nor did many libraries collect the cheap reprints when they first appeared. Rather, they might have volumes made up of the individual parts, but usually with the covers and advertisement pages stripped out. The only way to determine even an approximate dating, thus, is by how many titles the advertised lists contain, since the more titles on the list, the later in the century the individual texts or bound volume was published.[25]

None of this makes much difference if all you want is to see the play (frequently available only in a Dicks format which is why 'Dicks' Standard Plays' is arguably the most important of his reprint series) or novel (though not many novels from 'Dicks' English Novels' series are in libraries), since the work will probably be catalogued by the individual author's name. But if you are interested in sorting out the publication history of the Dicks reprint series and analysing the target audience, you have a thorny problem indeed, as Andrew King points out in his blog about Dicks's Library of Standard Works.[26]

Further complicating matters is that the numbering of the individual entries may differ as different texts—usually just out of copyright[27]—are inserted not at the end or the beginning of the list, but in the middle, a practice that is central to my thesis about the democratizing impact of the advertisements for Dicks's reprint series. In 'Dicks' Standard Plays', for example, most of the reprints in the very beginning were plays dating from the eighteenth century and earlier.[28] This was not necessarily because that is what Dicks thought his readers might want—though they might have—but mainly because copyright could be an obstacle to the production of cheap reprints of contemporary work. As Altick notes '[in] the latter half of the century there were some eighty or ninety inexpensive series consisting chiefly, if not exclusively, of reprints of the English classics. One reason for this phenomenon was that classics, being out of copyright, were cheaper to publish' (Altick, 1957, p. 308).

Thus, Dickens's novels come onto 'Dicks' English Novels' advertisements a decade or so after the series begins. But they are not added at the end or the beginning of the list but rather inserted individually into the middle of the list. So *Nicholas Nickleby* came in as number 84 (out of copyright in 1881); *Oliver Twist* as number 85 (out of copyright in 1880), and *Barnaby Rudge* as number 86 (out of copyright in 1883).[29] However, Harrison Ainsworth's novels were part of 'Dicks' English Novels' while they were still in copyright because Dicks bought Ainsworth's copyrights (Ainsworth's contract for selling the rights to *The South Sea Bubble* to Dicks in 1868 for £400 is one of the few business records of Dicks's publishing house that has survived [Guy Dicks, 2015, p. 37]). It is also probably no accident that quite a few of the serialized novels published in Dicks's periodical *Bow Bells* (1862–97) became part of the 'English Novels' series since they were copyrighted through publication in Dicks's journal, and in many cases appear in no other print form than the Dicks imprint.

Plays could be another matter in terms of copyright. Though Dicks began his 'Standard Plays' reprint series with plays out of copyright, as the series went on, titles were added that could technically still be in copyright, like number 82 *Under the Earth, or, the Sons of Toil* by Frederick Fox Cooper (1867) and based on *Hard Times*.[30] Dicks could have used actors' copies of contemporary plays rather than the official copies submitted to the Lord Chancellor for copyright protection; acting copies could technically escape copyright through being revised and changed by the actors and managers.

Also, as with Harrison Ainsworth, Dicks could have bought other copyrights which would have allowed him to reprint works still in copyright. A note added to an advertisement for 'Dicks' Standard Plays' on the back cover of number 7 *A New Way to Pay Old Debts* by Philip Massinger states 'AUTHORS desirous of selling the Copyrights of their Pieces are requested to apply by letter to Mr. J. Dicks, 313 Strand. As it is intended to confine this Publication to the superior productions of the stage, it will be needless to offer anything that has not been eminently successful.' Unfortunately we have no business records to indicate if indeed Dicks bought the copyrights for any plays or novels other than Ainsworth's, though since he bought those, it is reasonable to assume he bought others.

However, though copyright undoubtedly determined some of the ordering of the plays and novels in Dicks's reprint series, that does not necessarily change how readers might have gained an enlarged view of what constituted standard English literature through reading the advertisements in which the lists were made up of apparently equally worthy popular, standard, and classic literature. In other words the advertised lists of numbered works with their miscellaneous collection of texts created a canon not just of the literature the working classes might aspire to (Shakespeare), but rather one in which that literature was implicitly valued no more nor more less than the many popular works which were actually written for the working classes and many of which were published by Dicks himself.

THE ADVERTISEMENTS FOR DICKS'S REPRINT SERIES OF PLAYS AND NOVELS

To illustrate how the advertised lists of Dicks's reprint series would have looked to its readers, I will focus on some of the advertisements of two of Dicks's early series, the 'Standard Plays' started in 1864 and continuing through the end of the century, and the 'English Novels' beginning at the end of the 1860s and continuing for two decades.

Publishing two plays a week (for the most part) for over 40 years, Dicks's Standard Plays ultimately contained 1074 titles[31] (see Fig. 6.1).

When Shakespeare texts enter the series list, most are scattered throughout the advertisement surrounded by eighteenth-century popular plays and some nineteenth-century melodramas. For example, in a post-1874 advertisement for Dicks's Standard Plays list,[32] *King Lear* at Number 6 comes between *The Gamester* (by Edward Moore [1793]) at Number 5, and *A New Way to Pay Old Debts* (by Philip Massinger [1626]) at Number 7. Then Number 8 is the melodrama *The Road to Ruin* (by Thomas Holcraft [1792]) which is followed by Number 9 Shakespeare's *Merry Wives of Windsor*. Number 10 is another melodrama by George Colman *The Iron Chest* (1796), followed by Number 11 *Hamlet* which is followed by a third melodrama Number 12 (by Benjamin Thompson *The Stranger* [1820]) and then at Number 13 *The Merchant of Venice* (incomplete, however, with no fifth act) followed by Number 14, a five-act comedy *The Honeymoon* (by John Tobin [1804])[33] and so on. Thus, this advertisement for Dicks's Standard Plays presents its readers with a grouping of 'Standard Plays' in which the melodramatic writers Moore and Holcroft are on the face of it equal to Shakespeare, a levelling (or enhancing) emphasized by the lack of authors' names. The reader of the advertisement has only the

ADVERTISEMENTS.

Now Publishing, Price One Penny, Weekly,

DICKS' STANDARD PLAYS,

AND

FREE ACTING DRAMA.

FOR THE REPRESENTATION OF WHICH THERE IS NO LEGAL CHARGE.

1 Othello
2 School for Scandal
3 Werner
4 She Stoops to Conquer
5 The Gamester
6 King Lear
7 New way to Pay old Debts
8 Road to Ruin
9 Merry wives of Windsor
10 The Iron Chest
11 Hamlet
12 The Stranger
13 Merchant of Venice
14 The Honeymoon
15 Pizarro
16 Man of the World
17 Much Ado about Nothing
18 The Rivals
19 Damon and Pythias
20 Macbeth
21 John Bull
22 Fazio
23 Speed the Plough
24 Jane Shore
25 Evadne
26 Antony and Cleopatra
27 The Wonder
28 The miller and his men
29 The Jealous Wife
30 Therese
31 Brutus
32 The Maid of Honour
33 A Winter's Tale
34 The Poor Gentleman
35 The Castle Spectre
36 The Heir-at-Law
37 Love in a Village
38 A Tale of mystery
39 Douglas
40 The Critic
41 George Barnwell
42 Grecian Daughter
43 As You Like it
44 Cato
45 The Beggars' Opera
46 Isabella
47 The Revenge
48 Lord of the Manor
49 Romeo and Juliet
50 Sardanapalus
51 The Hypocrite
52 Venice Preserved
53 The Provoked Husband
54 Clandestine marriage
55 Fair Penitent
56 Two Gentlemen of Verona
57 Fatal Curiosity
58 Belle's Stratagem
59 Manfred
60 Rule a Wife, &c.
61 Bertram
62 Wheel of Fortune
63 The Duke of Milan
64 Good-Natured Man
65 King John
66 Beaux' Stratagem
67 Arden of Faversham
68 Trip to Scarborough
69 Lady Jane Grey
70 Rob Roy
71 [illegible] Father
72 The Provoked wife
73 The Two Foscari
74 Foundling of the Forest
75 All the World's a Stage
76 Richard III
77 Bold Stroke for a wife
78 Castle of Sorrento
[illegible]

85 The Brothers
86 Way of the world
87 Cymbeline
88 She Would, &c.
89 Deserted Daughter
90 Wives as They Were, and maids as They Are
91 Every man in his humour
92 Midsummer Night's Dream
93 Tamerlane
94 Bold Stroke for a husband
95 Julius Cæsar
96 All for Love
97 The Tempest
98 Richard Cœur de Lion
99 The Mourning Bride
100 The bashful man
101 Barbarossa
102 The Curfew
103 Merchant of Bruges
104 Giovanni in London
105 Timon of Athens
106 Honest Thieves
107 West Indian
108 The Earl of Essex
109 The Irish Widow
110 The Farmer's Wife
111 Tancred and Sigismunda
112 The Panel
113 Deformed Transformed
114 The Soldier's Daughter
115 Monsieur Tonson
116 The Black Prince
117 School for Wives
118 Coriolanus
119 The Citizen
120 The First Floor
121 The Foundling
122 Oroonoko
123 Love a-la-Mode
124 Richard II
125 Siege of Belgrade
126 Samson Agonistes
127 Maid of the mill
128 One o'Clock
129 Who's the Dupe?
130 Mahomet
131 Duplicity
132 The Devil to Pay
133 Troilus and Cressida
134 Ways and means
135 All in the Wrong
136 Cross Purposes
137 The Orphan
138 Bon Ton
139 Tender Husband
140 El Hyder
141 The Country Girl
142 Midas
143 Castle of Andalusia
144 Two Strings to your Bow
145 Measure for measure
146 The miser
147 Haunted Tower
148 The Tailors
149 Love for Love
150 [illegible] of Calabria
151 Zara
152 High Life below Stairs
153 [illegible]
154 The [illegible]
155 [illegible]
156 The [illegible]
157 [illegible]
158 The [illegible]
159 [illegible]
160 [illegible]
161 [illegible]

168 Recruiting Sergeant
169 Animal magnetism
170 The Confederacy
171 The Carmelite
172 The Chances
173 Follies of a Day
174 Titus Andronicus
175 Paul and Virginia
176 Know your own mind
177 The Padlock
178 Constant Couple
179 Better Late than Never
180 My Spouse and I
181 Every One has his Fault
182 The Deuce is in him
183 Adopted Child
184 Lovers' Vows
185 Maid of the Oaks
186 The Duenna
187 Turnpike Gate
188 Lady of Lyons
189 Miss in her Teens
190 Twelfth Night
191 Lodoiska
192 Earl of Warwick
193 Fortune's Frolics
194 Way to keep him
195 Braganza
196 No Song no Supper
197 Taming of the Shrew
198 Spanish Student
199 Double Dealer
200 Mock Doctor
201 Fashionable lover
202 The Guardian
203 Cain
204 Rosina
205 Love's Labour Lost
206 The Hunchback
207 The Apprentice
208 Raising the Wind
209 Lovers' Quarrels
210 Rent Day
211 Crononhotonthologos
212 His first champagne
213 Pericles
214 Robinson Crusoe
215 He's much to Blame
216 Ella Rosenberg
217 The Quaker
218 School of Reform
219 King Henry IV (1)
220 Fifteen Years of a Drunkard's Life
221 Thomas and Sally
222 Bombastes Furioso
223 First Love
224 Somnambulist
225 All's Well that Ends Well
226 Lottery Ticket
227 Gustavus Vasa
228 Sweethearts and Wives
229 Miller of Mansfield
230 Black-Eyed Susan
231 King Henry IV (2)
232 The Station-House
233 Recruiting Officer
234 The Tower of Nesle
235 King Henry V
236 The Rendezvous
237 Appearances is Against Them
238 William Tell
239 [illegible]
240 The [illegible] Progress
241 King Henry VI [illegible]
242 [illegible]
243 [illegible]

250 Mrs. Wiggins
251 Mysterious husband
252 Heart of Midlothian
253 King Henry VI. (3)
254 Illustrious Stranger
255 Register Office
256 Dominique
257 Chapter of Accidents
258 Descarte
259 Hero and Leander
260 Cure for Heartache
261 Siege of Damascus
262 The Secret
263 Deaf and Dumb
264 Banks of the Hudson
265 The Wedding Day
266 Laugh when you can
267 What Next?
268 Raymond and Agnes
269 Lionel and Clarissa
270 Red crow
271 The Contrivance
272 Broken Sword
273 Polly Honeycomb
274 Nell Gwynne
275 Cymon
276 Perfection
277 Count of Narbonne
278 Of Age To-morrow
279 Orphan of China
280 Pedlar's Acre
281 Mogul's Tale
282 Othello Travestie
283 Law of Lombardy
284 Day after the wedding
285 The Jew
286 Irish Tutor
287 Such Things Are
288 The Wife
289 Dragon of Wantley
290 Suil Dhuv
291 Lying Valet
292 Lily of St. Leonards
293 Oliver Twist
294 The Housekeeper
295 Child of Nature
296 Home, Sweet Home
297 Which is the man?
298 Caius Gracchus
299 Mayor of Garratt
300 Woodman
301 Midnight Hour
302 Woman's Wit
303 The Purse
304 Votary of Wealth
305 Life Buoy
306 Wild Oats
307 Rookwood
308 Gambler's Fate
309 Herne the Hunter
310 "Yes!" and "No!"
311 The Sea-captain
312 Eugene Aram
313 Wrecker's Daughter
314 Alfred the Great
315 (Virginia mummy / Intrigue
316 (My Neighbour's wife / Married Bachelor
317 Richelieu
318 Money
319 Ion
320 The Bridal
321 Paul Pry
322 Love-chase
323 [illegible]
324 [illegible]

Fig. 6.1 John Dicks's Standard Plays List

titles with which to construct what is 'standard' dramatic literature. When Fox Cooper's dramatic adaptation of *Hard Times* comes in as number 87, probably in 1871 or 1872, this enlarged list of 'standard plays' expands again to include a popular contemporary play. The advertisement suggests not only a rich particularly English dramatic heritage, but one in which Shakespeare is just one of many 'standard' English playwrights.

Another example of this interweaving of Dicks's heterogeneous advertised lists are those for the 'Dicks' English Novels' series. From the 1870s through the 1890s, the works on this list remain more or less in the same order, though as works by Dickens and others come out of copyright they are inserted into the middle of the list, thus throwing the numbering off but not the order. Montague Summers thought there were probably 243 titles in the 'Standard English Novels' series though he added '[It] is difficult to estimate exactly how many romances were published by Dicks since, towards the end, one or two novels were printed, but for reasons (presumably difficulties of copyright) never published, whilst some titles were announced but never printed' (Summers, 1942, p. 552). In a later (probably 1890s) advertisement for 'Dicks' English Novels', listing 225 titles, the longest advertised list I have found and 18 short of Summers's estimate, *Pickwick Papers* (at Number 60) is squeezed in between *Playing to Win* by Manville Fenn at Number 59 (serially published *Bow Bells* beginning 14 April 1875) and *Doom of the Dancing Master* by C.H. Ross (also published serially in *Bow Bells*, beginning 22 September 1875) at Number 61 while three other Dickens novels are sandwiched between *Splendid Misery* by Colin Henry Hazlewood (Number 83)[34] and Number 87 *Ingaretha* by M.E.O. Malen (serially published in *Bow Bells* beginning 16 August 1871), the only one of these particular novels that are in the British Library catalogue, in fact in a one volume version that is part of 'Dicks' Standard English Novels' dated in the British Library catalogue as 1875.

Other examples of this democratic mixing in the advertisements for the 'Standard English Novels' list include Thackeray's *Paris Sketchbook* (1840) at Number 115 which is surrounded by a novel by Charles Lever, Number 112 *Charles O'Malley* (1841); a two-part novel by Bulwer Lytton (Numbers 113, *Ernest Maltravers* 1837 and 114 *Alice, or the Mysteries* 1838), and Number 116 *Jacob Faithful* by Captain Marryat (1834), Lord Lytton's *Night and Morning* (1841) at Number 117, and 118 G.W.M. Reynolds's *Rosa Lambert* (1854). Whether or not the readers of the advertisements read any of these works in this order, their perusing the advertisement would, it seems to me, have suggested a levelling of all these heterogeneous novels to one plane of standard English literature.

The advertised lists thus present a new kind of canon of standard texts, not one organized by the classics, not one organized chronologically, but one of a heterogeneous mixture of all types from all periods. We might describe this canon as Jon Klancher in his 1983 article 'From "Crowd" to "Audience": The Making of and English Mass Readership in the Nineteenth Century' tried to do for the nature of the organization of material in cheap nineteenth-century periodicals like *Chambers Edinburgh Journal*. He argues that these cheap journals contributed to the construction of a mass reading audience by reflecting the readership's varied and mixed experience of modern urbanized world. The overall impression created by these journals was, as he says, a 'collage', a '*bricolage*', a '*mélange*', 'encyclopedic', and an 'anthology'.[35] These descriptive words also sum up the effect Dicks's advertisements could have had on his working-class readers, whatever commercial purposes or legal or other restraints were involved in the reprint series' development, namely, a classless, heterogeneous, and inclusive idea of what is 'standard' in English literature.

One further point about the possible impact of these advertisements. The pressures of empire building and the anxieties about the British out in the empire 'going native' in the last decades of the nineteenth century contributed to a late-century move to codify what being 'English' might mean. For example, at the same time as Dicks's advertisements for the 'English' series of Standard Plays and English Novels are constructing an inclusive 'canon' of English literature that includes dozens (and in the case of the 'Standard Plays' hundreds) of works by popular writers, some of them inevitably hacks, the universities were in the process of working out what the course of study for 'English' literature might be, establishing a canon of classics we all know.[36] By periodically adding the actual word 'English' to his series' titles, Dicks in his advertisements extends the democratic inclusiveness of their contents to the very notion of 'Englishness'[37] as constructed by literature. They project a kind of alternative 'canon' of 'English' literature, an interweave of the 'classics' of the past and more contemporary popular works, many of whose titles and authors are almost completely forgotten today.

Even further, the advertisements of Dicks's reprint series could have opened up a question even as to what English literature might mean not only for those putative British working-class readers, but also for the far-flung colonists and their subjects. For Dicks's reprint series, along with their advertisements, were exported, according to Guy Dicks, via colonial agents to New York, Bombay, Toronto, Melbourne, Cape Town, New Zealand, Jamaica, and Nova Scotia (Dicks, 2001, p. 39) where they were likely to be widely read. Though I have found no comments from Dicks's readers abroad, we do know at least that the novels of G.W.M. Reynolds, published and reprinted by the John Dicks Press and listed in his 'English Novels' series, were more popular and influential than those of Dickens or any other imported English novel in India.[38]

Dicks's advertisements for his various reprint series brought to the attention of a large reading public that could sometimes cut across class (middle-class readers like Montague Summers were also customers of his reprint series) and national lines through their export to the colonies not only a variety of 'the classics', but hundreds of popular plays and dozens of novels not known to us now. However the nineteenth-century readers of Dicks's reprint series might have construed what was 'standard' and what was 'classic' English literature from Dicks's advertisements, these advertisements, at the very least, provide scholars of nineteenth-century literature a broader publishing and cultural context for the canonized works we know. But these advertisements also give us a glimpse of what the successful owner and publisher of, as Montague Summers has it, 'one of the largest and busiest printing and publishing offices in England in the 19th century' (Summers, 1942, p. 552) sensed the 'unknown public' wanted and would buy—an alternate canon of English literature which gave equal weight to the aspirational classics they (and others both contemporary and modern) thought they ought to read and the popular texts that in fact made up the bulk of nineteenth-century working-class reading.

Notes

1. According to the *Bookseller* (18 July 1868, p. 447), Reynolds was 'the most popular writer in England'. His *Mysteries of London* reputedly sold over a million copies.
2. William St. Clair, *The Reading Nation in the Romantic Period* (Cambridge: Cambridge University Press, 2004) p. 645.
3. Jonathan Rose, *The Intellectual Life of the British Working Class* (New Haven: Yale University Press, 2001), p. 121.
4. Quoted in Andrew Murphy, *Shakespeare for the People: Working-class Readers, 1800–1900* (Cambridge: Cambridge University Press, 2008), pp. 83–86. The quotations come from Thomas Okey, *A Basketful of Memories: An Autobiographical Sketch* (London: Dent, 1930) and Thomas Burt, *An Autobiography* (London: T. Fisher Unwin, 1924).
5. Quoted in Richard Altick, *The English Common Reader: A Social History of the Mass Reading Public: 1800–1900* (Chicago: University of Chicago Press, 1957), p. 315.
6. Murphy, p. 86.

7. *The British Working-Class Reader, 1790–1848* (London: George Allen and Unwin, 1955), p. 31.
8. Jonathan Rose notes that in 1863 the following collections of classics were in print: Charles Knight's Library of Classics, Bentley's Standard Novels, Bohn's Standard Classics, W. and R. Chambers People's Editions, Chapman and Hall's Standard Editions of Popular Authors, Murray's British Classics, Routledge's British Poets and Standard Novels. All these sold for between 3s.6d. and 5s. (Rose, 2001, p. 131). Dicks's reprint series sold for lower prices, as he promised in 1866. St. Clair also lists a number of collections of plays prior to Dicks' in Appendix 6 (St. Clair, 2004, p. 538).
9. In Green's series, Shakespeare's works were priced at six shillings and sixpence, not a price a working-class reader could afford (Dicks's Complete Shakespere was initially priced at two shillings, ultimately at 1s.)
10. See Meredith McGill, *American Literature and the Culture of Reprinting, 1834–1857* (Philadelphia: University of Pennsylvania Press, 2007), pp. 97–98 for a discussion of the ways stereotyping impacted on the cheap reprint trade in the United States.
11. *Literacy and Popular Culture: England 1750–1914* (Cambridge: Cambridge University Press, 1989), pp. 109–11. Vincent says of Milner that 'his Cottage Library [published in 1836] was soon imitated, particularly by John Dicks's Library of Standard Works, and by mid-century, most of the standard repertoire up to and including the Romantics was available in shilling editions.'
12. See Guy Dicks, *The John Dicks Press* (Lulu.com 2015) for a history of the press after the death of Dicks and Reynolds. Available on Amazon. This history of John Dicks Press by a descendent of Dicks contains the most complete information we have to date about the Press.
13. Montague Summers, 'John Dicks, Publisher', *Times Literary Supplement*, 7 November 1942, p. 552.
14. Dicks published a Catalogue of his publications dated 1875 which lists 34 entries for Dicks's English Novels and 48 entries for Dicks's Standard Plays. In addition he includes lists of publications of several authors—Malcolm Errym, Edward Ellis, Gabriel Alexander, G.W.M. Reynolds, and Walter Scott. Though not a series per se, this listing of various series of works by individual authors shows the heterogeneous nature of Dicks' reprints—from the hack writer Malcolm Errym to Walter Scott. Dicks also advertises in this catalogue several other series: the Illustrated Standard Authors (which I have not located or seen advertised elsewhere, though this may be the Standard Works referred to by Vincent in note 11). Dicks's English Classics (all canonized authors), and other series of prints, music and other miscellaneous publications. *John Dicks' Catalogue* (London: John Dicks Press, 1874). A later edition in 1896 (dated by hand) includes a number of other series probably put together by his sons after his death.

15. The advertisement for the first 151 novels reads 'The following List of Complete Illustrated Novels, by Eminent Authors, are verbatim copies of the original editions, and are now issued to the public without any abridgement whatever, although in a cheap form.' Later Dicks's advertisements for the English Novels still contain only 150 titles.
16. Watts Phillips (16 November 1825–2 December1874) was a British illustrator, novelist, and playwright best known for his play *The Dead Heart* which reputedly served as a model for Charles Dickens's *A Tale of Two Cities*.
17. 'The Mysteries of Reading: Text and Illustration in the Fiction of G.W.M. Reynolds', in Anne Humpherys and Louis James, eds., *G.W.M. Reynolds: Nineteenth-Century Fiction, Politics, and the Press* (Aldenham: Ashgate, 2008), p. 227.
18. The British Library has Dicks's Complete Shakespere in one volume and some bound volumes of the Standard Plays but apparently no individual numbers with their covers and advertising. Other libraries I have consulted may have a handful of individual plays but also some scattered bound volumes.
19. Recent books on the subject of Victorian readers in addition to those already referenced in this chapter include Rachel Ablow, *The Feeling of Reading* (Ann Arbor: University of Michigan Press, 2010); Matthew Bradley and Juliet John, eds., *Reading and the Victorians* (Farnham, Surrey: Ashgate, 2015); Patrick Brantlinger, *The Reading Lesson* (Bloomington: Indiana University Press, 1998); Nicholas Dames, *The Physiology of the Novel: Reading, Neural Science, and the Form of Victorian Fiction* (Oxford; New York: Oxford University Press, 2007); Kate Flint, *The Woman Reader* (Oxford: Clarendon Press, 1993); Leah Price, *The Anthology and the Rise of the Novel* (Cambridge: Cambridge University Press, 2000). See also the review essay "Victorian Readers" by Miriam Bailin in *Victorian Literature and Culture* (forthcoming).
20. Stephen Colclough in his *Consuming Texts: Readers and Reading Communities 1695–1870* (Basingstoke: Palgrave/Macmillan, 2007) describes Rose's main thesis this way.
21. Rose recounts the experience of one working-class reader of the Walter Scott Library: 'For one grocer's boy [John Birch Thomas (b. 1860)] Scott's work (in the 3d Dicks' editions) were studies in social history, and he came away feeling that Rebecca not Rowena was the right girl for Ivanhoe' (Rose, 2001, p. 40).
22. Charles Henry Ross (1835–97) was an illustrator and novelist and the creator of the popular figure Ally Sloper, one of the earliest comic strip characters.
23. The OED defines 'classic' as 'judged over a period of time to be of the highest quality and outstanding of its kind'. It defines 'standard' as 'a

required or agreed level of quality or attainment'. Dicks, like many other publishers of cheap reprints, makes a distinction between 'classics' (older works) and 'standard' (including newer works) in determining the contents of his reprint series. The contents of 'English Classics' (published late in the century) are the canonized writers—Shakespeare, Milton, Pope, Wordsworth, and so forth. But the title, 'Standard Plays' allows Dicks to include not only the 'classics' but a wide range of other works. In Wilkie Collins's *The Moonstone* (1868), Ezra Jennings writes in his journal about finding Franklin Blake surrounded by 'classics' including Samuel Richardson's *Pamela*, but ends his journal entry by referring contemptuously to all Blake's reading as 'standard' literature. *The Moonstone* (Oxford: Oxford University Press, 1999), p. 414.

24. Colclough's final section in *Consuming Texts* points out that 'the undisciplined nature of street advertising often leads to strange and amusing conjunctions' (173) and argues that the reading of advertisements can lead to a variety of different narrative constructions, one of which I am arguing for here.

25. For example, the British Library catalogued *Dicks' English Library of Standard Works* in 1896 though it was probably issued in the early 1880s. Also the British Library's bound volume of Dicks's Standard Plays carry dates of 1874, 1894, and 1907, though the weekly publication of the individual plays began in the mid-1860s.

26. 'John Dicks, Publisher, and "Dicks' English Library of Standard Works."' Blogs.gre.ac.uk/andrewking/?p=453. King comments 'What one has to do is try to establish the publishing history of a series. Adverts are always useful this."

27. The Talford Copyright Bill of 1842 set copyright at 42 years or the author's life plus 7 years, whichever is longer.

28. The first play was *The Gambler* by Edward Moore (1753) which is followed by *Jane Shore* (1714) by Nicolas Rowe and *The Man of the World* (1792) by Charles Macklin. Many of the next numbered plays are early nineteenth-century plays (Lord Byron is a favourite). Victorian era plays begin to come on the list beginning in numbers 200 (probably sometime in late 1860s or early 1870s). Douglas Jerrold's *Rent Day* (1832) is Number 210.

29. Number 6 in the earlier list (*Heiress of the Mount* by S. Dunn) is replaced later with *Sketches by Boz*. In a later list, five of 26 titles in the original list are replaced by works by authors like Dickens, Lord Lytton, G.W.M. Reynolds, and George Augustus Sala. These insertions and replacements do not affect the order of the remaining titles which remain consistent with earlier advertised lists. Nor arguably do they affect the sense that the advertisements construct an enlarged democratic sense of what is standard literature.

30. This play is numbered 82 in an 1870s advertisement for Dicks's Standard Plays (listing 308 plays), but in a much later one it does not appear at all. H. Philip Bolton in *Dickens Dramatized* (Boston: G.K. Hall, 1987) says the play was written by W.H.C. Nation and F. Fox Cooper and was produced at Astley's on 22 April 1867.
31. There were two different series for Dicks's reprints of plays, though the titles and formats are the same. The first was Dicks's Standard Plays, the parts of which were published weekly. The second format was Dicks's English Drama which consisted of 12 bound volumes of 20 plays each volume (thus containing only a total of 240 plays) which sold for a shilling a volume, probably beginning sometime in the late 1870s. The contents of the two volumes and order of the plays does not change at all over the century. Neither of the two series of drama includes the names of the authors.
32. The advertisement is on the back cover of Number 701, *The Forced Marriage* by Mrs. T.P. Cook. The Bodleian Library at Oxford catalogued this play on 29 July 1886. There is a scanned volume of 21 plays (Numbers 681–702) plus some unnumbered items from the collections of the Bodleian, nearly all of which have their covers and advertisements intact. This volume is available through Amazon under the title of *Dicks' Standard Plays*. The publisher is listed as Nabu Public Domain Rights, n.d.
33. John Tobin (1770–1804) was an unsuccessful playwright until the year of his death when he had a success with this comedy which was on the stage for the next 20 years.
34. This may be a play rather than a novel which Hazlewood wrote based on Mary Elizabeth Braddon's *Barbara and her Splendid Misery and Splendid Cage* (1880). This item demonstrates only too clearly the difficulties in sorting out Dicks' publications. The various advertisements for Dicks' Standard English Novels continue to list this title under Hazlewood's name, though a word search of *Bow Bells* turns up no such work. In the British Library Catalogue there is a novel *Splendid Misery* by Thomas Skinner SURR (T. Hurst 1801). C.H. Hazlewood has many entries in the British Library Catalogue, all plays, but none called *Splendid Misery*.
35. J. Klancher 'From "Crowd" To "Audience": The Making of an English Mass Readership in the Nineteenth Century.' ELH 50.1 (1983) 155–73.
36. James Donald in 'How English Is It? Popular Literature and National Culture' (*New Formations* No. 6 (Winter 1988), 31–47), though he is writing about contemporary Britain, makes several points that are also relevant to the nineteenth century. He devises a model for a reading culture that can enable a way to include the 'popular' (his case is the movies) into an understanding of the culture that emerges from Literature with a capital L.

37. Dicks's series of 'English Classics' (in the 1874 Catalogue) was issued again after Dicks's death in a small print version with double columns, illustrated by Victorian artists, bound in cloth or paper, five shillings in cloth, one shilling in paper. Added to this late advertised list of English Classics was Felicia Hemans, who had not appeared in the lists earlier. The texts in this late version were, as the advertisement had it, 'profusely illustrated, neatly printed, and stitched in coloured paper. Pronounced to be the cheapest books ever published.' Andrew King in his blog argues that the 'reissue of these texts cannot be taken to be an unalloyed index of popularity amongst readers of cheap publications ... it is a mark of what the public *should* aspire to." Blogs.gre.ac.uk/andrewking/?p=453.
38. See Priya Joshi, *In Another Country: Colonialism, Culture, and the English Novel in India* (New York: Columbia University Press, 2002) in which she establishes the importance of Reynolds's novels in creating the Indian novel, and Sucheta Bhattacharya, 'G.W.M. Reynolds: Rewritten in Nineteenth-century Bengal', in *G.W.M. Reynolds: Politics, Literature and the Press*, in which she analyses the Bengali translations of some of Reynolds's novels (pp. 247–60).

CHAPTER 7

Serialization and Story-Telling Illustrations: R.L. Stevenson Window-Shopping for Penny Dreadfuls

Marie Léger-St-Jean

The following chapter considers the practice of 'reading' illustrated serials in shop-windows during the second half of nineteenth-century Britain. It relies on two magazine articles published 15 years apart and retelling events separated by two decades. The first, published in 1873 by children's author and journalist James Greenwood (1832–1929) in the shilling monthly *Saint Paul's Magazine*, is partly a cautionary tale about two lower-class boys. It warns against the evils of penny dreadfuls, the cheap illustrated serial literature of the day. The second, published in 1888 in the American monthly *Scribner's*, features the autobiographical reminiscences of Robert Louis Stevenson (1850–94) looking back on his childhood readings.

I would like to thank John Adcock for allowing me to initially work this material into a post on his blog, Yesterday's Papers. I first presented on window-shop reading at a symposium entitled 'Authors, Publishers and Readers: Selling and Distributing Literary Cultures, 1880–1940' held at the University of Reading in 2012

M. Léger-St-Jean (✉)
University of Cambridge, Cambridge, UK

© The Author(s) 2016 111
P.R. Rooney, A. Gasperini (eds.), *Media and Print Culture Consumption in Nineteenth-Century Britain*, New Directions in Book History, DOI 10.1057/978-1-137-58761-9_7

This chapter investigates a reading practice through the lens of the stories of only three boys. The motherless brothers Charley and Bill from London's East End featured in Greenwood's article are certainly very different from the Scottish boy christened Robert Lewis Balfour who grew up to write *Treasure Island* and *The Strange Case of Dr Jekyll and Mr Hyde*. Nonetheless, there were countless more, and probably girls too, but written records of shop-window serial reading are few and far apart. I will demonstrate, by contrasting his account with that of Greenwood's poor London boys, that Stevenson wrongfully universalizes his childhood reading experiences. I thus wish to stress that reading experiences cannot be extrapolated from a descriptive presentation of a reading practice.

Furthermore, I will point to how the distinction Stevenson draws between lower- and upper-class escapist reading is artificial. In the end, I will show that his particularly class-based understanding of reading attitudes is flawed, though class, and its corollary education, are certainly worthy factors to take into account. This analysis therefore leads to the conclusion that individuality will always remain an important factor in reading experiences, thwarting any generalization when a large enough sample of evidence is not available.

We shall first consider the case of the two poor brothers. Bill was illiterate. In charge of his younger siblings, he had not had his brother's luck: Charley attended the Ragged School on Hatton-Garden. A ten-minute walk away from the school, on Rosamund Street, now the Spa Fields Park, stood a newsvendor. The power of illustration seems forgotten nowadays that adult literacy in England is 97% rather than roughly 60% around 1840 (41 % among working classes).[1] Our experience of being unable to read is mainly confined to childhood and foreign countries. However, Billy's interest in the newsvendor is akin to that of a child in 'reading' only the illustrations in a comic or a graphic novel. Indeed, the shop windows of newsvendors and libraries alike displayed the first page of the week's number for a variety of penny dreadfuls, and each one contained an elaborate woodcut.

Nowadays, if one consults a penny dreadful, or one of its penny blood predecessors—most likely in the Rare Books Room of a research library unless one is fortunate enough to be acquainted with a collector—it will more often than not come in a single volume, hardly distinguishable from a 'normal' book. The binding masks seriality except for the predictable presence, every eight page, of a woodcut.[2] This removal of the physical object from its original setting is what makes Bill's story so important for book historians: it brings to life the context in which penny dreadfuls were encountered when they were first published.

Illiteracy is an important barrier to the transmission of alternative reading practices and experiences. Presumably, if Billy could not read, he could not write.³ Thence, his story was passed down the annals of history second-hand, or rather third-hand, assuming it is actually true.⁴ According to '"Penny Awfuls"', the article produced by Greenwood, Billy's brother Charley recounted the events in a Thieves Anonymous meeting, which the journalist attended.⁵

According to his younger brother Charley, Billy managed to reconstruct the greater part of the narrative in the highwaymen serials by 'reading' the illustration on the front cover. Illustrations, however, can be ambiguous, generating suspense. In these instances, Billy would call upon his brother to use his newly acquired reading skills to decipher the text beneath the illustration. Perhaps it could tell if Tyburn Dick had successfully escaped from the gallows or failed to do so.⁶ However, the text printed on the first page would not always settle the matter. Presumably, the answer lay in the seven hidden pages, but the two boys' pockets were empty.

Though social critics denounced or celebrated penny fiction as horrendously or triumphantly cheap, Billy had to steal and pawn a hammer to acquire the prized jewel. The following week, it was his younger brother's turn. Theft was the only recourse to obtain the boys' weekly mental sustenance, and as Charley told in the Thieves Anonymous meeting, how could it be wrong to steal tools when, week after week, Jonathan Wild was appropriating luxurious jewelry?

Therefore, Greenwood and other detractors of penny dreadfuls found substantiation for their arguments in stories such as that of Charley. Penny dreadfuls caused petty criminality, both by creating an addiction and by disseminating bad examples. By displaying the first page and its engraving in their shop windows, newsvendors were offering insidious advertising. How else were boys expected to react to the enticing snippet but to want to know what happened next? Such went Greenwood and others' argument against penny dreadfuls.

Greenwood occupied an interesting position.⁷ He was an investigative journalist and social critic who wrote against the perils of 'pernicious literature', including penny dreadfuls. Therefore, his account of the story of Billy and his brother is from the point of view of a detractor of cheap serialized fiction. Yet, in the first half of the 1860s, Samuel Orchart Beeton (1830–77) published not only investigative journalism and slum novels by Greenwood, but also adventure stories.⁸ These novels, sometimes serialized in *The Boy's Own Volume*, were more upmarket than penny dreadfuls, but no less violent.⁹ Afterwards, Greenwood started writing in the penny weekly counterparts to *The Boy's Own* published by former Chartist Edwin John Brett (1827–95): *The Boys of England, Young Men of Great Britain* and *Wedding Bells*, marketed to young ladies.¹⁰

How can one be at once an author *and* a detractor of novels issued in penny numbers by the same publisher? Indeed, 'A Short Way to Newgate', a chapter from Greenwood's *The Wilds of London* (1874), offers a scathing critique of *The Skeleton Crew, or, Wildfire Ned*, issued in 1866–67 by Brett through his Newsagents' Publishing Company. Many Victorian writers were certainly trying to string together a living as hard-working low-earning men of letters, otherwise known as literary hacks. The published diaries of bohemian Edward Litt Leman Blanchard (1820–89) offer a sense of how versatile and indiscriminate 1840s writers needed to be should they wish to pay the rent, veering from advertising to 're-originated' (as the magazine insisted in its section titles) plagiarisms.¹¹ The files of the Royal Literary Fund are filled with applications from young men, and fewer young women, attempting to enter the new profession of writer.¹² Greenwood was therefore possibly working to order, as the other 'obliging writer[s]' that he describes unflatteringly at the end of '"Penny Awfuls"'.¹³

Christopher Banham and Elizabeth Stearns discuss Greenwood's duplicitous position in their introduction to *The Skeleton Crew, or, Wildfire Ned*. They dismiss the possibility that Greenwood was simply a hack by underscoring 'the sincerity and consistency of his social conscience'.¹⁴ They suggest that Greenwood distinguished between the publications of the Newsagents' Publishing Company and the literature published in the pages of *The Boys of England*, despite being both published by Brett in penny numbers. Banham and Stearns believe that Greenwood's harsh criticism of the former publications was meant to convince Brett to definitely move away from that style and to concentrate on that found in the pages of the periodicals in which he wrote.

Brett was part of the new publishers entering the scene in the 1860s, along with the Emmett brothers and their Hogarth House. Previously, between 1835 and 1860, during the penny blood era, another set of older publishers—some veterans of the Unstamped Wars, others newcomers, such as the tremendously successful Edward Lloyd (1815–90)—experimented to find the best design and format for their new media: cheap novels. They settled on the eight-page double-column large octavo format that lasted all through the penny dreadful era for number-books (as opposed to periodicals).

Periodicals went through even more experimentations, and the non-illustrated periodicals of the mid-1840s—*Lloyd's Penny Weekly Miscellany* (1842–46) and *The London Pioneer* (1846–48), for instance—did not survive the growing popularity of the illustrated *Family Herald* (1842–1940), *London Journal* (1845–83), and *Reynolds's Miscellany* (1846–69). In 'Popular Authors', Stevenson refers to both the *London Journal* and the lavishly illustrated *Cassell's Family Paper* (1853–65). Illustration was thus firmly entrenched as a key component of penny serial literature as early as the 1840s.[15] The shift from penny bloods to penny dreadfuls is therefore not materially apparent: it is a shift in targeted audience. Despite a clear-cut change in the industry in 1860, the term 'penny dreadful' only appeared in the late 1860s, as shown on Fig. 7.1.

Because library collections are at best specialized in Victorian penny publications, spanning several decades, the distinction between penny bloods and penny dreadfuls has never really emerged in scholarship, except in John Springhall's thoroughly researched *Youth, Popular Culture and Moral Panics* (1998).[16] He insists on the change in publishers and on the younger audience to mark the shift, but does not attempt to give an explanation. I conjecture that growing readerships - and numbers of buyers - allowed for segmentation and specialization of the market for cheap fiction: penny magazines moved towards a more female audience and penny-issue novels towards a juvenile niche.[17] Indeed, during the penny-blood era, penny-number publications catered to an undifferentiated audience of men, women, and children of all classes.

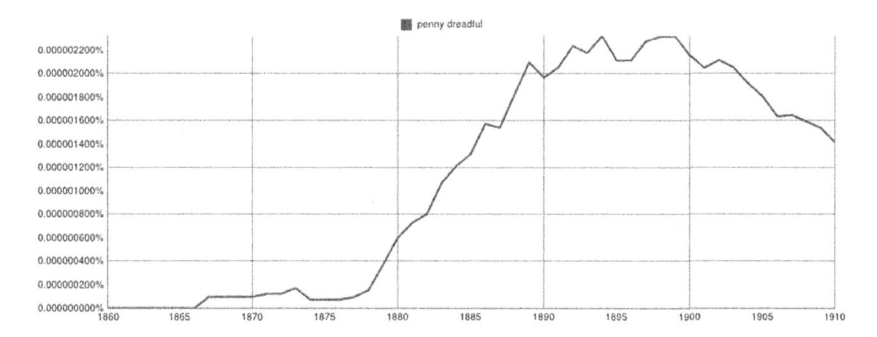

Fig. 7.1 Google Ngram chronicling historical patterns of use of the term 'Penny Dreadful'. *Source*: Google Books Ngram Viewer, 19 March 2012, http://books.google.com/ngrams

By the late 1860s, in addition to penny dreadfuls in stand-alone numbers, new periodicals appeared: the title of Brett's flagship publication, *The Boys of England* (1866–99), inscribes clearly the targeted audience. When Greenwood started contributing, his name was greatly advertised as it brought respectability. His 'Joe Sterling: or, A Ragged Fortune', serialized in *The Boys of England* starting in the summer of 1870 and adapted in November of the same year for the stage at the Victoria, is a testament to the cross-class appeal of certain penny dreadfuls.[18]

Whether the thieving consequences of reading in shop windows illustrated in Greenwood's article are fabricated or not, there is little reason to believe that the journalist would have also made up the reading practice itself since it is illustrated in other Victorian instances. Not all boys, however, resorted to theft to provide themselves with penny literature, and not just because some had better morals or showed more self-restraint than Billy and his brother. Robert Lewis needed nothing more than the illustration and its caption to set his imagination going and reconstruct the narrative. In 'Popular Authors', Stevenson even claims that an entire paper could be written on the relative merits of reading a story only by looking at the pictures.[19] He never penned down such a paper, hence the present essay is my own attempt at delving into 'reading' only illustrations.

There were many different reading practices in the nineteenth century, just as nowadays reading comes in many different shapes and forms, not to mention attitudes to or modes of reading, such as absorption, duty, and so on. Stevenson describes three in 'Popular Authors'. The most common among literary scholars, and therefore the assumed de facto practice, is reading the full text, from cover to cover. How widespread it actually was among contemporary readers of Victorian cheap literature is probably impossible to know, but I would venture to guess that it was not the main form of reading. Another fairly common and often discussed practice is reading aloud to an audience. Stevenson's nanny Alison Cunningham ('Cummie') read him tales from *Cassell's Family Paper*, but the true force of words was impressed upon him by his mother reading *Macbeth*, the sounds of the storm raging outdoors uplifting the power of words.[20]

Stevenson's two examples, however, present reading aloud as confined to the domestic space, yet it can also be a public activity, performed outside of the home. Indeed, Henry Mayhew describes in his sociological account *London Labour and the London Poor* (1861) how costermongers have those who are 'schollard[s]' read to them aloud the latest instalment of *Mysteries of the Court of London* by George W.M. Reynolds (1814–79).[21]

Stevenson also refers to 'public story-tellers' and 'word-of-mouth recitation' in the first part of his 'Popular Authors' essay to describe the sort of tale produced by William Stephens Hayward (1835–70), the author of a penny dreadful he recalls very fondly: 'They were the unhatched eggs of Arab tales; made for word-of-mouth recitation, certain (if thus told) to captivate an audience of boys or any simple people—certain, on the lips of a generation or two of public story-tellers, to take on new merit and become cherished lore'.[22] The reference to 'simple people' signals a class distinction between public and domestic reading aloud. Class-based differentiation persists when Stevenson attempts to link up his account of his own reading experience while window-shopping and his interpretation of reading in the lower classes.

Representations of newsvendor shop windows are difficult to find. An engraving of William Strange's 21 Paternoster-row shop—which appears in one of his catalogues, a copy of which was bound into a copy of the new edition of *Master Timothy's Book-Case* (1847)—offers a glimpse of what the window-shopping reading practice might have looked like. A man is hunched, examining the publications in the bottom of the window. Another man is holding a child's hand. The engraving signed Walmsley does not give details of the publications in the windows, insisting rather on the lettering above the shop and the insignia '21 | STRANGE | Bookseller and Publisher'.[23] It does nonetheless offer a visual representation of window-shopping as a practice in 1840s London, complementary to book-buying and book-lending.

The practice is also featured in Albert Smith's novel *The Struggles and Adventures of Christopher Tadpole at Home and Abroad* (1848): 'There was always somebody looking into the window of "Smedlar's Library" as it was now called: for there was plenty to see.' A library instead of a newsvendor, the display includes '[w]ell thumbed novels ... opened enticingly at exciting pages' in addition to cheap periodicals and seasonal publications, such as comic Valentines, song books, cheap steamboat guides, and Christmas specials.[24] It is worth noting that publishers' bindings were just being introduced in the 1840s. Therefore, bound books, as opposed to just sheets, would be an unlikely occurrence at a newsvendor's shop.[25]

In his essay 'Popular Authors', Stevenson describes his experience of window-shopping for romance in an attempt to link up this reading practice with the disregard for style of 'uneducated readers' in their choice of reading as well as their propensity to find improbable tales true to life. His chosen practice evidently requires dipping in and out of stories from week to week, using illustrations and 'exposed columns' of text as material from which to playfully reconstruct stories to one's liking.[26] He argues that the lower classes read with the same 'selective partiality' as children, while the upper classes have inexplicably evolved.[27] The problems with the argument put forth by Stevenson will become apparent once his perception of his own experience as universal is contrasted with that of East End boys Charlie and Bill as related by Greenwood.

As stated earlier, before resorting to shop-window reading, Robert Lewis, the young Stevenson, was introduced to penny fiction through his nurse reading aloud from *Cassell's Family Paper*. It is noteworthy that Stevenson makes a distinction between appropriate 'Family Tales' on the one hand and the offensive 'novels' on the other hand, which Stevenson is probably only sarcastically borrowing from Cummie.[28] When that was no longer acceptable reading for his strict Calvinist caregiver, he started doing weekly rounds of the shop windows.

After having listened to his nurse read stories to him aloud and then having reconstructed them through their illustrated weekly front covers (the practice we shall turn to shortly), the young Stevenson stumbled upon his first complete numbers of penny novels abandoned in the romantic setting of Neidweith Castle. The tales sparked his interest, and only then did he become addicted to penny dreadfuls in their full form, complete with images and text.[29] As the article unfolds, it becomes clear that only after discovering the power of words through Shakespeare was Stevenson prepared for the genius of Viles, Rymer, & cie. Only then did it seem that authors might actually tell a better story than he could from the illustrations. His privileged storytelling abilities appear to set him apart from the poor London boys even more than his class. Indeed, Stevenson could not at first afford to buy any complete numbers and had to content himself, like Billy and his brother, with the first page before finding the abandoned stash in Neidweith Castle. However, unlike them, he did not seem to mind: he took what he wanted and constructed his own stories. Stevenson does describe his window-shopping as 'lusting after' a work of fiction, yet it does not seem a painful experience, in contrast with that of Billy.[30] Young brother Charley recounts that the catalyst for Billy's first theft, perpetrated in order to buy their first number, was their inability to make out from the first page alone whether Tyburn Dick's escape had been successful:

He [Billy] wasn't a swearin' boy, take him altogether, but this time he did let out, he was so savage at not being able to turn over [the page]. He was like a mad cove, and without any reason punched me [Charley] about till I run [sic] away from him and went to school again.[31]

Faced with the impossibility of knowing what happened next, Billy appears to be lacking the imaginative resources to make up his own story. The poor boy is therefore not only challenged by his illiteracy, but by the lesser imaginative powers that Stevenson ascribes to all lower-class readers, be they readers of illustrations or words.

In contrast with Billy's stark feelings of dispossession, Stevenson described himself as 'master of the weekly gallery'. How can one be a master while having access to only incomplete tatters? Stevenson says he 'thoroughly digested' the serials, meaning, as he explains further, taking 'that which pleases us, leaving the rest aside', using the 'material' while 'act[ing] as our own artists'. The young Stevenson did not need the writer's skill to access stories, he could 'realiz[e]' them himself.[32] This capacity seems lacking in Billy, who is left to throw a fit and beat his brother, filled with the rage of being unable to continue experiencing the story.

Reflecting on these 'early years', Stevenson comes to the brash conclusion that 'those books that we have (in such a way) avoided reading, [sic] are all so excellently written!'[33] In an unpublished essay written earlier, in 1882, and uncovered by Kevin Carpenter, Stevenson had explained more clearly that first readings, whether pictorial or textual, become the 'true perusal' of a work.[34] Illustrations generate high expectations when a story is encountered first through them: no matter how skilled a writer Newgate novelist William Harrison Ainsworth (1805–82) might have been, the Jonathan Wild in his *Jack Sheppard* (1839–40) 'was nothing, he was not my [Stevenson's] old love, he was not that startling figure with the bludgeon that stood in the prints'.[35] Even the powerful experience of hearing Shakespeare's words spoken by his mother did not seem agreeable compared to 'the ditch-water stories that a child could dip and skip and doze over, stealing at times materials for play'.[36] Yet all do not share this capacity to use stories as building blocks from which one can pick and choose.

The comparison between Stevenson's reading experience and that of Billy shows that Stevenson's own experience is wrongfully universalized. His recollections do not carry the frustration found in Greenwood's account of Billy, the illiterate boy. In addition to frustration over having to rely on his younger brother Charley to make sense of the illustrations with the help of the words on the page, he is enraged when the first page, the only one on display in the shop-window, is not enough to make out the outcome of the event illustrated.

Hence, Stevenson does not recognize his own privilege in being able to simply dip into stories and play with them, what he calls the 'selective partiality' of children's reading. He understands it as a 'weakness to create', failing to see how creative a practice it actually is.[37] The flip-side of this weakness is a 'power of adoption' which he identifies not only in children, but also in 'uneducated readers'. Indeed, throughout the essay, Stevenson is attempting to understand how lower-class readers of popular literature can be so insensitive to how 'always acutely untrue to life as it is' penny fiction is that they understand it as a 'true picture' of reality.[38]

Stevenson is also puzzled by the public's lack of discrimination with regards to style: he himself would 'read for pleasure' John Frederick Smith (1806–90), James Malcolm Rymer (1814–84, which he calls by one of his pen-names, the anagram 'Errym'), and William Stephens Hayward at varying stages of his life. Nonetheless, he felt that the very high-selling Samuel Bracebridge Hemyng (1841–1901), George W.M. Reynolds ('the dull ruffian') and the American Sylvanus Cobb (1823–87, often reprinted in the *London Journal*) had absolutely no talent.[39] Given this discrepancy between upper-class Stevenson's taste and that of the masses, the self-reflective reader of popular literature posits that the character set and setting is all that counts for the later group.

While very aptly describing escapist literature, Stevenson fails to register that popular upper-class reading operates identically, the sole difference being that higher-class readers escape to different settings, guided by different characters. Indeed, he draws attention to the escapist qualities of penny literature: the reader 'escapes the narrow prison of the individual career' through works that dress up his or her 'naked fancies', his or her 'ardently but impotently preconceived' hopes for 'changed situation'.[40] Diving into penny literature allows one to adopt the position one always wished for, thus popular narratives are 'often pleasantly coincident with childish hopes of what life ought to be'.[41] These are the very qualities of 'formulaic literature' described by John G. Cawelti in his wonderful analysis of later twentieth-century popular fiction, both on the page and on the screen.

Stevenson then speaks of upper-class readers, now including himself in the group: 'when the scene of a romance is laid on any distant soil, we look with eagerness and confidence for the coming of the English traveller'.[42] What he fails to realize is that the function of 'the English traveller' is identical to the one of 'the poor governesses supplied' to make lower-class readers 'feel at home in the houses of fraudulent bankers and the wicked dukes'.[43] This blind spot is indicative of Stevenson's class bias.

There is thus no universal way in which 'fancy works in children'— allowing him or her to 'dip and skip and doze over' stories—which remains unchanged in 'uneducated readers' but evolves in 'readers of an upper class'.[44] Though a child, Billy is unable, unlike Stevenson, to be his own artist. The engraver and the writer are not sufficient to provide him the scenery for 'autobiographical romancing': he requires a complete narrative. Therefore, Stevenson was exceptionally imaginative. Greenwood's account potentially hints at the role of education in fostering such imaginative skills, as Charley, who is lucky enough to attend a ragged school, is certainly not as impacted as Billy by the impossibility of turning over the page. Nonetheless, it could also be chalked up to individual differences.

These discrepancies further my main argument: the same reading practices can be experienced very differently from one person to the other, be it because of age, class, education, or individual variability. Studying material formats was an important first step towards understanding how Victorians read. Studying reading practices in all their diversity is the next step. Just as material formats do not determine reading experiences (they are but a factor among others), reading practices can also lead to very different reading experiences. Therefore, avoiding generalizations is key in interpreting the available evidence.

Histories of reading and readers have not discussed so far the reading practice, consisting chiefly of image reading on a weekly basis, highlighted by the stories of Billy, his brother, and Stevenson. It was at least common throughout the United Kingdom in the second half of the nineteenth century: a journalist surveyed the shop windows of London, Edinburgh, and Newcastle for the 'gruesome covers' of penny dreadfuls in 1888.[45] It endures today in check-out lines in the Western world, with fictionalized accounts of robbery being replaced by the reported woes of Hollywood stars. It has certainly existed in other times and places in which serials have been on display.

As the available reading material changes, worries about the danger of illustrations morph. Joseph Stamper, an ironmoulder-turned-writer, reminisced in 1960 about 'the lower part of the newsagent's windows' which contained 'the journals that catered for' him when he was a boy at the beginning of the twentieth century: *Deadwood Dick*, *Bronco Bill*, and *Jack Wright*. He does not speak of reading illustrations through shop windows, however, since he bought his reading material, sometimes having to 'ponder whether to buy Thomas à Kempis or *Deadwood Dick*'.[46] Penny fiction and poetry were not the only wares on display: crime-related news and pornography also came in illustrated periodicals.

These journals printed on pink newsprint included *Police News*, *Police Budget*, *Sketchy Bits*, and *Photo Bits*. The later two displayed 'huge nude thighs and huge, almost nude, bosoms, with the absolute minimum of clothing'. The two former were equally graphic, but depicted violence rather than sex: 'The most sensational crime of the previous week was always given on the front page; and if it was murder by knife or gunshot, there was always oceans of blood sloshed about the picture, and the dying man's face was horrific with his agony.'[47] It is therefore no surprise that around the same time Stamper was purchasing these journals at the newsagent or second-hand, a working-class woman warned against the dangers of daily news being displayed in such a fashion, ironically preferring that boys read penny dreadfuls instead of 'records of the Divorce Court, details of revolting murder cases, seduction cases, and society scandals of every kind'.[48]

Attitudes towards penny-dreadful display therefore seemed to have changed in the half-century following Greenwood's article because of the appearance of potentially worse illustrations in the public space. However, caution must be applied when extrapolating from only two pieces of evidence. It is noteworthy nonetheless that they converge in their description of the illustrated periodicals available in the first decades of the twentieth century for the consumption not only of adults, but also of youth.

Despite the moral panics about the images that could be casually 'read' in public, the diverging accounts of Stevenson and Greenwood bring attention to the fact that one cannot abstract a reader's attitude from retail and distribution strategies. It is important to bring to light the different ways in which fiction was encountered by Victorian audiences and to break the uniform mould of the three-decker novel. This is true for any historical period and all geographic locations. However, taking into account the varied publishing formats is not enough to understand actual reading experiences: they are variable, pluralistic, in some cases counterintuitive, and should never be generalized.

The history of Victorian reading has taken very long strides thanks to the rediscovery—facilitated by the Research Society for Victorian Periodicals (RSVP)—that many canonical texts on both sides of the Atlantic (and of the Channel) were first published serially. Seriality is still nonetheless hailed as a Victorian invention, often attributed to Dickens. This misconception obscures the eighteenth-century history of seriality, which informs the unusual way in which penny bloods and penny dreadfuls are sliced up into numbers. Nonetheless, book historians now acknowledge that readers can encounter texts in many different shapes and forms. First editions and later reprints, in periodicals or in bound volumes, in sheets or in publisher's bindings, on cheap newspaper paper or on expensive vellum, in type so small it strains the eyes or in specially designed fonts, with old and reused woodcuts, lovely engravings, fancy lithographs or no illustrations at all.

The importance of the physical object's mediation having been firmly established, the history of reading must widen its field of enquiry to encompass the mediation of the material conditions in which this physical object is encountered. The *Reading Experience Database* (*RED*), *1450–1945*, spearheaded since 2006 by the Open University, invites us precisely into this novel and impossibly expansive territory. It contains over 30,000 records of reading experiences in the British world over five centuries.[49] People read at home, by the fireside or in brightly lit private libraries, in public spaces such as coffeehouses, pubs, and circulating libraries, and in the new non-places of public transportation such as railway stations and onboard trains and steamboats.[50]

Similarly, penny dreadfuls, like any type of literature, not only can be encountered in different formats, but also read in many different ways. They can be read aloud to an assembled group, eagerly hanging on to the storyteller's every word; they can be read dutifully each week when it hits the stands; they can be poured over, once complete and bound, or skimmed through searching for the naughty bits; they can be read through the front-page of each weekly number displayed in the shop-window; and this is not even counting on penny gaffs and other theatrical adaptations.[51]

Each of the reading practices outlined above will shift the focus to a different locus in the text, from episodic cliff-hangers to the complete (and seemingly incoherent) narrative. The difference for Victorian readers is therefore analogous to that of contemporary television viewers, whose habits may veer between binge-watching a Netflix series and painfully waiting for each weekly episode to air. Whatever the medium, different consumption practices produce different experiences, but also different interpretations. In the realm of printed literature, some reading practices focus on discrete incidents, made easier to find by the illustrations, or even disregard the text entirely to 'read' only the illustrations.

Thus, most reading practices completely break down the beautiful gem of the complete and integral text fetishized by literary studies.[52]

The reading practice highlighted in this chapter only applies to illustrated serial story-telling, but this is not restricted to penny dreadfuls and their penny blood predecessors. Comics are certainly the most easily identifiable descendent, but gossip magazines operate identically, with the snapshots and puzzling headlines on their cover allegedly telling the lives of stars over multiple weeks. The contrast this chapter draws between two accounts of window-shopping demonstrates how the same reading practice can produce widely differing reading experiences, from delightfully playful to painfully infuriating.

Variability is true in all contexts. I myself am content, much like Stevenson, in looking at the paparazzi shots on the cover of the people press and inferring what they depict from the headlines it contains, but others will be compelled to buy the issue at hand. These differing attitudes are informed by the reader's age, class, education, (gender and ethnicity too, presumably, though these variables have not been studied in this chapter), but also his or her individuality.

NOTES

1. D.F. Mitch, The Rise of Popular Literacy in Victorian England (Philadelphia: University of Pennsylvania Press), p. 217; p. 75. Victorian literacy rates are based on signature rates in marriage registers. Literacy is very different, though, when defined as the ability to understand texts: PIAAC defines it as 'the ability to identify, understand, interpret, create, communicate and compute, using printed and written materials associated with varying contexts'. OECD, 'Adult Literacy', *Innovation in Education*, http://www.oecd.org/edu/innovation-education/adultliteracy.htm, date accessed 13 November 2015. According to the final report of the International Adult Literacy Survey, 'Level 3 is considered a suitable minimum for coping with the demands of everyday life and work in a complex, advanced society', and half the English population still does not meet this standard. OECD and Statistics Canada, *Literacy in the Information Age*, 2000, p. xi, http://www.oecd.org/edu/skills-beyond-school/41529765.pdf; Department for Business, Innovation and Skills, *The International Survey of Adult Skills 2012: Adult Literacy, Numeracy and Problem*

Solving Skills in England, UK Government, October 2013, p. 56, https://www.gov.uk/government/uploads/system/uploads/ attachment_data/file/246534/bis-13-1221-international-survey-of-adult-skills-2012.pdf

2. It took me three weeks to realize that the penny bloods I was consulting at the Cambridge University Library were not later reprints, despite numbers finishing and starting in the middle of a sentence, or even of a word.
3. Importantly for literacy rate estimates, the reverse—that someone who cannot write therefore cannot read—could not be assumed to be true. On the difficulties of measuring literacy and relating literacy to reading, see R. Chartier, trans. A. Goldhammer, 'The Practical Impact of Writing', *A History of Private Life: III. Passions of the Renaissance* (Cambridge, MA and London, England: Belknap Press of Harvard University Press, 1993), pp. 111–12; translated from 'Les pratiques de l'écrit', *Histoire de la vie privée: Tome 3. De la Renaissance aux Lumières* (Paris: Seuil, 1986), pp. 113–61.
4. Greenwood is suspected of having fabricated an account of a fight organized between a dog and a man in one of his reports for the *Daily Telegraph* signed 'One of the Crowd'. It was published in July 1874, a year and a half after the publication of '"Penny Awfuls"'. See P.J. Keating, 'James Greenwood', *Into Unknown England, 1866–1913: Selections from the Social Explorers* (Manchester: Manchester University Press, 1976), pp. 33–64.
5. J. Greenwood, '"Penny Awfuls"', *Saint Paul's Magazine* 12 (1873), 161–68 (pp. 165–67).
6. Greenwood, '"Penny Awfuls"', p. 166. Greenwood mentioned the narrative indeterminacy of illustrations five years earlier in *The Seven Curses of London*, using instead the example of a doorkeeper either shutting or opening the door to let the highwayman through or to bar his way. See J. Greenwood, *The Seven Curses of London* (London: Rivers, 1869), pp. 70–72.
7. The ODNB biography focuses on Greenwood's journalistic work, A. Tomkins, 'Greenwood, James William (bap. 1835, d. 1927)', *Oxford Dictionary of National Biography* (Oxford University Press, 2010) http://www.oxforddnb.com/view/article/41224, date accessed 13 November 2015. For a more complete picture including his children's literature, see a partial bibliography put together by cheap periodical specialist John Adcock, 'Works of the Amateur Casual (ca. 1835–1927)', *Yesterday's Papers*, 2011, http://johnadcock.blogspot.ca/2011/02/works-of-amateur-casual-1832-1929.html
8. For more on Greenwood's slum literature, see S. Koven, 'Workhouse Nights: Homelessness, Homosexuality, and Cross-Class Masquerades', *Slumming: Sexual and Social Politics in Victorian London* (Princeton, NJ and Oxford: Princeton University Press, 2004), pp. 25–93.

9. John Adcock selects the following passage from *The Adventures of Reuben Davidger* (serialized in 1863, stand-alone edition in 1865) as 'outdo[ing]' all that this profuse penny-blood and -dreadful reader has read:

> Topmost of the buried pile was the head of our lady passenger, and so it was well placed, as its beautiful long brown curls (which many a time, as I waited at the captain's table, had caused my heart to flutter with admiration) hung down and over the other ghastly heads, partly concealing the features. Attached to the brown ringlets by a long copper hair-pin was a tag of red cloth, placed there, as I suppose, by the ruffian whose spoil the lady's head was, that he might know his own.

10. J. Greenwood, *The Adventures of Reuben Davidger* (London: S.O. Beeton, 1865), p. 89.
11. C. Banham, '*Boys of England* and Edwin J. Brett, 1866–99', unpublished dissertation, University of Leeds, 2006, p. 37.
12. C. Scott and C. Howard, *The Life and Reminiscences of E. L. Blanchard* (London: Hutchison & Co., 1891), pp. 31–32. The term 're-originated' is used in *Parley's Penny Library* to describe Blanchard's summaries of favourite novels of the day by Dickens or Edward Lytton Bulwer, for instance. See M. Léger-St-Jean, *Price One Penny: A Database of Cheap Literature, 1837–1860*, http://www.priceonepenny.info/database/show_periodical.php?periodical_id=27. In 1845, Dickens sued following the 're-origination' of *A Christmas Carol*, see E.T. Jaques, *Charles Dickens in Chancery; being an Account of his Proceedings in Respect of the 'Christmas Carol', with some Gossip in Relation to the Old Law Courts at Westminster* (London: Longmans, Green and Co., 1914).
13. The files of the Royal Literary Fund are currently housed at the British Library, but also available in microfilm and online as part of the *Nineteenth-Century Collections Online*. On the development of the profession, see N. Cross, *The Common Writer: Life in Nineteenth-Century Grub Street* (Cambridge: Cambridge University Press, 1985) and L.H. Peterson, *Becoming a Woman of Letters: Victorian Myths of Authorship, Facts of the Market* (Princeton, NJ and Woodstock: Princeton University Press, 2009).
14. Greenwood, '"Penny Awfuls"', p. 168.
15. C. Banham and E. Stearns, 'Introduction', *The Skeleton Crew, or, Wildfire Ned* (Brighton: Victorian Secrets, 2015), p. 10.
16. For more on the importance of illustration in Victorian penny publications, see P.J. Anderson, *The Printed Image and the Transformation of Popular Culture 1790–1860* (Oxford: Clarendon Press, 1991).
17. J. Springhall, *Youth, Popular Culture and Moral Panics: Penny Gaffs to Gangsta-Rap, 1830–1996* (New York: St. Martin's Press, 1998),

pp. 42–43. Louis James's seminal work *Fiction for the Working Man* (1973) concentrates on only two decades, the 1830s and 1840s: he thus cannot offer a complete picture of the evolution of penny publishing up to its 1860 transformation.

18. At the same time, non-serial cheap formats, such as the single-volume novel and the yellowback, were appearing for adults. William Roberts, writing in the 1920s and 1930s in general publications such as *The Nineteenth Century and After* and the *Times Literary Supplement*, was the first to draw attention to the distinction between bloods and dreadfuls. He also addresses translation in penny numbers, usually absent from discussions, though it is a distinctive feature of penny bloods as opposed to penny dreadfuls. Ronald Arthur Brimmell (1917–93), an English bookseller and specialist of children's books and rare detective fiction, wrote a very perceptive article on penny bloods and penny dreadfuls, published in two parts in 1982 and 1983. He offers two suggestions for the rupture between bloods and dreadfuls: (1) that yellowbacks would have replaced the former in the market, (2) that blood authors were dying out and being replaced by a new generation. See R.A. Brimmell, 'Old Bloods & Penny Dreadfuls Part 2', *Antiquarian Book Monthly Review* 10.3 (1983), 80–83 (p. 80). Blood authors were not all dying, however: the most prolific, including James Malcolm Rymer (1814–84) and Pierce Egan (1814–80), referred to in Stevenson's 'Popular Authors', kept on writing for the magazines, including *Reynolds's Miscellany* and the *London Journal*. Nonetheless, there were certainly a new generation of authors, who had never written bloods, such as Samuel Bracebridge Hemyng (1841–1901) and William Stephens Hayward (1835–70), whom Stevenson cites in 'Popular Authors'.

19. For a manuscript copy of the play, see Lord Chamberlain's Plays, Add MS 53089 I at the British Library. On the relationship between penny dreadfuls and the London theatre, see C. Banham, and E. Stearns, 'Introduction', pp. 11–12.

20. R.L. Stevenson, 'Popular Authors', *Scribner's Magazine* 4.1 (1888), 122–28 (p. 125).

21. Stevenson, 'Popular Authors', p. 125.

22. H. Mayhew, *London Labour and the London Poor*, Vol. I (London: Griffin, Bohn, and Company, 1861), p. 28. For *The Mysteries of the Court of London*, M. Léger-St-Jean, *Price One Penny: A Database of Cheap Literature, 1837–1860*, http://www.priceonepenny.info/database/show_title.php?work_id=582 and sequels.

23. Stevenson, 'Popular Authors', p. 122.

24. Illustration of Strange's shop at 21 Paternoster-row, c. 1847 on the front page of his catalogue, tucked in classmark Mas.1044(15) at the National Library of Scotland.
25. A. Smith, *The Struggles and Adventures of Christopher Tadpole at Home and Abroad* (London: Richard Bentley, 1848), pp. 178–79. On comic Valentines, see the curators of the John Johnson Collection's explanation: 'Comic Valentines: Topical Ephemera 2' (2012), *The John Johnson Collection: Now and Then*, http://johnjohnsoncollectionnowandthen.wordpress.com/2012/02/13/comic-valentines/, date accessed 7 December 2015; *A Selection of Valentines from the John Johnson Collection of Printed Ephemera* (2010), Bodleian Library, University of Oxford, http://www.bodleian.ox.ac.uk/__data/assets/pdf_file/0009/81387/season-for-love-leaflet.pdf, p. [3].
26. Despite being a neglected reading space to which I wish to bring attention, I would not want to give the impression that shop windows only contained literary matter. In 1851, publisher Edwin Dipple placed an advertisement for betting men in Bell's Life in London, offering advertising space in his Holywell-street shop window: : 'Any respectable party wishing to exhibit lists can hear of a situation in one of the leading thoroughfares in town by applying (if by letter prepaid) to E. Dipple, publisher, Holywell-street, Strand. References given and expected', *Bell's Life in London and Sporting Chronicle*, 20 April 1851, p. 1.
27. Stevenson, 'Popular Authors', p. 125.
28. Stevenson, 'Popular Authors', p. 127.
29. Stevenson, 'Popular Authors', p. 125.
30. Unlike Charlie in his Thieves Anonymous meeting, Stevenson does not mention in his article how he procured himself the means of sustaining his addiction.
31. Stevenson, 'Popular Authors', p. 125.
32. Greenwood, '"Penny Awfuls"', p. 166.
33. Stevenson, 'Popular Authors', p. 125.
34. Stevenson, 'Popular Authors', p. 125.
35. K. Carpenter, 'R. L. Stevenson on the *Treasure Island* Illustrations', *Notes and Queries* 29.4 (1982), 322–25 (p. 324).
36. Carpenter, 'R. L. Stevenson', p. 324.
37. Stevenson, 'Popular Authors', p. 125.
38. Stevenson, 'Popular Authors', p. 127.
39. Stevenson, 'Popular Authors', p. 123; p. 122.
40. Stevenson, 'Popular Authors', p. 126.
41. Stevenson, 'Popular Authors', p. 127.
42. Stevenson, 'Popular Authors', p. 123.
43. Stevenson, 'Popular Authors', p. 127.

44. Stevenson, 'Popular Authors', p. 128.
45. Stevenson, 'Popular Authors', p. 127; p. 125; p. 127; p. 127.
46. T. Mackay, 'Penny Dreadfuls', *Time* 19.44 (1888), 218–25 (p. 218).
47. J. Stamper, *So Long Ago* (London: Hutchinson, 1960), p. 162.
48. Stamper, *So Long Ago*, p. 161; p. 160. Quoted in UK RED, records 11533 and 11531, http://www.open.ac.uk/Arts/reading/UK/record_details.php?id=11533 and http://www.open.ac.uk/Arts/reading/UK/record_details.php?id=11531, date accessed 6 December 2015.
49. P.E. Moulder, 'The Morals of the Coming Generation', *Westminster Review* 180.3 (1913), 299–301 (p. 300).
50. *UK Reading Experience Database* (RED), http://www.open.ac.uk/Arts/reading/UK/The RED will be expanding in the next years into a pan-European project and will record readers' marks and responses in all types of media: http://eured.univ-lemans.fr/ and https://eured.hypotheses.org/
51. Regarding the term 'non-places', see M. Augé, *Non-Lieux, introduction à une anthropologie de la surmodernité* (Paris: Le Seuil, 1992); *Non-Places: Introduction to an Anthropology of Supermodernity* (London and New York: Verso, 1995).
52. For more on penny gaffs, see J. Springhall, 'Penny Theatre Panic: Anxiety over Juvenile Working-Class Leisure', *Youth, Popular Culture and Moral Panics*, pp. 11–37.
53. As translation scholar Itamar Even-Zohar notes, 'the direct consumption of integral texts has been, and remains, peripheral to the largest part of "direct," let alone "indirect," consumers of "literature."' I. Even-Zohar, 'The "Literary System"', Poetics Today 11.1 (1990), 27–44 (p. 36).

BIBLIOGRAPHY

Cawelti, J.G. (1976) *Adventure, Mystery, and Romance: Formula Stories as Art and Popular Culture* (Chicago: University of Chicago Press).

Greenwood, J. (1874) 'A Short Way to Newgate', *The Wilds of London* (London: Chatto and Windus), 158–172.

Léger-St-Jean, M. (2012) '"long for the penny number and weekly woodcut": Stevenson on Reading and Writing Popular Fiction', *Journal of Stevenson Studies*, 9, 207–232.

Michel, J.-B., Shen, Y.K., Presser Aiden, A., Veres, A., Gray, M.K. et al (2011) 'Quantitative Analysis of Culture Using Millions of Digitized Books', *Science*, 331, 176–182.

CHAPTER 8

Sensation and Song: Street Ballad Consumption in Nineteenth-Century England

Isabel Corfe

Nineteenth-century street ballads have often been identified as an early form of tabloid press that provided news of sensational events—especially murders and executions—in verse form. This association with topical news has led to their comparison with contemporaneous newspapers. In particular, the cheap price of street literature and ballads compared to newspapers in the first half of the century has been cited as a reason for street balladry being popular at this time. A correlation has been made between a population eager to purchase news in a burgeoning public sphere, and its consumption of the only affordable type of newsprint available. As a result of this identification of street ballads with newsprint, there has been a perception that the drop in price of newspapers in the 1850s and 1860s caused a corresponding fall in the consumption of street ballads. The assumption has often been that the subsequent market for street ballads was somehow a nostalgic one—aware of its patronage of a dying textual form.[1] The validity of this view of nineteenth-century street-ballad consumption will be explored here primarily through an exploration of the nature of the street ballads themselves.

I. Corfe (✉)
National University of Ireland, Galway, Ireland

When James Catnach and his rival John Pitts dominated the printing trade of the Seven Dials (but were by no means the only ballad printers) in the 1820s and 30s, they no doubt satisfied a mass audience of buyers who enjoyed street ballads as a truly popular print form. James Catnach (trading between 1813 and 1837) was said to have made 'upwards of 10,000*l*.' over the course of his career, and to have 'made the greater part of this sum during the trial of Queen Caroline' (in 1820).[2] Charles Hindley, writing what could already be described in 1869 as a nostalgic look back at the history of the 'Jemmy' Catnach press, gave a description of the type of material printed and the way in which it was traded. In doing so, Hindley conveyed a trading environment that was indeed reminiscent of the tabloid press or of the flurries of textual material disseminated on social media: 'Great as was the demand, the printers of street literature were equal to the occasion, and all were actively engaged in getting out "papers," squibs, lists of various trade deputations to the Queen's levées, lampoons and songs, that were almost hourly published, on the subject of the Queen's trial.'[3] While this trial was an unusual event, it was indicative of the excitement that surrounded all public events at the time, and that was most commonly manifested in the sales of 'last dying speeches' and 'sorrowful lamentations'. In 1857 Charles Manby Smith pointed out 'so strong is the morbid craving of the multitude for details connected with the gallows, that the sale of these gloomy sheets far exceeds that of any other production of the press throughout the world'.[4] Mayhew gave sale figures for copies of last-dying speeches of the Rush hanging in 1849, as two and a half million copies, and quoted the same high figure for the hanging of the Mannings that occurred in the same year.[5] He was keen to state that the 'publications which relate to the hanging of malefactors', was 'not of any minor importance', because a 'very extensive … portion of the reading of the poor' was supplied by the '"Sorrowful Lamentations" and "Last Dying Speech, Confession, and Execution" of criminals'. Reading, as an act, is significant in this description because while the sheets were often described as 'ballads', they often included a passage of prose alongside the verse—as well as the decorative woodcut, usually the image of a hanging man, or a 'true likeness' portrait of the criminal.

However, 'gallows literature' by no means constituted the entirety of the street ballad repertoire, and did not form the primary focus of all those in the ballad trade—as one of Mayhew's street authors of ballads and poems lamented 'the printers like hanging subjects best, and I don't'.[6]

Evidence from our extant collections of nineteenth-century street ballads suggests that in fact, throughout the nineteenth century, the vast majority of the street ballads sold were ordinary song sheets rather than sheets pertaining to the gallows.[7] This seeming contradiction between the material in extant collections, and commentary, both contemporary and subsequent, is not easy to explain. Printers of street literature were notoriously bad record-keepers, so sales figures for the different types of ballads do not exist, and the contradiction could be easily dismissed as the result of individual collectors placing more value on the less topical, more universally appealing material. The one type of evidence that printers did provide, however, were printers' catalogues consisting of lists of songs available for purchase. These catalogues reveal lists of ballads roughly correspondent in content to ballads found in extant collections – supporting the idea that our extant collections are a relatively true representation of the ballads produced and sold. And, what these printers' catalogues from London, Manchester, and Glasgow contain, are hundreds of what could be described as ordinary songs and ballads, rather than the oft-analysed murder and execution ballads. Moreover, many of these songs remained in print across almost the entirety of the nineteenth century, from the time during which public hangings still took place (the last public execution occurred in 1868), to the end of the century. For example, 'Poor Dog Tray' by Thomas Campbell appears in catalogues of the following dates: 1832 (the Catnach catalogue), 1836 (Pitts), 1836 (T. Birt), 1872 (Thomas Pearson), and 1890 (H.P. Such). 'Bay of Biscay' by Limerick-born Andrew Cherry occurs in all but the Pitts catalogue, 'Last Rose of Summer' by Thomas Moore appears in the Pitts catalogue (1836), the Pearson catalogue (1872), and the Such catalogue (1890). And the 'Wild Rover' appears in the catalogues of Birt (1836), Pearson (1872), and Such (1890). What these examples seem to show, is that while the more topical ballads evidently sold in large numbers at times of high public excitement, they were outweighed—at least in variety of choice if not in sheets sold—by what could be described as ordinary songs. A revealing note on the back of Catnach's 1832 catalogue states that in addition to the listed songs in the catalogue, there are a 'number of Sheets and Half-Sheets, which being only of temporary interest, are not enumerated in the above Catalogue'.[8]

However, definitive conclusions about proportions of the various ballad types that were sold, are difficult to make. Contemporary accounts such as those related by Mayhew can help to build a picture, but are often contradictory. In Mayhew's work alone there are many accounts of ballad sellers and/or patterers reminiscing about the profitability of certain high-profile murders and tragedies, but there are also many others that reveal an ongoing reliance by ballad sellers on song sheets. Some examples of the former include one patterer who informed Mayhew that he lived on Rush's execution (which occurred in 1849) 'for a month or more' and that he managed to astonish 'the wise men in the east' by paying his landlord the full 14s. he owed him.[9] Another patterer 'Irish Jem, the Ambassador', apparently 'never went to bed without blessing the memory of that truculent farmer', that is, the hanged Rush.[10] Another example originating with Irish Jem relates to a ballad about the tragedy of Sarah Holmes in Lincoln, which he sold 'every winter' for five years. Other tragedies, such as 'The Scarborough Tragedy' (about a clergyman's daughter and a rich, young naval officer), were 'in work' for 20 years.[11] These examples paint a picture of a street ballad trade heavily reliant on true crime, tragedy and murder despite the fact that tragedies such as these, and high-profile hangings such as the Mannings's were not regular occurrences.

Less discussed in later nineteenth-century accounts as well as in scholarship thus far, are those accounts that reveal the significance of song sheets. Another patterer interviewed by Mayhew, for example, told him that he 'never works a last dying speech on any other than the day of execution—all the edge is taken off of it after that'[12]—indicating that for the rest of the time he relied on other material. Mayhew also wrote of a ballad seller who said that although 'a good murder will cut out the lot of them', he was still eventually 'driven into the comic standing patters'.[13] He elaborated by saying a 'foolish nonsensical thing will sell twice as fast as a good moral sentimental one', and that he found customers for these 'nonsensical things' among 'footmen, the grooms, and the maid-servants' in the West End, and among the dock men in 'the east end of town' (which was 'best on Friday and Saturday evenings'). As for what else these customers were buying, Mayhew provides what he describes as a 'curious' list of ballad titles in his section on street poets and authors. He writes that 'though not all' the ballads in this list were written expressly for the purpose of being sold and sung in the street, 'they presented a curious study enough', being 'of every class'. The list is worth exploring because as a representative sample, and like the printers' catalogues discussed above, it corresponds closely to the type of material found in extant collections. It names 17 songs and ends the list with an '&c. &c.'—itself indicative of the familiarity that Mayhew and his readership had with the type of material being discussed. It contains songs by well-regarded popular poets and writers (although authors were rarely listed on the sheets themselves), national songs, romantic songs, comedic songs, satirical songs, songs of Irish and Scottish origin and one example of blackface minstrelsy. The emblematic nature of the list can be quickly verified by the fact that many are extant in the Bodleian Broadside Ballads collection (Broadside Ballads Online) and their popularity evidenced by their presence in multiple print forms, that is, from various printers in different towns, operating at different times.

The list contains two songs by Thomas Moore, 'Remember the Glories of Brian the Brave' and 'The Young May Moon'—the latter being relatively popular with 12 results in Broadside Ballads Online—from multiple printings originating in London, Manchester, York, Birmingham, and one from Dublin. Another song with an Irish theme, 'Erin Go Bragh', was one of the most popular on the list (with at least 18 versions in the Bodleian collection), and remained popular throughout the nineteenth century. There are three or four distinctly different versions of the song. The first is that in which 'Duncan Campbell' or 'Pat Murphy' achieves just revenge on a policeman who gives him some 'jaw' (for he knows he's a 'Pat' by the 'twist of [his] hair').[14] Another version is one of ambiguous loyalties and begins 'Oh! I sing of sweet Erin my country admiring', but continues to extol the virtues of unity with 'Albion'. All copies of this last version are London printings (R. March and Co., J. Pitts., T. Birt, and W.S. Fortey) and most likely originated as anti-repeal (of the 1801 Act of Union) propaganda. Apart from the songs with Irish sentiment, the most obviously patriotic song is 'The Death of Nelson', of which there are nearly 30 results in the Bodleian that include a number of different versions. 'There's a good Time coming, Boys' (extant in around 18 versions in the Bodleian) was another very popular song by well-known songwriter Charles Mackay, which spurned a number of alternative versions—'There's a good time coming Girls', and 'Comic Version of there's a good time coming boys'. 'The Girls of ____shire' was a popular format in street literature, and an example of the kind of song that was likely written especially for street-ballad dissemination. The space before the 'shire' is left blank in order to extol the virtues and praise the girls of whichever shire the ballad seller is currently peddling in. 'Ye Banks and Braes o' Bonnie Doun' by Robert Burns was also very popular—with approximately 17 printed versions in Bodleian Ballads (when the different spellings of 'Doun'/ 'Doon' are factored). Versions were printed in London, Liverpool, Chester, Gateshead, Preston, Worcester, and as ever, there are one or two versions with no printer imprint. 'Nix, my Dolly' first appeared in W.H. Ainsworth's novel *Rookwood*, in 1834, and was later popularized—various printings are extant in the Bodleian database—for example from Paul, J. Sharp, T. Birt in London, W. Jackson and son in Birmingham, W. and T. Fordyce in Newcastle and others in Nottingham, Pocklington, and Carlisle. Another very popular ballad praises Tyrol in 'Hail to the Tyrol' and yields 14 results in the Bodleian collection. The list's example of Blackface Minstrelsy is the song named 'Lucy Long'—a particularly racist and misogynistic example in which the narrator sings that 'if he had a scolding wife', he'd 'take her down to New Orleans, / And trade her away for corn'.[15] A casual flippancy about marital violence in comic songs was relatively common, albeit far outweighed by comic and sentimental songs. Another song with a similar sentiment is 'Clementina Clemmins'(a comedic take on an overly-modest sweetheart) of which there are four printings in London, Manchester, and Leeds. Mayhew's interview with the 'street author or poet' in the same section, gives further insight. This poet wrote 'Demon of the Sea' (three extant versions contained in the Bodleian collection from printers in London, Nottingham, and Preston) and sold this song not to a ballad printer, but to a concert-room manager in the hope of better remuneration. In true pirating style, however, the song was 'soon in the streets, and ran the whole winter'. He also wrote 'Pirate of the Isles' (six extant versions in the Bodleian—London, Manchester, Preston, and printer unknown), and 'other ballads of that sort' including 'Husband's Dream' (with which the teetotallers were 'very much pleased', and on account of which the printer once sent him 5 shillings).[16] The poet added that usually 'The concert-rooms pay no better than the printers for the streets'—1 shilling.[17]

That this eclectic list of songs was produced during the period around 1850 when gallows literature was at its height, is further evidence of the fact that gallows literature may not have dominated the trade to the extent that might at first be assumed from their oft-quoted sales figures. During the 1850s, gallows literature indeed declined, although it was still being produced in the 1860s. In his 1871 publication *Curiosities of Street Literature*, Charles Hindley gave a number of examples of the various types of street literature, along with sales figures, but stated that as 'far as can be ascertained, the sale of Broad-sheets in the Mannings and Rush's case far exceed that of any now before us.' He further speculated that 'this difference is no doubt to be explained by the fact that since Mannings and Rush's day [1849] the daily penny newspapers have almost forestalled the "Dying Speeches and confessions"—with or without the "copy of verses"—by giving a full account of the different enormities in all their minute and hideous details'.[18] This example of the comparison of street ballads with the 'daily penny newspapers' was due to the focus of Hindley's work being solely on those 'curiosities', 'squibs', 'cocks' and 'catchpennies', and dying-speeches, that he perceived to have been especially composed for street sale. So, while Hindley's work remains an essential resource for scholars of street literature, it should not be viewed as a representative sample of the ballads produced and sold on the streets.

One type of ballad that would have been included in Hindley's collection, however, were those new ballads on topical subjects that were still being composed. Examples include those songs that were composed about Fenians (such as 'Lamentation for the four unfortunate Men at Manchester' and 'The Lamentation and Last Farewell to the World of Michael Barrett'—two sympathetic examples printed by H. Disley). These songs include the familiar tropes of 'old Erin' and 'Erin's children' found so often in Irish-themed songs. A song on the 'Sentence of Death on Michael Barrett for the Clerkenwell Explosion' (which occurred in 1867) printed by W.S. Fortey, follows the more usual format for gallows literature—relating the 'dreadful crime—horrible to tell', the last verse ending with the usual 'we hope all men will a warning take'. One extant version (BBO) with a less sympathetic stance, is that published by a virtually unknown London printer K.J. Ford. Named 'A Special Song' by 'A Special', to the tune of 'Hearts of Oak', it begins 'Come neighbours and join, 'tis for orders we're here / To shew the Fenians how little we fear', and ends 'But to put down the Fenians who soil ERIN'S GREEN / Soldiers, Sailors and Specials will stand by our QUEEN' (capitals original). These are just a few examples of newer printed material in verse form— Shepard also quotes one of printer E. Hodges's imprints (successor to J. Pitts who operated between 1855 and 1861) that claimed 'two or three New Songs are published every week'.[19]

Some of what were described in the nineteenth century as 'ancient ballads' were also sold on the streets and can be found in extant collections, although they are found in far fewer numbers than the newly composed ballads. Mayhew gives a sample of these songs that includes 'Children in the Wood', 'Chevy Chase', 'Barbara Allen' and 'Gilderoy was a Bonnie boy'. That the list also includes the authored 'My Days have been so wondrous Free' by Thomas Parnell, shows that 'ancient' was not necessarily synonymous with the later term 'folk-song'.

What these examples from the second half of the century, as well as those slightly earlier examples given by Mayhew show, is that (in Mayhew's own words) the ballads 'sold and sung on the street', are 'of every class', and include many varieties in addition to the 'gallows literature'. And the evidence that the street-ballads as a whole were still printed and sold in the 1860s, 70s and 80s, negates the widely held assumption that the ballad trade died after the drop in the price of newspapers that occurred in the early 1860s. As discussed earlier, this assumption seems natural if viewing the ballads as another form of printed news and making comparisons based on price. The stamp tax had been fully repealed in 1855 and the abolition of the paper duty occurred in 1861, so the price of newspapers gradually but steadily declined to a norm of between 1d. and 3d. from the 1860s onwards—which compared to previous highs of between 5d. and 7d. in the 1840s and 1850s. In 1861, the *Penny Illustrated Paper* was founded, consisting of 16 pages, 7 of which contained large and elaborate engravings. If viewing the broadsides purely as a form of print and source for reading, logic would suggest that people would rather spend scant earnings on a publication such as the *Penny Illustrated*, rather than on a half-penny ballad consisting only of a single-sided sheet and two or three songs and one or two (if you were lucky) very poorly printed woodcuts. One *Chambers's Journal* author, evidently frustrated by the seeming perverseness of this fact wrote:

> From what has been shewn [*sic*] … it would appear inexplicable, on the face of it, that in these days, when good and serviceable literature is so cheap and abundant, there should be found a paying market for what not only *is* unquestionable rubbish, but looks what it is, and scorns to assume the appearance of anything better … The paper is so vile that no decent shopkeeper would condescend to use it to wrap up copper change. The print is indescribably villainous—rarely legible for three lines together, and teeming with blunders and omissions where it is legible … What, then, is the secret of the large and continuous sale … ?[20]

As discussed above, a straightforward correlation between the price of newspapers compared to ballads cannot be made. Partly, this was due to the fact that previous to the decline in cost of newspapers, the average member of public had more contact with newspaper content than might at first be supposed. In 1829, an article in the *Westminster Review* calculated that on average, 'every copy of a newspaper in Great Britain ... was read by perhaps twenty-five persons on average'—with the average in the London area being higher still—at around 30 people.[21] With this in mind, if people already had access to newspapers in the first half of the nineteenth century, then the argument that they bought ballads merely as cheap forms of print becomes inadequate. The author of the *Chambers's Journal* quote above, argues that the answer lies in the trade itself, and in the practicalities distribution in particular:

> 'Oh,' says the philosopher, 'the reason is plain enough—it is the corrupt taste of the masses, who will feed on garbage, and prefer it to wholesome mental food.' [But] as practical inquirers, we look at facts, and we find this single one to be worth more than a bushel of theories: The distribution-agent of the Seven Dials literature pockets as profit four-fifths of his receipts. The chanter, the patterer, the pinner-up, the cock-crower, the small shop-keeper—all buy their sheet-ballads, lamentations, crows, &c., at 2*d*. to 2 ½ *d*. the long dozen. The trade thus yields the agent from 200 to 300 per cent. on his outlay ... [So] ... trumpeted as it is by hundreds of bawling vagabonds and audacious wags in the ears of the ignorant populace, it creates its own market wherever it goes; and the Seven Dials press flourishes, thanks to its paternal care of its agents.[22]

What this article reveals is not only that ballad singers (or 'bawling vagabonds') were still numerous in 1856, but it also highlights the importance of the distribution method. At a time when the rural poor travelled little, or never, street ballads may indeed still have been one of the only forms of cheap, new print available. Newspapers certainly had a variety of forms of dissemination, for example: shopkeepers in market towns employing hawkers to disseminate papers in rural areas; the rental of newspapers; or, the joint purchase of newspapers amongst families. The simplicity of the ballads however—their size, the universal nature of their content, and the cheapness of their wholesale price—meant that they were far more likely to be found in pedlars' baskets than newspapers. And, this was in addition to the fact that they were sold on streets far more frequently than were newspapers. Ballads were portable in a way that newspapers weren't. They were found on city streets, in towns on market days and at sporting events, as well as peddled door-to-door. These modes of dissemination therefore came closer to the daily lives of the urban and rural poor, even during the 1860s and 1870s, than newspapers yet did.

A 'paper-worker' who often visited 'small and obscure villages in Norfolk' gave Mayhew the following anecdote:

> one evening after dark, through the uncurtained cottage window, eleven persons, young and old, gathered round a scanty fire, which was made to blaze by being fed with a few sticks. An old man was reading, to an attentive audience, a broad-sheet of Rush's execution [1849], which my informant had sold to him; he read by the fire-light; for the very poor in those villages, I was told, rarely lighted a candle on a spring evening, saying that 'a bit o' fire was good enough to talk by.[23]

An appetite for sensation and murder is revealed here, but what is also described is the type of gathering that would have taken place in rural areas long after the mid century, and that were likely to have included readings of all kinds—as well as song. And, what the above examples of street ballads show, is that the bulk of broadside material, even in the nineteenth century, was what Leslie Shepard described as 'good singable material'. More than just reading matter, these were 'songs to be sung'.[24] During a period in which there was still only semi-literacy, and when other forms of entertainment were generally still prohibitively expensive (especially in rural areas), access to cheap song-material was not just a nostalgic novelty, but was central to the way in which people occupied their spare time.

In 1857, Charles Manby Smith wrote that to half the population 'it matters nothing that the theatres, the music-halls, the casinos, the gala-gardens, the panoramas, or the free-and-easies, the public-houses, and the gin shops, stand perpetually open. They have no money to expend for purposes of amusement.'[25] 'Penny Gaffs' had existed for some decades in urban areas like London but were primarily frequented by children and youths.[26] In 1852, the entrance fee for the Canterbury Hall in Lambeth was via a 'sixpenny refreshment ticket'. In 1856, a new hall was built on the site and the new fee was sixpence or nine-pence to the gallery—refreshments being charged for separately.[27] Compared to this, listening to a ballad on the street and taking home a half-penny song as souvenir, provided free entertainment as well as the means to produce one's own. Another article from the mid-1850s, 'Amusements of the Moneyless', gives an account of ballad singers and patterers—'bawling the last new political ballad, with interlocutory explanations—or a lament for the Crimean army—or a dirge for Nicholas, from which we learn that the czar lies "buried in a hole in famed Sebastypol" [*sic*].' This example reveals that the newly printed material did not only include literature that would prove lucrative at the emotionally charged events of public hangings, but also included newly produced topical balladry on political and state subjects—and was therefore still a means of disseminating news stories. Especially for the urban poor, this method of accessing the news through busked song and 'patter' on the street, was still an important way of engaging with the public sphere at a time before universal education, radio, or other cheap forms of entertainment. The mix of song, humour and topicality in this form of street literature, provided a compelling combination that was truly affordable to the poorest for the first time in the nineteenth century. Buying a ballad such as this was an act that combined an entertaining communal experience, with a later private reading, or further oral and/or musical dissemination. So while it resembled tabloid print in price, it provided more than a reading experience. Ballad culture throughout the nineteenth century straddled the space between oral tradition and communal entertainment, print culture and private reading, and a sense of individual engagement with the burgeoning public sphere that was later fulfilled by radio and television. Some of the other activities described in 'Amusements of the Moneyless' such as observing the soldiers' exercises in Hyde Park, the launch of a steamer in the Thames, the 'grand rowing-match', and visiting state buildings such as the Courts of Chancery or the House of Commons,[28] illustrate how listening to a ballad provided oral commentary on city and public life not provided elsewhere.

Evidently, street ballads in the nineteenth century provided a range of thematic experiences in spoken and sung form, and it was in their orality and musicality that their uniqueness lay. While they were important as an early print form, print and the association we now attach with print—the act of individual reading—was not their primary function. Anecdotes about ballads as print text—manifesting most obviously in their being used as literacy tools in poor household—are plenty, Walter Scott and John Clare being notable examples, and there are many more including a street author quoted by Mayhew who stated 'I certainly knew my letters before I left home, and I have got the rest of the dead walls and out of the ballads and papers I have been selling'.[29] All of these anecdotes, however, occur in the last decades of the eighteenth and the first half of the nineteenth century, and are virtually nonexistent after around 1850. These examples indicate that street ballads were used less for this purpose when the price of newspapers fell, but they also raise questions around what they *were* purchased for; the argument that their primary function related to their function as cheap print no longer seems valid. The same conclusion as that drawn from the ballad lists above seems to be valid here—that it was the ballads' function as song throughout the entirety of the nineteenth century that ensured their ongoing popularity. This was reiterated by one of Mayhew's chaunters who emphasized the importance of a good chorus. Declaring it essential for a successful street song, he told Mayhew that a 'ballad on a subject' had to have verses of at least eight lines and, 'a four-line chorus to every verse; and, if it's the right sort, it'll sell the ballad'.[30]

Further evidence that these street ballads were indeed sung after purchase comes from an unlikely source—from those song collectors in the 1890s and early decades of the twentieth century who sought to find and preserve songs from what they perceived to have been an unbroken oral tradition dating back to previous centuries. The perception was that rural areas, being freer of the corrupting influences of print culture, still contained an oral tradition consisting of old songs never before written down. However, undoubtedly disappointed, these collectors sometimes discovered songs collected in rural areas that had in fact been originally learned from broadsides. One example is that of singer John Woodbridge from whom Sabine Baring-Gould collected a number of songs. While having indeed learned songs passed down from his grandmother, he had also learned a number of songs from broadsides, including 'The Buxom Young Tailor'.[31] Another example from the same collector was that of singer Samuel Fone who was able to read, but not to write well, who had learned a 'very high proportion of his repertoire' from broadside ballads.[32] Sabine Baring-Gould became increasingly accepting of the idea that broadside ballads played an important role in the dissemination of songs— songs that themselves sometimes returned to, or entered for the first time into oral 'tradition'.[33] This was not necessarily an easy concession to make for a scholar/collector coming from the romantic, antiquarian tradition of Francis James Child who drew a clear distinction between broadsides (which he described as 'vulgar ... despicable and worthless'[34]), and those ancient songs unsullied by contact with print.

Child's frustration at the content and quality of some street verse of the gallows type was understandable, but in dismissing the whole street ballad genre, he missed an exploration of those songs that were truly popular amongst large sections of the population. A similar narrowness of focus, however, has been displayed by those scholars who have placed too heavy an emphasis on works written specifically for the street trade (by street poets), to the detriment of other material sold on the street or in rural areas. This polarized discourse has meant that the middle spectrum consisting of a vast array of songs printed with their consumption as song in mind, has been entirely ignored. The existence of these ballads in such large numbers in extant collections suggests that they formed part of a living song culture well into the second half of the century. And, that these ballads have the potential to provide insight into nineteenth-century attitudes and tastes that has thus far only been marginally explored.

NOTES

1. For further discussion and examples see the following: James Hepburn's *A Book of Scattered Leaves* (Lewisburg: Bucknell University Press, 2000) for a questioning of the assumption that gallows literature was the 'chief literature of the broadside trade' (pp. 74–75); Charles Hindley's *Curiosities of Street Literature Comprising 'Cocks,' or 'Catchpennies'* (London: Reeves and Turner, 1871) for a contemporary work that focuses solely on topical street ballads and 'cocks'; Ellen L. O'Brien's article 'Every Man Who Is Hanged Leaves a Poem': Criminal Poets in Victorian Street Ballads by Ellen L. O'Brien in *Victorian Poetry* 39, no. 2 (Summer 2001) for a closer examination of Victorian trial and execution ballads; Sheila O'Connell's *The Popular Print in England: 1550–1850* (London: British Museum Press, 1999) for an exploration of a wide range of popular print and newsprint; and Leslie Shepard's book *John Pitts: Ballad Printer* (London: Private Libraries Association, 1969) for an example of a work that reiterates the decline of the ballad trade after the mid-nineteenth century.
2. Henry Mayhew, *London Labour and the London Poor*, Vol. I (London: Charles Griffin and Company, 1861), p. 234.
3. Charles Hindley, *The History of the Catnach Press, at Berwick-upon-Tweed, Alnwich and Newcastle-upon Tyne, in Northumberland, and Seven Dials, London* (London: Charles Hindley (The Younger), 1886), p. 47.
4. Charles Manby Smith, *The Little World of London; or, Pictures in Little of London Life* (London: Arthur Hall, Virtue and Co., 1857), p. 258.
5. Henry Mayhew, *London Labour and the London Poor*, Vol. I (London: Charles Griffin and Company, 1861), p. 308.
6. Henry Mayhew, *London Labour and the London Poor*, Vol. I (London: Charles Griffin and Company, 1861), p. 302.
7. See James Hepburn, *A Book of Scattered Leaves: Poetry of Poverty in Broadside Ballads of Nineteenth-Century England*, Vol. 1 (Lewisburg: Bucknell University Press, 2000), pp. 74–75.
8. *Catalogue of Songs and Song Books, Sheets, Half-Sheets, Christmas Carols, Children's Books, &c. Printed and Published by J. Catnach* (1832). Madden Papers, University of Cambridge Library, Cambridge, 1 September 2015.

9. Henry Mayhew, *London Labour and the London Poor*, Vol. I (London: Charles Griffin and Company, 1861), p. 237.
10. 'A Literary Bohemia', *The St. James's Magazine* 1 (April 1868), 431–48. *British Periodicals*, Web, 12 December 2015, p. 437.
11. Henry Mayhew, *London Labour and the London Poor*, Vol. I (London: Charles Griffin and Company, 1861), p. 236.
12. Henry Mayhew, *London Labour and the London Poor*, Vol. I (London: Charles Griffin and Company, 1861), p. 250.
13. Henry Mayhew, *London Labour and the London Poor*, Vol. I (London: Charles Griffin and Company, 1861), p. 251.
14. *Erin Go Bragh & Tom Bowling* c. 1863–1885 (London: H.P. Such), *Broadside Ballads Online* Edition—Bod11450, Harding B11(1084), Web, 14 February 2016, http://ballads.bodleian.ox.ac.uk/static/images/sheets/05000/01975.gif
15. *Miss Lucy Long & Travelling Tinker.* c. 1845 (London: J. Sharp) *Broadside Ballads Online*, Edition—Bod12505, Harding B11(2442), Web, 14 February 2016, http://ballads.bodleian.ox.ac.uk/static/images/sheets/05000/03343.gif
16. Henry Mayhew, *London Labour and the London Poor*, Vol. I (London: Charles Griffin and Company, 1861), p. 302.
17. Henry Mayhew, *London Labour and the London Poor*, Vol. I (London: Charles Griffin and Company, 1861), p. 301.
18. Charles Hindley, *Curiosities of Street Literature: Comprising 'Cocks', or 'Catchpennies', a Large and Curious Assortment of Street-drolleries, Squibs, Histories, Comic Tales in Prose and Verse, Broadsides on the Royal Family, Political Litanies, Dialogues, Catechisms, acts of Parliament, Street Political Papers, a Variety of 'Ballads on a Subject', Dying Speeches and Confessions* (London: Reeves and Turner, 1871), p. 160.
19. Leslie Shepard, *John Pitts Ballad Printer of Seven Dials, London 1765–1844: With a Short Account of his Predecessors in the Ballad and Chapbook Trade* (London: Private Libraries Association, 1969), p. 85.
20. 'The Press of the Seven Dials', *Chambers's Journal of Popular Literature, Science and Arts* 130 (1856), 401–05, *ProQuest British Periodicals*, Web, 30 October 2013, p. 404.
21. A. Aspinall, 'The Circulation of Newspapers in the Early Nineteenth Century', *The Review of English Studies* 22.85 (1946), 29–43, p. 30.
22. 'The Press of the Seven Dials', *Chambers's Journal of Popular Literature, Science and Arts* 130 (1856), 401–405, *ProQuest British Periodicals*, Web, 30 October 2013, p. 404.
23. Henry Mayhew, *London Labour and the London Poor*, Vol. I (London: Charles Griffin and Company, 1861), p. 302.

24. Leslie Shepard, *John Pitts Ballad Printer of Seven Dials, London 1765–1844: With a Short Account of his Predecessors in the Ballad and Chapbook Trade* (London: Private Libraries Association, 1969), pp. 44–45.
25. Charles Manby Smith, *The Little World of London; or, Pictures in Little of London Life* (London: Arthur Hall, Virtue and Co., 1857), p. 2.
26. Henry Mayhew, *London Labour and the London Poor*, Vol. I (London: Charles Griffin and Company, 1861), p. 42.
27. 'The Story of Music Hall; The Origins of Music Hall', *Victoria and Albert Museum*, http://www.vam.ac.uk/content/articles/t/the-story-of-music-halls/, Web, 14 December 2016.
28. 'Amusements of the Moneyless', *Chambers's Journal of Popular Literature, Science and Arts* 72 (1855), 401–05. *ProQuest British Periodicals*. Web, 31 October 2013.
29. Henry Mayhew, *London Labour and the London Poor*, Vol. III (London: Charles Griffin and Company, 1861), p. 206.
30. Henry Mayhew, *London Labour and the London Poor*, Vol. I (London: Charles Griffin and Company, 1861), p. 297.
31. Martin Graebe, '"I'd Have You to Buy It and Learn It": Sabine Baring-Gould, his Fellow Collectors, and Street Literature', in D. Atkinson and S. Roud, eds., *Street Ballads in Nineteenth-Century Britain, Ireland and North America: The Interface between Print and Oral Tradition* (Farnham: Ashgate, 2014), p. 187.
32. David Atkinson and Steve Roud, eds., *Street Ballads in Nineteenth-Century Britain, Ireland, and North America: The Interface between Print and Oral Traditions* (Farnham: Ashgate, 2014), p. 187.
33. Martin Graebe, '"I'd Have You to Buy It and Learn It": Sabine Baring-Gould, his Fellow Collectors, and Street Literature', in D. Atkinson and S. Roud, eds., *Street Ballads in Nineteenth-Century Britain, Ireland and North America: The Interface between Print and Oral Tradition* (Farnham: Ashgate, 2014), p. 177.
34. Francis J. Child, '"Ballad Poetry", *Johnson's Universal Cyclopedia*, 1900', *Journal of Folklore Research* 31.1/3 (1994), 214–22, p. 218.

CHAPTER 9

Reading Reynolds: *The Mysteries of London* as 'Microscopic Survey'

Ruth Doherty

George William Macarthur Reynolds: even to those with an interest in Victorian literature and culture, this is an unfamiliar name, but Reynolds's obituarist in 1879 described him as the most popular writer of his time.[1] Described in the *Dictionary of National Biography* as 'novelist, journalist and radical', Reynolds presents an interesting case history in terms of the history of reading, with a prodigious written output produced and consumed over a relatively short period of time.[2] Anne Humphreys has estimated that he wrote between 35 and 40 *million* words over a 12-year period.[3] E.F. Bleiler notes that though '[o]ther writers in the popular traditions of England, France and America have written comparable amounts', this monumental word-count was usually accomplished over many more years.[4] Jonathan Rose contrasts Reynolds's legacy with that of a better-remembered contemporary: 'It has been argued that the sensational novelist GWM Reynolds (1814–79) outsold Dickens in his day, but his books had no staying power.'[5] Thus, Reynolds's readership belonged to a particular time. Though there is some evidence of his cross-class appeal, he aimed his work largely at a working-class audience, and in terms of sales was hugely successful. Louis James has claimed that Reynolds's serial

R. Doherty (✉)
Trinity College, Dublin, Ireland

© The Author(s) 2016
P.R. Rooney, A. Gasperini (eds.), *Media and Print Culture Consumption in Nineteenth-Century Britain*, New Directions in Book History, DOI 10.1057/978-1-137-58761-9_9

147

fiction *The Mysteries of London* was 'almost certainly the most widely read single work of fiction in mid-nineteenth century Britain, and attracted more readers than did the novels of Dickens, Bulwer-Lytton or Trollope.'[6]

Reynolds has not been widely studied in academic circles, though recent years have witnessed a resurgence in interest.[7] This essay focuses on *The Mysteries of London*, the series that brought Reynolds fame, *that* began publication in 1844.[8] Just over 170 years later, *Mysteries* has once again become widely accessible. When Trefor Thomas published an abridged edition of Volumes 1 and 2 in 1996, he noted that the complete original text had never been reprinted in the twentieth century; now, however, these volumes are available online, and in annotated editions from Valancourt Press.[9] Concentrating on Volume 1 of *Mysteries*, and mindful of the caution of Stephen James Carver that 'any reading of *The Mysteries of London* is either reductive or ambivalent, ultimately falling ... into the language of paradox', this essay demonstrates how Reynolds's use of readers and reading helps him to achieve his aim of creating a 'microscopic survey' of London.[10]

The 'microscopic survey' is shown to be an organizing principle for a long, detailed narrative that aims to represent the life of a huge city. Reynolds changes narrative point of view to bring his readers both minutely detailed scenes and sweeping overviews of nineteenth-century London. His characters tell stories, becoming narrators within narration, and speak of their own reading, situating their individual experience within a grand narrative which also involves the reader of *Mysteries*. The attempt to represent such a huge field of experience with words on a page requires a combination of particular formal, stylistic and narrative techniques. This essay explores Reynolds's use of characters' reading habits as a way to allow his readers to sense a wider world of literature, allowing his own text to stand metonymically for a much larger narrative: 'LONDON'.[11]

In the Epilogue to the first volume, Reynolds's narrator states that 'the word "LONDON" constitutes a theme whose details, whether of good or evil, are inexhaustible: nor knew we, when we took up our pen to enter upon the subject, how vast—how mighty—how comprehensive it might be!'[12] The attempt to present a microscopic view of London life threatens to create an infinitely detailed, never-to-be-completed text. Richard Maxwell has written that 'there can be no satisfactory method for ending *The Mysteries of London*'.[13] Maxwell also claimed that '*The Mysteries of London* is one of those books which works only when one has read too much, when situations have been repeated so that they echo painfully in the head'.[14] The pain caused by reading Reynolds is also a result of the constant shifts in point of view, from microscopic detail to wide survey, and the consequent shifts in viewer/reader position.

THE MICROSCOPE IN REYNOLDS

> The visitor to the Polytechnic Institution or the Adelaide Gallery, has doubtless seen the exhibition of the microscope. A drop of the purest water, magnified by that instrument some thousands of times, appears filled with horrible reptiles and monsters of revolting forms.
> Such is London.
> Fair and attractive as the mighty metropolis may appear to the superficial observer, it swarms with disgusting, loathsome, and venomous objects, wearing human shapes.
> Oh! London is a city of strange contrasts![15]

This image appears in Chapter 23 of *Mysteries*, first published in 1844.[16] The Adelaide and the Polytechnic were actual London institutions that had opened in the 1830s, providing access to scientific and technical devices, models and lectures for the general public for a 1 shilling entrance fee. One of the attractions on offer at these institutions was 'large-scale projections of microscopic images'.[17] Richard D. Altick provides a confirmation of the scene described by Reynolds: 'The Polytechnic had its own gas microscope, projecting on a 425-square-foot screen the animal life present in the rich broth that was the metropolitan water supply.'[18] The apparently innocuous drop of water does provide a 'strange contrast' to the creatures within it, microscopically tiny but projected large-scale. Figure 9.1 gives us a nightmarish interpretation of the kind of projection that might have been displayed.

Figure 9.1 shows 'Microcosm, dedicated to the London Water Companies': the text along the bottom of the image reads 'Monster soup commonly called Thames Water, being a correct representation of that precious stuff doled out to us'.[19] This cartoon illustrates concerns in 1828 about dirty London water.[20] The viewer of Fig. 9.1 has the whole picture: the woman with the teacup and the close-up of the creatures within the Thames water that has been used to prepare the tea. The woman herself, by contrast, is experiencing what Isobel Armstrong has called 'a strange double vision',

Fig. 9.1 'Microcosm, dedicated to the London Water Companies "Monster soup commonly called Thames Water, being a correct representation of that precious stuff doled out to us "' (1828)

> as the peering microscopist adjusted to one set of proportions under the microscope and to another outside it. The disproportion of two worlds, concurrently existing in seething activity but oddly independent of one another, is nothing like so evident in the telescope, which brings distant things close but makes them commensurate with objects seen by the naked eye. Pullulating and diaphanous, the world of the microscope seemed to offer up the secret of the origin of life in a way that the telescope did not.[21]

The woman in the image, granted a view of the hidden world within her drink, recoils: the drop of water filled with monsters is still *there*, but its proportions relative to its viewer have suddenly adjusted. There are two worlds coexisting, each ignorant of the other, except when the microscope brings their relationship into focus. Reynolds, in his description of a similar moment of revelation, is arguing that the city of London appears to a 'superficial observer' as a drop of water might: apparently pure and wholesome. After reading *The Mysteries of London*, however, it will be impossible to look at the city in this way, as this text grants the reader a closer view of the hidden monsters. After reciting a litany of the strange contrasts offered by the city, the narrator of *Mysteries* makes the following pronouncement: 'all the features, all the characteristics, all the morals, of a great city, must occupy the attention of him who *surveys London with microscopic eye*' (emphasis added).[22] This remarkable image collapses together two opposing senses of the verb 'survey': to scrutinize in detail, and to look at from a high or commanding position.[23] The viewer who can survey with microscopic eye is in a powerful position, but how could such a totalizing vision be represented?

How to Read Reynolds: The Microscope and the Map

The huge serial novel (such as *Mysteries*) was one nineteenth-century innovation for the representation of the huge city; another was the Ordnance Survey map. Reynolds wrote about the microscopic survey in 1844: in 1850 the first Ordnance Survey map of London was published. The microscopic image in Fig. 9.1 illustrates contemporary fears about how safe it was to drink Thames water; the map, too, was a response to sanitation concerns. Lynda Nead notes that, up until the mid-nineteenth century, maps of London had prioritized 'aesthetic or historical landmarks'.[24] However, as Judith Flanders explains, with the 1848 cholera epidemic, it was clear that something more *practical* was needed. Overcrowding and poor sanitation fed the fury of repeated outbreaks of cholera, while the Metropolitan Board of Works lacked the basic information necessary to combat the disease, such as the exact locations of the city's sewers.[25] Proposals were put forward to cobble together a map of London from previously existing maps, but the Commission of Sewers, led by Edwin Chadwick, proposed that the Royal Corps of Sappers and Miners should undertake to draw up a new, technically accurate map.[26] Ordnance Survey maps derive their name from the making of this first official map of London, as the ordnance division of the army set up scaffolding around Westminster Abbey, from which point all London could be surveyed.[27]

The production of a map of a constantly growing city was a huge undertaking, since, as Judith Flanders has neatly described it, 'London was, to many, a great map that mapped out the impossibility of mapping.'[28] When complete, the map was printed on 847 sheets: truly a mammoth piece of work.[29] In its physicality, this map seems to have a kind of affinity with the original parts of the *Mysteries*: multiple parts, multiple pieces of paper, boldly claiming to add up to a coherent whole. To survey with a microscopic eye is to achieve a very particular kind of view, echoing the double vision noted by Armstrong: it is to see everything there is to see, all at once. How is this kind of view possible, and what does it do to the viewer? The woman in Heath's image is horrified: the world she thought she knew contains other, hidden worlds, which in their turn are full of monsters. The sanitary reformer with a new Ordnance Survey map may have felt daunted by its huge, unwieldy size, or he may have felt a sense of control: finally, he has the whole city at his fingertips, and can begin to make a plan. What Reynolds does in *Mysteries* is to try and give the reader both kinds of views: detailed particulars and vast sweeping survey. Shifts in narrative focus and writing about reading are just two ways of achieving this.

In Volume 1 of *Mysteries*, expansions and contractions and sudden zooms from the general to the particular insistently call the reader's attention to the fact that he/she is reading a narrative, while also reminding him/her of just what narrative is capable of doing. The Prologue blithely skims the history of 'Civilisation' from Egypt and Syria in the tenth century to London in 1831; the narrative can expend as much space explaining what has been omitted as describing what has been included: 'Perhaps a dozen pages of laboured description will not afford the reader a better idea of the characters and dispositions of the two brothers than that which has already been conveyed by their conversation and conduct detailed in the preceding chapter.'[30] This sentence, typical of Reynolds's style, is both large and small at the same time—as an individual sentence it may be periergiac, but it claims to replace 12 pages of flabby sentences. Characters, too, explain themselves in terms of what they are not, as for example when Eliza rebuffs George Montague's attempted seduction: 'I repeat, I am not the heroine of a novel in her teens—I am a woman of certain age, and can reflect calmly in order to act decidedly.'[31] Eliza, and by extension Reynolds, presumes that Montague, and thus the reader, will know how a teenage heroine usually behaves: they draw on our previous reading to help us interpret the text. Certain narrative qualities of *Mysteries* are produced by its format and intended audience: Reynolds posts clear signposts to guide the reader, but also leaves deliberate omissions, designed to encourage the reader to interpret, intuit, and work with the text. As I will show, *Mysteries* both steers the reader and also trusts him/her to find his/her own way.

Almost every chapter opens with the exact date, time and location of its action; there are frequent recaps of previous events. These serve as signposts to the reader/listener, to help steer him/her through this long narrative. Mary L. Shannon has noted the roots of penny fiction in the oral tradition, and gives examples of the rhetorical effects used in *Mysteries*; recapitulation and repetition are crucial tools in a long oral narrative or speech. Another of the rhetorical techniques Shannon points to is 'the deliberate withholding of information that the reader has already begun to guess'.[32] The purpose of this silent encouragement to interpret the text is to draw the readers in, allowing them to participate in the narrative.

The participation proposed by the text is a demanding one. Maxwell counts 'fifty or sixty interlocking stories'.[33] Stephen Knight notes that it was normal for two narrative strands to appear in one weekly issue of *Mysteries*, thus creating 'the sense of a multiple story dealing with different social classes and locations'.[34] 'By the time the serial reaches its halfway point,' Maxwell argues, 'these situations and many others have accumulated; they weigh on the mind all at once.'[35] Nor is this all: it becomes clear that some of the characters are not who they claim to be on first encounter. Indeed, Maxwell reckons that over half of the characters are impostors, 'and so one falsehood constantly confronts or creates another'.[36] The doubling of names and identities transforms a huge cast of characters into the illusion of an absolutely enormous one, with the reader encountering the same characters over and over again in different guises.[37] Again, it is at once large and small, microscopically detailed and yet amenable to overview by the surveying eye. This doubling and disguise allows Reynolds to create the sense of a huge, densely populated city whilst retaining an essential element of character recognition, so that his readers do not find themselves utterly awash in the unknown.

Repeated 'resurrections' of characters (most notably, and appropriately, the Resurrection Man himself, Tony Tidkins) perform a similar structural function. Characters are dispatched by being thrown down trapdoors (Eliza/Walter), imprisoned (Bill Bolter), or entombed alive (Meg Flathers/the Rattlesnake), but somehow manage to escape and return to the story's main action. There are also more startling resurrections, in which characters presumed dead come back to life. The graverobbing Resurrection Man is believed by other characters to be dead on several occasions, but each time he resurrects himself back into the narrative.[38] His physicality points to his liminal state between life and death:

he is repeatedly described as 'cadaverous'. So singular is his appearance that occasionally the narrative does not even refer to him by name—the physical clues offered indicate to the reader that the person referred to can only be the Resurrection Man. To give one example, in Chapter 109, the Resurrection Man enters the office of James Tomlinson. Tidkins does not introduce himself to Tomlinson, who has never met him before, and the narrative likewise does not refer to him by name: he is described variously as 'a person', 'a man of cadaverous countenance', 'the man', 'the stranger', 'a resurrectionist', 'the body-snatcher'.[39] The reader is offered these hints and trusted to come to the correct conclusion. Though this may be only a minor example of reader participation, it contributes to readerly satisfaction at successfully following a long narrative, and at knowing more than Tomlinson does. The reader feels that s/he has become, in Walter Nash's terms, 'an insider, an accurate and qualified observer'.[40] Decoding and understanding the text gives the illusion of decoding and understanding the city.

THE HOUSE IN SMITHFIELD

Returning again to the beginning of *Mysteries*, we encounter a character who must also learn to decode this mysterious city. At the beginning of Volume 1 the reader is introduced to a youth named Walter, who is actually a young girl named Eliza. Eliza has been posing as her deceased brother Walter in order to inherit the family estate, and in Chapter 1, she wanders through insalubrious London streets in disguise:

> He [i.e. Walter] was evidently shocked at the idea that human beings could dwell in such fetid and unwholesome dens; for he gazed with wonder, disgust, and alarm upon the houses on either side. It seemed as if he had never beheld till now a labyrinth of dwellings whose very aspect appeared to speak of hideous poverty and fearful crime.[41]

The reader and narrator watch this young man looking around at this overcrowded neighbourhood—just as we gaze on Heath's woman in 'Monster Soup', here we watch Walter's fear. In an attempt to shelter from the storm which has broken out, he enters an apparently deserted house—the house of the chapter's title. The narrator sets the scene:

> He was alone—in an uninhabited house, in the midst of a horrible neighbourhood; and all the fearful tales of midnight murders which he had ever

heard or read, rushed to his memory; then, by a strange but natural freak of the fancy, those appalling deeds of blood and crime were suddenly associated with that incomprehensible but ominous black square upon the floor.[42] (emphasis added)

Whilst focusing in on this one character in this one house, the narrative simultaneously spreads out; by suggesting stories that this young man has heard and texts that he has read, *Mysteries* calls to the reader's mind other texts that he/she has read, tales he/she has heard. In her article on oral effects in Reynolds, Mary L. Shannon argues that Reynolds must have been conscious that his works were both consumed by individual readers and read aloud to groups; she notes the effects of *hearing* as well as of reading this story.[43] For the reader or auditor of this passage, the prompt is equally effective. There is no need here for the 'dozen pages of laboured description': by recalling our own reading, our minds have set the scene for us.[44] Just as quickly as the text expands the reader's thoughts, however, the focus is drawn back in to one particular spot: the black square on the floor.[45] Sure enough, Walter ends up down that hole; however, by a lucky chance, he lives to tell the tale, six chapters later.[46]

In Chapter 9, we get a first-person account of the same event from Eliza, who is still dressed as Walter, but whose auditors are aware that she is really Eliza (the narrative registers the ambiguity of this position by referring to Eliza as 'Walter' and 'she'). Both the narrator and the reader are present at a telling of the tale which has earlier been related by the narrator.

> But, oh! the revolting streets which branch off from that Smithfield. It seemed to me that I was wandering amongst all the haunts of crime and appalling penury of which I had *read in romances*, but which I never could have believed to exist in the very heart of the metropolis of the world. Civilisation appeared to me to have chosen particular places which it condescended to visit, and to have passed others by without even leaving a footprint to denote its presence.[47] (emphasis added)

This confirms the narrator's statement in Chapter 1 that Walter's thoughts immediately ran to previous reading to help interpret what was happening to him. We, as readers of *Mysteries*, also have our own previous reading of the events as they happened to Walter to help us interpret it. Of course, as well as being a reader of stories, Walter/Eliza is a character in a story, and so the escape from this predicament is suitably dramatic. Walter escapes from the house, is caught up in a crowd watching a street brawl and carried along to a lodging-house, where he is granted a rather grim guided tour by the mistress of the house.[48] Eliza recalls:

> On the third floor and in the attics were the most horrible scenes of wretchedness which I had yet beheld. Those dens were filled with straw beds, separated from each other only by pieces of plank about eight or ten inches in height. Men, women, and children were all crowded together—sleeping pell-mell. Oh! it was a horrible, horrible spectacle.[49]

From the street, to the house, to this room full of people: just as the microscope reveals the hidden world in a drop of water, the zooming in of the narrative has revealed more life in a small space than could previously have been believed possible. Through Walter, the reader has experienced the claustrophobic horror of poor London as an outsider. This horror comes not only from being hemmed in with too many people, but from being trapped with too many of the *wrong kind* of people. This sudden proximity with a large number of unfamiliar bodies—bodies that fight, bodies that are almost naked, bodies that are pressed close together without discrimination of age or gender, bodies that are *dirty*—creates a feeling of overwhelming disgust. However, narrative point of view modulates the horror. As Trefor Thomas notes, four years have passed since these events: the distance is temporal as well as physical.[50] Eliza distances herself from this crowded room by describing it as a 'scene' or a 'spectacle' which she 'beheld'; she positions herself as an observer rather than a participant, as the person looking through the microscope rather than one of the powerless microbes underneath the lens. She is now the narrator of this experience, not just the hapless victim of it, and she exercises her narrative control of the story by hurriedly changing the scene: 'To be brief, I escaped from that moral plague-house; and in a few moments was traversing Smithfield once more.'[51] In contrast with the sentence quoted earlier that took up space while claiming to save space, this narrative jump cuts out a whole sequence of action. Walter's experience of uncomfortable proximity with the teeming, sickly life of London has been translated into a tale to be told by Eliza, safe within the domestic space: it has become like one of the stories Walter recalled to himself at the moment he was first trapped in the old house. And, indeed, the reader of *Mysteries* can enjoy this episode as a tale, as he/she experiences only imaginary danger; Walter, Eliza, and their stories can be kept at arm's length.

Further drama is in store for Eliza in later chapters: after her impersonation of her brother is revealed, she spends two years in Newgate prison. On her release, she is happy to leave England, telling Richard Markham, the hero of the story,

> ... there is but little to wed the sensitive mind to England. Since my release *I have passed nearly all my time in reading*; and I am shocked to perceive, from the information I have gleaned, that England is the only civilized country in the world where death from starvation—literal starvation, is common. Indeed, it is an event of such frequent occurrence, that it actually ceases to create astonishment, and almost fails to excite dismay. There must be something radically wrong in that system of society where all the wealth is in the hands of a few, and all the misery is shared by millions.[52] (emphasis added)

Eliza has moved from romances and bloodcurdling tales of horror to a different kind of disturbing reading: she is now delving into 'information'. She has had first-hand experience of the crowded lodging-house in Smithfield and the horrors of prison, but it is only by reading 'information' that she becomes convinced of the injustice of the current system. In the flesh, the people of Smithfield were a 'horrible spectacle'; hidden behind statistics, they can become objects of compassion.

Reading places Eliza at one remove from real danger. Rather than replacing her direct experience, it may simply reframe it, so that it can be approached in a usable form. As readers, we might ponder whether the only way to deal with the overwhelming reality of life in London is to displace it onto 'information', to contain it within pages. *Mysteries* presents a sprawling city of endless misery within an enormous text: ways of framing and containing this microscopic survey must be found, so that it is both representable and bearable.

Eliza's next speech registers both the pain and the power of the surveying view:

> I sometimes look forth from the window, and survey that mighty city which stretches over plain, hill, and valley, and which is ever extending its mighty arms—as if in time it would embrace the entire island:—I gaze upon it at that hour in the morning when the eternal cloud is raised for a little space from its brow; and, as I mark the thousand spires which point up into the cool clear sky, I tremble—I feel oppressed as with a weight, when I reflect upon the hideous misery, the agonising woe, the appalling sorrow that want entails upon the sons and daughters of toil in that vast Babylon.[53]

Eliza can read the cityscape with an awareness of the individual suffering being endured by its crowded citizens. Both her life experience and her reading of 'information' have given her this awareness, and her ability to contextualize and discuss it. Reynolds chooses to show this contextualization by positioning Eliza's surveying view point at a window. As Susan Stewart has noted, '[i]nside or outside, the typical view of the city is through the window—a view within a definite frame and limited perspective, mediated and refracted through the glass of the city's abstraction of experience'.[54] Looking specifically at the nineteenth-century novel, Isobel Armstrong has noted the prevalence of 'the overdetermined "window moment" in prose fiction', a moment '[m]ostly though not always experienced overwhelmingly by women'.[55] Armstrong argues that in these texts the window 'is an inlet, particularly for women, into real and imagined space, and a moment where reading—since *we view the viewer*—becomes a reflective and textual act of seeing' (emphasis added).[56] Just as when we looked at Heath's image in Fig. 9.1, just as when we compare Walter's and Eliza's experience of the House in Smithfield, just as when we realize that Tomlinson's unnamed visitor is Tony Tidkins, by reading Eliza's words we see the woman *and* we see what she is seeing.

But what does Eliza see? Again, the distance is physical, temporal, and verbal. What we have here is not a real-time 'window moment'—Eliza is narrating her past experience of such a moment. Referring to London as 'Babylon' was one of the clichés of the nineteenth century: talking about the city by talking about another, historical, city removes us from the present.[57] Mention of cloud recalls the Prologue of *Mysteries*, which referred to constant cloud hanging over London, while Eliza's vision of London's future again creates distance.[58] It is a pessimistic view: the spread of the city, with the city as it is, cannot be a good thing. For the time being, however, London is contained within her personal 'survey' of it from her window. The wide survey of the city must be framed; the microscopic detail of horror must be placed within a wider context so that it does not become overwhelming.

CONCLUSION

When first confronted with an image of the microscopic world blown up on a 425-square-foot screen, the visitor to the Polytechnic was faced with a challenge to his/her sense of proportion: the huge creatures on the screen are tiny enough to fit in a drop of water—and perhaps every drop of water in the Thames was similarly populated. When first encountering *Mysteries*, the reader/auditor was faced with a narrative which promised to reveal the many mysteries of London, to simultaneously provide an overview of the huge city and a detailed account of the goings-on within it. After reading this text, *Mysteries* claims, you will no longer be the casual observer who sees only the superficial appearance of the city; you will be able to see the city as it really is. In order to accomplish this huge task, the text co-opts its audience's knowledge of generic and narrative conventions and clichés to set a scene or create an implicit back-story, focusing the audience's attention on the story at hand even as it distracts them with reminders of other stories—simultaneously expanding and contracting. The use of rhetorical devices, and the references to stories that characters have heard as well as those that they have read, allows *Mysteries* to be enjoyed by auditors as well as silent readers. The narrative, and by extension the city, becomes navigable and understandable. As we view the viewer in Fig. 9.1 once more, however, we may question whether it is desirable to see so much, all at once.

Notes

1. Obituary in the *Bookseller*, quoted in L. James, 'G[eorge] W[illiam] M[acarthur] Reynolds (1814–79)', in *The Victorian Novel* (Malden, MA, Oxford, and Victoria: Blackwell, 2006), p. 136.
2. L. James, 'Reynolds, George William MacArthur (1814–1879)', *Oxford Dictionary of National Biography*, 2004; online ed. 2008, Oxford University Press, http://www.oxforddnb.com/view/article/23414, date accessed 11 January 2015.
3. A. Humpherys, 'The Geometry of the Modern City: G.W.M. Reynolds and *The Mysteries of London*', *Browning Institute Studies* 11 (1983), 70.
4. E.F. Bleiler, 'Introduction to the Dover Edition', in E.F. Bleiler, ed., *Wagner the Wehr-Wolf*, Dover Classics (New York: Dover; London: Constable, 1975), p. xi.
5. J. Rose, *The Intellectual Life of the British Working Classes*, 2nd ed. (New Haven and London: Yale University Press, 2010), p. 111.
6. L. James, foreword to G.W.M. Reynolds, *The Mysteries of London*, Vol. 1 (Kansas City: Valancourt Books, 2013), p. v (all references are to this edition, hereafter referred to as *Mysteries*, unless otherwise stated). However, Sally Ledger notes that Dickens's popular *reach* was greater than that of Reynolds, as Reynolds targeted an exclusively working-class readership (see Sally Ledger, *Dickens and the Popular Radical Imagination*, Cambridge

Studies in Nineteenth-Century Literature and Culture (Cambridge and New York: Cambridge University Press, 2007), p. 169). Reynolds's *The Mysteries of London* was published by John Vickers from 1844–48; Vickers then continued the serial using the writers Thomas Miller and E. Leman Blanchard instead of Reynolds, who had no involvement with their series. Reynolds went on to publish the serial *The Mysteries of the Court of London* from 1848–55/6 with the publisher John Dicks. See A. Humpherys and L. James, 'Dating Reynolds's Serial Publications', in A. Humpherys and L. James, eds., *G.W.M. Reynolds: Nineteenth-Century Fiction, Politics, and the Press* (Aldershot and Burlington, VT: Ashgate, 2008), p. xvii.

7. Stephen Knight attributes the lack of study of various titles in the Mysteries genre to 'the hostility of the literary and academic elite in the past and present to such essentially popular fiction'. Knight also suggests that Reynolds's text was, in its time, both too radical for the literary and too fictional for serious Marxist circles to take an interest. See S. Knight, *The Mysteries of the Cities: Urban Crime Fiction in the Nineteenth Century* (Jefferson, NC and London: McFarland, 2012), pp. 7, 110. The introduction to A. Humpherys and L. James, eds., *Fiction, Politics, and the Press*, pp. 1–15, gives a summary of critical responses to Reynolds.

8. L. James, 'Reynolds'. Information on the publication history of *Mysteries* can be found in A. Humpherys and L. James, 'Dating Reynolds's Serial Publications' (2008), pp. xvii–xviii.

9. T. Thomas, 'Introduction to G.W.M. Reynolds', in T. Thomas, ed., *The Mysteries of London*, (Keele: Keele University Press, 1996), p. vii. The online edition of *Mysteries* is available at http://www.victorianlondon.org/mysteries/mysteries-00-chapters.htm. The Valancourt editions of Volumes 1 and 2 of *Mysteries* have forewords by Louis James and Mary L. Shannon, respectively.

10. See S.J. Carver, 'The Wrongs and Crimes of the Poor: The Urban Underworld of *The Mysteries of London* in Context', p. 161, in A. Humpherys and L. James, eds., *Fiction, Politics, and the Press* (2008).

11. G.W.M. Reynolds, 'Epilogue' in *Mysteries* (2013), p. 1162.

12. G.W.M. Reynolds, 'Epilogue' in *Mysteries*, p. 1162.

13. R. Maxwell, *The Mysteries of Paris and London*, Victorian Literature and Culture series (Charlottesville and London: University Press of Virginia, 1992), p. 165.

14. R.C. Maxwell, Jr., 'G. M. Reynolds, Dickens, and the Mysteries of London', *Nineteenth-Century Fiction* 32.2 (September 1977), 193.

15. G.W.M. Reynolds, *Mysteries*, ch. 23, p. 156.

16. I am grateful to Jessica Hindes for sharing her work on dating the original weekly parts of *Mysteries*. Hindes has calculated the date of the first publication of Volume 1, Chapter 23 of *Mysteries* as 16 November 1844 (personal communication, 17 April 2015).

17. L. Jackson, 'Polytechnic Institution, Regent St', in *The Victorian Dictionary*, http://www.victorianlondon.org/index-2012.htm, date accessed 12 June 2014.
18. R.D. Altick, *The Shows of London* (London, England and Cambridge, MA: The Belknap Press of Harvard University Press, 1978), p. 383, available at quod.lib.umich.edu, date accessed 25 September 2015. The reader of *Mysteries* in the mid-1840s would likely have been limited to the public shows of the Adelaide and the Polytechnic; by the 1850s, the microscope was an affordable piece of equipment for the middle-class purchaser. See I. Armstrong, 'The Microscope: Mediations of the Sub-visible World', in R. Luckhurst and J. McDonagh, eds., *Transactions and Encounters: Science and Culture in the Nineteenth Century* (Manchester and New York: Manchester University Press, 2002), p. 30.
19. 'Front Matter' (1 November 2005) *Clinical Infectious Diseases* 41.9, inside front cover, http://www.jstor.org/stable/4463497, date accessed 15 August 2013. Image reproduced by kind permission of London Metropolitan Archives.
20. This cartoon was drawn by William Heath, known as 'Paul Pry': see C. Horrocks (Spring 2003) 'The Personification of "Father Thames": Reconsidering the Role of the Victorian Periodical Press in the "Verbal and Visual Campaign" for Public Health Reform', *Victorian Periodicals Review* 36.1, 3, available at http://www.jstor.org/stable/20083907, date accessed 15 August 2013.
21. I. Armstrong, 'The Microscope', 2002, p. 31.
22. GWM Reynolds, *Mysteries*, ch. 23, p. 157.
23. See 'survey, v.', 3, 4a, and 4b, in *Oxford English Dictionary*, www.oed.com, date accessed 15 August 2013. Section 3 notes that 'survey' in the sense of 'view in detail' is now rare or obsolete, but the last example given dates from 1871, and so this sense was still current in Reynolds's time.
24. L. Nead, *Victorian Babylon: People, Streets and Images in Nineteenth-Century London* (New Haven and London: Yale University Press, 2000), p. 21.
25. J. Flanders, *The Victorian City: Everyday Life in Dickens's London* (London: Atlantic, 2012), p. 59.
26. L. Nead, *Victorian Babylon*, p. 19.
27. J. Flanders, *The Victorian City*, p. 59.
28. J. Flanders, *The Victorian City*, p. 59.
29. J. Flanders, *The Victorian City*, p. 59.
30. L. James notes the span of time covered by the Prologue: foreword to GWM Reynolds, *Mysteries*, p. ix; G.W.M. Reynolds, *Mysteries*, ch. 5, p. 28.
31. G.W.M. Reynolds, *Mysteries*, ch. 22, pp. 153–54.
32. M.L. Shannon, 'Spoken Word and Printed Page: G.W.M. Reynolds and "The Charing-Cross Revolution", 1848', *19: Interdisciplinary Studies in*

the Long Nineteenth Century 18 (2014), 7, http://bbk.ac.uk, date accessed 7 June 2014.
33. R. Maxwell, *The Mysteries of Paris and London*, p. 161.
34. S. Knight, *The Mysteries of the Cities*, p. 102.
35. R. Maxwell, *The Mysteries of Paris and London*, p. 162.
36. R. Maxwell, *The Mysteries of Paris and London*, p. 162.
37. Many characters have more than one name over the course of the first two volumes of the *Mysteries*, whether because they gain titles (the men) or get married (the women), or because they have reasons to pretend to be someone else. S.J. Carver notes that almost every central character has an alter ego (see 'Wrongs and Crimes', p. 154).
38. A. Humpherys, 'The Geometry of the Modern City', p. 74.
39. G.W.M. Reynolds, *Mysteries*, ch. 109, pp. 942–48.
40. W. Nash, *Language in Popular Fiction*, The Interface Series (London and New York: Routledge, 1990), p. 66.
41. G.W.M. Reynolds, *Mysteries*, ch. 1, p. 7.
42. G.W.M. Reynolds, *Mysteries*, ch. 1, p. 8.
43. M.L. Shannon, 'Spoken Word and Printed Page', 2. Shannon notes that many Reynolds scholars have picked up on a passage in Henry Mayhew's *London Labour and the London Poor* which gives some indication of Reynolds's audience: 'the costermongers are very fond of hearing anyone read aloud to them, and listen very attentively. […] Of all London, Reynolds is the most popular man among them.' Quoted in M.L. Shannon, *Dickens, Reynolds, and Mayhew on Wellington Street: The Print Culture of a Victorian Street* (Farnham and Burlington, VT: Ashgate, 2015), p. 79.
44. G.W.M. Reynolds, *Mysteries*, ch. 5, p. 28.
45. See Robert Mighall on the narrative's contraction of focus onto this one black square: R. Mighall, *A Geography of Victorian Gothic Fiction: Mapping History's Nightmares* (Oxford: Oxford University Press, 1999), p. 29.
46. G.W.M. Reynolds, *Mysteries*, ch. 4, p. 18.
47. G.W.M. Reynolds, *Mysteries*, ch. 9, p. 58.
48. G.W.M. Reynolds, *Mysteries*, ch. 9, pp. 59–62.
49. G.W.M. Reynolds, *Mysteries*, ch. 9, p. 62.
50. Note to Volume 1, Chapter 9, in G.W.M. Reynolds, *The Mysteries of London*, edited by T. Thomas (1996), p. 24.
51. G.W.M. Reynolds, *Mysteries*, ch. 9, p. 62.
52. G.W.M. Reynolds, *Mysteries*, ch. 50, p. 418.
53. G.W.M. Reynolds, *Mysteries*, ch. 50, p. 418.
54. S. Stewart, *On Longing: Narratives of the Miniature, the Gigantic, the Souvenir, the Collection* (Durham and London: Duke University Press, 1993), p. 79.

55. I. Armstrong, *Victorian Glassworlds: Glass Culture and the Imagination 1830–1880* (Oxford and elsewhere: OUP, 2008), pp. 124, 131.
56. I. Armstrong, *Victorian Glassworlds*, p. 124.
57. See L. Nead, *Victorian Babylon*, p. 3 for a discussion of London as Babylon.
58. G.W.M. Reynolds, 'Prologue', in *Mysteries*, p. 2.

Acknowledgements I am indebted to Richard Maxwell's 1992 *The Mysteries of Paris and London*, Victorian Literature and Culture series (Charlottesville and London: University Press of Virginia) for first prompting my thinking on this topic. This essay is based on research originally conducted for my unpublished PhD dissertation, produced in Trinity College Dublin, the University of Dublin, and funded by the Irish Research Council.

CHAPTER 10

Cross-Media Cultural Consumption and Oscillating Reader Experiences of Late-Victorian Dramatizations of the Novel: The Case of Fergus Hume's *Madame Midas* (1888)

Paul Raphael Rooney

The context that the narrator of John Fowles's *The French Lieutenant's Woman* (1969) offers when introducing the manservant character of Sam Farrow, describes how Farrow's familiarity with his Dickensian forbearer and/or counterpart was derived in very particular circumstances—'he even knew of Sam Weller, not from the book [*The Pickwick Papers*], but from a stage version of it'.[1] Granted, this allusion occurs within the postmodern setting of a work of neo-Victorian literature. However, the significance of this reference for the study of nineteenth-century reading lies in its highlighting of a set of circumstances where audiences consumed literature that had originally circulated via the medium of print by engaging with affiliated versions of this cultural matter encountered within other categories of media. With this chapter, I wish to look at this broader sphere of intra-media experiences and examine Victorian audiences' cultural consumption

P.R. Rooney (✉)
Trinity College, Dublin, Ireland

© The Author(s) 2016
P.R. Rooney, A. Gasperini (Eds.), *Media and Print Culture Consumption in Nineteenth-Century Britain*, New Directions in Book History, DOI 10.1057/978-1-137-58761-9_10

that encompassed both incarnations of such artefacts or properties—the print media text via which the novel was disseminated and a performance of the stage adaptation that was founded upon the novel.

This is not a scholarly endeavour upon which I will embark in a vacuum; the long-established and vibrant field of adaptation studies offers a framework for this examination. This body of scholarship focuses in the main on the present-day media environment, and explores the cultural experiences that transpositions of specific books to the medium of film or television furnish for readers who become viewers.[2] In exploring Victorian readers' encounters with stage adaptations of novels that formed part of their reading histories (or to use the categorization commonly deployed in nineteenth-century critical parlance, dramatizations), I will build upon the existing scholarship within this broader area produced by Nicholas Daly and by Andrew Maunder. In particular, I wish to explore further the significance of exposure to what Daly has rather brilliantly conceptualized as 'amphibious' nineteenth-century literary matter, which he defines as the sort of cultural content capable of 'gliding from novel to stage, and more rarely, from stage to novel'.[3] Furthermore, in a number of respects, I conceive of my present study, which will focus on such questions in the context of late nineteenth-century consumption of popular fiction, as a companion piece to Andrew Maunder's 2013 book chapter, 'Sensation Fiction on the Stage'.[4] Maunder's excellent and thought-provoking study of this mid-nineteenth-century genre of popular literature affords particular attention to the hierarchies of cultural value that defined the adapted text-adaptation relationship with reference to the output of the genre's major writers and the cultural anxieties elicited by drama trading in narratives of crime. Most pertinently for my present purposes, he also spotlights some of the more high profile examples of theatrical stagecraft employed in these dramas that looked to induce reactions of awe and amazement in their audiences. Granted, the most obvious audience trajectory in this realm of cultural consumption was from book to playhouse and this has informed the predominant course of scholarly enquiry upon this topic. However, I would venture that it is also necessary to widen the remit of the examination to consider other permutations and their significance. Maunder's closing statement, which observes 'stage adaptations did not damage novels but transformed them, affecting the audience's interpretations of them',[5] gestures towards such a kindred class of nineteenth-century audience experience where the ways readers approached a particular novel was shaped by earlier contact with the transposed versions of this literature encountered within the theatre.

My choice of subject matter for the case study, which I wish to undertake in order to illuminate how Victorian reader engagement with print culture artefacts disseminating popular literature were framed by prior and subsequent contact with related matter from interconnected media, is informed by the particular insight this work can offer on such questions. Thus, this chapter considers audience experiences of the novel, *Madame Midas* (1888) by the Antipodean writer Fergus Hume, and the stage adaptation of this book Hume co-authored with the dramatist Philip Beck, which toured extensively the playhouses of provincial England across 1888–89 as a production performed by Balsir Chatterton's theatre company. Hume is primarily remembered today for his bestselling debut work, *The Mystery of a Hansom Cab* (1887)—a Melbourne-based crime fiction novel that reputedly realized nineteenth-century sales of in excess of several hundred thousand copies.[6] Much of the scholarly discussion this title has attracted has focused on this work and the book's place in the cultural history of the detective novel.[7] Interestingly, in the context of this present discussion, the favour that *The Mystery of a Hansom Cab* found with readers precipitated a number of different stage adaptations.[8] Thus, it is very possible that the frame of reference that characterized many consumers' contact with *Madame Midas* was informed by exposure to Hume's prior work within the context of the playhouse. Here, I argue that the publication history and fabric of *Madame Midas* suggest a work that was envisaged as furnishing entertainment readers across multiple platforms. In some respects, a partial sequel to the enormously successful title that had launched Hume's career, *Madame Midas* was a tale of Australian mining and urban life, which in the main exchanged the sensation and detection that marked Hume's debut for a more obviously melodramatic canvas. Therefore, in this essay, I will begin by examining where consumer experiences of the book and the play could conceivably converge. I then chart the particular status of *Madame Midas* as what I term a 'bi-media' cultural commodity and, finally, explore the ways in which the two principal classes of reader encounters with this book were conditioned by contact with the play founded upon the novel.

Media Convergences: The Book and the Play

In order to illuminate fully the paradigm within which Hume and the publisher founded with the express purpose of disseminating his work, the Hansom Cab Publishing Company, envisaged *Madame Midas* reaching audiences, it is necessary to consider the immediate pre-history of Hume's output. 'Hugh Conway' (Frederick John Fargus) was an important forerunner of Hume in this field of cheap plot-driven literature. Such works initially reached readers within the medium of print via ephemeral single-volume publishing formats like 'the shilling shocker' before subsequently or concurrently crossing over to the stage where nineteenth-century audiences could take in a dramatization. *Called Back* (1883), Fargus's novel of adventure and mystery, which evoked the spirit of Wilkie Collins's 1860s writing, was the surprise literary sensation of the late 1883–early 1884 period. It registered a comparable degree of impact as the commercial success that Hume went on to achieve with *The Mystery of a Hansom Cab* and to a somewhat lesser extent, *Madame Midas*.[9] It should be noted that the insight we possess about the commercial performance of the book, *Madame Midas*, suggests it was a fastseller whose prominence was shorter, compared to the more enduring success of the bestselling *The Mystery of a Hansom Cab*.[10] The interconnected book-stage adaptation release strategy that had characterized the issue of *Dark Days* (1884), which was Fargus's less strikingly successful attempt to repeat the triumph of *Called Back*, charted the path that *Madame Midas* would follow. Crucially for this present examination, amidst the extensive lampoonery that the success of *Called Back* and its subsequent stage adaptation elicited in the pages of *Punch*, there appeared an observation of significance, which underscored the importance of viewing novels like the early output of Fargus and Hume within the context of a reading environment encompassing multiple media. Interwoven within the humour of an 1884 sketch entitled 'Letters to Some People' where an imagined correspondent purported to detail his experience of attending a dramatization of *Called Back*, one encounters a succinct pronouncement on this particular class of media synergy—'Those who have read the book will go to see the Play, just to "see how it is done," and those who haven't read the book will see the Play and then order the novel, so it's good for the bookseller anyhow.'[11] In this respect, *Madame Midas* represented a distinctive class of entity relative to Hume's previous output given that such links were very much to the fore when readers encountered this book. Whereas the cover art adorning *The Mystery of a Hansom Cab* was of a markedly literal character in its use of an image of the titular vehicle, *Madame Midas* was, by contrast, a print culture artefact that manifestly signalled its affinity with cultural content that belonged to another medium. The eye-catching and decidedly lurid illustration that appeared on the front cover of the 1888 Hansom Cab Publishing Company edition of *Madame Midas* (Figure 10.1) was a

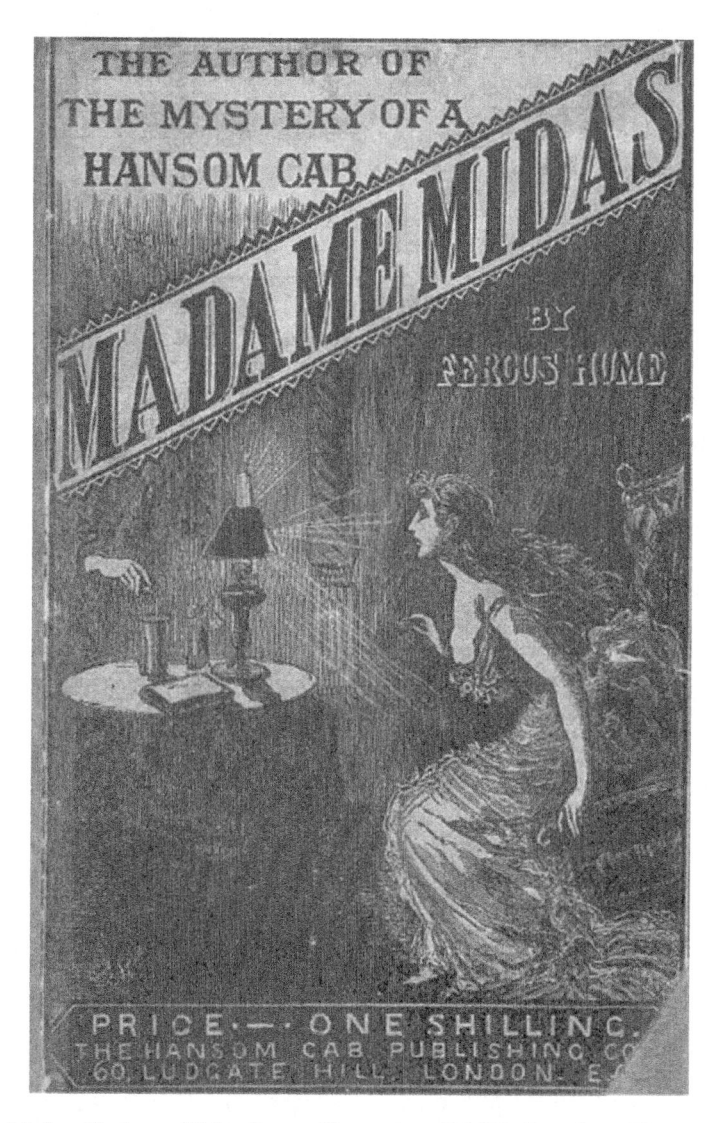

Fig. 10.1 *Madame Midas* Cover Illustration (1888) (London: Hansom Cab Publishing Company). Image reproduced courtesy of © The British Library Board, DRT lsidyv3ad542cb

curious choice as the female figure depicted is in fact not the eponymous heroine but rather the visual was characterized by a very definite sense of what one might term interpictoriality.[12]

Although it should be acknowledged that the scene depicted in this image did not exactly mis-sell Hume's novel (a poisoning case that is orchestrated in precisely this fashion figures relatively prominently in the latter half of the novel), the larger significance of this illustration lay in the fact that it represents a very deliberate allusion to *The Hidden Hand* by Tom Taylor, a famed mid-Victorian stage melodrama. The play was first staged in 1864 and largely remained a staple of nineteenth-century theatre in the intervening years.[13] Thus, we might speculate that conversance with this visual or merely just the core conceit of Taylor's drama would figure on the cultural radar of a significant proportion of contemporary readers. Moreover, the use of this specific illustration can be interpreted as an effort on the part of Hume's publisher to capitalize on the likely resonances the image would evoke. This particular allusion was also significant in the context of *Madame Midas* as it gestured toward the fact that there was further scope to engage with this novel beyond the book within the medium where *The Hidden Hand* had come to prominence.

MADAME MIDAS AS BI-MEDIA CULTURAL COMMODITY

Therefore, one key avenue through which we might initiate a recovery of the experiences of audiences who consumed hybrid texts like *Madame Midas* via a pattern of traversing between print and performance (or indeed from theatre to book) is by considering their exploits through the lens of the concept of the cross-media as articulated by Simone Murray with reference to present-day media 'pro-sumption'.[14] Work by such scholars concentrates on what Murray herself writing in collaboration with Alexis Weedon has elsewhere termed 'the migration [of content] across media formats [in] the twenty-first century media environment'[15] and is commonly concerned with digital and transmedia channels. That said, I would venture that the repurposing of this idea within the context of the nineteenth-century reading milieu has the potential to prove tremendously illuminating. Specifically, this framework will enable us to begin to unpack how historical audiences would process their navigation between formats. In turn, this will also facilitate an effort to conceptualize the intersections that emerged in the context of a work like Hume's *Madame Midas*, which I suggest should be regarded as a 'bi-media' cultural commodity.

It is evident that the specific facets of the circulation of the novel *Madame Midas* certainly ventured to stimulate such crossovers. The title page of the 1888 edition included a statement that 'The dramatic rights of the story are the property of the Author who, in conjunction with Mr PHILIP BECK, has written and produced a dramatic version.'[16] The implication here was plain; if one's experience of the novel were to prove pleasurable, a kindred stage play likely awaited where the author was an important creative force, which signalled a desirable commonality between the book and the drama. Moreover, the production to secure copyright that this declaration references, which was a semi-private or closet performance that staged an early draft of the script of this dramatization in the days directly prior to the novel's publication, actually formed part of the publicity strategy intended to stimulate reader interest in *Madame Midas*. An account of this one-off production was published in *The Era*, one of the leading newspapers that reported on goings-on related to the stage, the weekend prior to the book's publication. Doubtless, the rationale in admitting the article's writer to this performance at the Theatre Royal, Stratford East, was the expectation that the resulting write-up would kindle audience interest in both properties.[17] Interestingly, employing this kind of strategy in the promotional drive for Hume's novel, which also included more conventional devices such as announcements of the work's imminent publication in the main literary-cultural miscellanies along with newspaper interviews and puff pieces,[18] had the potential to frame many readers' first contact with the novel, *Madame Midas*, in a distinctly theatrical light. Although *The Era* writer took some pains to avoid what in present-day media terminology would be viewed as 'spoilers', the overview of the principal points of the piece's story conceptualized the three characters at the heart of *Madame Midas* in terms of the theatrical archetypes of the spirited heroine, the foreign villain, and the fallen woman or pathetic wronged heroine.

There is little doubt that one of the key determining factors in shaping the tenor of these kinds of print encounter and the broader literary experiences they occasioned would have been the trajectory according to which consumers moved between the interconnected forums of page and stage. Granted, it is important to acknowledge that there would be certain audience constituencies whose contact was bounded or incomplete in that they experienced only the novel or the drama. However, the allure of the kind of carryover delineated by *Punch* was sufficiently potent to ensure that the majority of those who derived satisfaction from their engagement with the text within the context of what for them represented 'medium a' (book or theatre), would be motivated to seek out and consume the affiliated version of *Madame Midas* in their individual 'medium b' (theatre or book). The appetite for taking in highly coloured literary works across their interconnected media manifestations was an enduring nineteenth-century phenomenon. For instance, there is compelling anecdotal evidence that points towards a strong synergistic (and indeed controversial) public demand for both the book and stage incarnations of Harrison Ainsworth's *Jack Sheppard* (1839) when this novel was first published during the early years of the Victorian period.[19]

The frame through which a consumer interpreted their engagement with the narrative, characters, themes, and places of this text was conditioned in large part by the sequence of their media orbit—in other words, was the Hume-Beck authored adaptation or alternatively, Hume's novel (the adapted text) their initial point of contact with *Madame Midas*? Specifically, the nature of the gateway medium could prove critical in determining the set of criteria brought to bear in 'reading' the personalities and scenarios encountered.

Although the underlying premise of A.B. Walkley's 1892 piece, 'Novel and Drama', somewhat overplays the gulf between the two genres, a number of Walkley's key contentions are particularly relevant to the present discussion. While noting the common intended audience impact that unites the two forms—'Each aims at exciting, the one in the reader, the other in the spectator, the same special sort of emotion, the aesthetic emotion',[20] Walkley emphasizes the stage can achieve an immediacy or visceral influence that the novel cannot. The essential qualities of each medium are said to underlie the variation in immersiveness according to Walkley. The 'mere fact that what you are regarding is a printed page, a collection of black signs on an oblong area of whiteness, is sufficient to assure [the reader of the fictitiousness of the novel]'.[21] Conversely, these 'correctives'[22] are diminished in the environment of the theatre auditorium, where spectators are conditioned to regard as real the events playing out on the stage. Thus, the printed page or auditorium beginnings of consumer experiences of a cross-media entity such as *Madame Midas* were considered to have the potential to temper the extent to which audiences invested in the narrative journeys of the three central figures at the core of Hume's novel.

Walkley's distinction between the formats of page and playhouse is also significant given its underlining of the need to consider other critical factors such as the shifts in media inherent in the crossovers of consuming adaptations, the altered modes of engagement consumers' transfers across media occasioned, and the resultant adjustments in the processes of signification. First, the temporal dynamics of taking in a stage play within a three-hour period over a single evening were fundamentally different to a phased reading of a shilling paperback novel like *Madame Midas* during intervals conducive to the consumption of print like journeying to and from work aboard a train or omnibus or during domestic periods of inactivity or leisure. There was an inevitable immediacy to a spectator's meaning making in the auditorium, without the interludes of latent reflection made possible by the everyday activities that punctuated a piecemeal reading of the novel. That said, it is also true that there would have been a certain degree of structural commonality. Both modes shared a quasi-episodic shape; however, while reading involved a partitioning of the novel's narrative into arbitrarily sized segments, taking in the play was marked by more symmetrically proportioned divisions arising from the dramatic conventions of scenes and acts. Second, the climate in which individuals now construed these stories was fundamentally altered. Reading silently to oneself in the domestic space or aboard public transport was a solitary exercise in meaning making. To experience the text in a communal environment like a theatre, which in the nineteenth century were not necessarily governed by the code of silent spectatorship that is the rule today, was to also be exposed to the responses of others. In addition, it is also important to emphasize that a darkened auditorium did not become the norm in British playhouses until the early twentieth century[23]; accordingly, the facial responses exhibited by neighbouring spectators to what was occurring on stage could also be discerned. While some theatregoers would have been more inured to what was happening front of house than others, this is a factor of which we need to be conscious, especially when considering a drama like *Madame Midas* that played exclusively to the senses owing to its very clear affinity with the genre of melodrama. Music would commonly have scored the various critical moments of tension, levity, or tragedy that unfold in the story of *Madame Midas*. Thus, these instrumental numbers played by the house's orchestra exercised an important influence in shaping the responses elicited from spectators in the playhouse. Readers, by contrast, would not generally have been subject to these specific emotional cues, which meant their experiences of the villain's machinations or the heroine's sufferings were not scaffolded or predetermined to the same extent. There was, however, an interesting musical intersection between novel and adaptation where *Madame Midas* was concerned. Hume depicts a scene in the book where the villain and his estranged lover dance to a waltz entitled 'One Summer's Night in Munich' and promotion for the Balsir Chatterton touring production of the state adaptation called attention to the fact that performances of their drama would feature an Alfred Cellier composition that bore this same name.[24]

CLOCKWISE AND COUNTER-CLOCKWISE AUDIENCE EXPERIENCES OF CROSS-MEDIA CONTENT

A cross-media lens has significant potential to advance efforts to illuminate how reader encounters with novels like *Madame Midas* were framed by exposure to contemporary dramatizations. On the other hand, adaptation studies proper, and in particular the ideas of Linda Hutcheon on these cultural forms, can also contribute to our understanding of the ways in which the medium of the stage conditioned nineteenth-century popular reading experiences of bi-media entities. Hutcheon contends 'we experience adaptations (*as adaptations*) as palimpsests through our memory of other works that resonate through repetition with variation'.[25] Hutcheon elaborates on the workings of this process noting that the adapted text 'oscillate[s] in [consumers'] memories with [the adaptation they] are experiencing'.[26] Moreover, the core tenet of her argument lies in the fact that such 'familiarity bred through repetition and memory [is] part of both the pleasure and frustration of experiencing an adaptation[27]; [it is an encounter combining] the comfort of ritual combined with the piquancy of surprise'.[28] It should be noted that Hutcheon's theorizations are articulated in the context of a postmodern cultural landscape. Yet, this diagnosis of the allure of this class of media consumption, which situated the appeal of such compound encounters in the opportunity to build upon a pleasurable reading experience by attending an affiliated theatrical performance that would be processed through the prism of prior contact with the book, was also in circulation within a nineteenth-century milieu. W. Davenport Adams's 1897 article, 'What is the Theatrical Public?', published in *The Theatre* highlighted the apparently substantial appetite for dramatizations of the novel amongst a notable constituency of the theatre-going public rooting this appeal in a very particular class of visual impulse. Although tinged with an undeniable element of cultural condescension, there is considerable significance in Adams's observation that 'works like *The Prisoner of Zenda* have charms, in particular, for that great section of the middle class which loves to see on the boards the people of whom it has read in books. The youngsters who delight above all in pictures develop into adults for whom the pictorial representation of a favourite fiction is a joy forever.'[29] His assessment underscores the extent to which consumption of Victorian popular fiction was frequently shadowed by a supplementary or adjunct experience where the audience mentally retraversed their reading of the novel as they subsequently took in a transposed or remediated iteration of the text staged at a playhouse. While Adams's analysis encapsulates the more obvious or clockwise category of oscillatory consumption, I would venture that it is also critical to consider this notion of blended gratification and frustration in the context of those parallel classes of experience where the playhouse attendee evolved into a reader, which we might conceive of as counter-clockwise in character. While there is little denying the comparative reductiveness of first-wave adaptation scholarship that was rooted in a discourse of fidelity criticism, it is necessary to confront the logical inference from this theorization of the allure of adaptation. Namely, certain types of adaptation had the potential to enhance the reading pleasure of consumers whose evening at the theatre precipitated a subsequent visit to the bookseller whereas other kinds of drama were liable to engender less satisfactory print encounters. In specific terms, the reading experience of the theatre patron inspired by word of mouth to attend a performance of the dramatization of a particular novel, which was currently then enjoying what might be termed 'book of the moment' status, and who was entertained by a play that qualified as a particularly 'loose' adaptation, might well be coloured by the dissimilarity encountered in the affiliated prose fiction work. If this same novel were encountered under alternative circumstances, cold and free of a prehistory that included acquaintance with an adaptation, the odds of the book furnishing a significantly more pleasing read might well be greater. However, this is not to suggest that all consumers would inevitably navigate cross-media experiences in this way; there was also scope for a less prosaic class of evaluation where fluency in the conventions of each respective mode would give rise to an oscillatory class of consumption that recognized the specific limits and possibilities of the two media. Considering the particular example of the bi-media work, *Madame Midas* will offer the opportunity to probe this question further and illuminate the workings of such acts of reading in practice.

Granted, the relationship between *Madame Midas*, the novel written by Fergus Hume, and *Madame Midas: The Gold Queen*, the drama co-authored by Hume in conjunction with Philip Beck, cannot be completely reconstructed today. However, it is clear that this was a hybrid cultural artefact marked by an apposite, potentially gratifying blend of familiarity and variance with the capacity to please both the reader who was moved to attend the play and the theatre patron inspired to consume the book. At their respective cores, both the print media text and the theatrical performance rested on three central pillars. First, there is the story of the eponymous wronged wife who, having escaped the cruelties of marriage to a husband who had squandered the fortune she inherits from her father, restores herself to a position of wealth through her extraordinarily lucky discoveries in the Australian goldfields. She must then navigate the challenges that result from her position as a woman of means in the Melbourne metropolis. Second, both play and novel also chart the 'fall' narrative arc of Madame Midas's ingénue friend who is transformed from an innocent clergyman's daughter to a discarded mistress to ruined outcast. Third, each text derives much of its momentum from the machinations of the scheming villain responsible for the secondary heroine's corruption; he is an escapee from a New Caledonian penal colony who conspires to gratify his monetary and sexual desires on the Australian mainland weaving a trail of destruction in the process.

The play was also a distinct entity in a number of critical respects such that both novel and drama would have held an element of surprise for the body of consumers for whom it constituted medium b (to reuse my earlier categorization). The introduction of a subtitle (*The Gold Queen*) in the billing under which the theatrical production played gestured toward its discrete qualities. In an intriguing example of convergence disruption and also sidestepping of a potentially exceedingly meta moment, the scenario of a murder mystery committed after the fashion of *The Hidden Hand*, which the book's cover imagery had spotlighted, was not a feature of the Hume-Beck stage drama. Moreover, the culpability in the reframed case of attempted poisoning that the play did dramatize is assigned to a different party entirely. There is also no whodunit scenario as the audience is never in any doubt about the individual who orchestrates the murder attempt, which centres on a contaminated drink at a party. This reassigning of guilt in scenarios involving criminality was a ploy that nineteenth-century dramatists working upon adaptations often enlisted to reintroduce an element of tension and astonishment for audiences who arrived at the playhouse conversant with the central 'reveal' of a book's climactic moments.[30] In the context of cross-media consumption, this had the potential to cut both ways as it meant that the dramatic revelation of the novel's denouement would also surprise those who had traversed from playhouse to print. My intention here is not to embark on an extended comparative examination that traces the assorted reorientations that Hume and his co-adapter instituted (although this is not to deny the possible merit in such an exercise). However, I would suggest that the tonal recoding that the dramatization introduced is significant given my earlier discussion of the punctuational or structural affinities and variances that distinguished the two modes of reading and spectatorship. Stage melodrama was inclined to blend light with shade by punctuating scenes of high drama with comedic relief.[31] The Hume-Beck play made very obvious use of this convention such that the two of the caricatured minor characters who had served as local colour in the novel figure much more prominently in the play and actually dominate the opening scene supplanting the embroidered descriptions of the Australian coastline that Hume had used to begin the novel.

'Melodrama is the sensation novel in acts,' observed J.M. Barrie in an 1889 theatre review for the periodical, *Time*.[32] Barrie's pronouncement was made in the context of a write-up of Robert Buchanan's play, *A Man's Shadow*. While there is little doubt that Barrie is generalizing to a rather significant degree with this assessment, the broad thrust of his observation is noteworthy when considering the experiences of readers moving between the dual incarnations of works like Hume's *Madame Midas*. Granted, the melodramatic credentials of both iterations were strong. The review of the novel that appeared in *The Graphic* went so far as to comment that 'the story reads as if it were written for the melodramatic stage'.[33] Although not intended as a compliment, the remark is interesting as it signalled a likely textual recognition on the part of a certain proportion of contemporary readers that this was a novel that had the potential to make a ready transfer to the playhouse. Interestingly, the other leading current in contemporary criticism of Hume's novel highlighted the work's affinity with sensational literature.[34] Sensation fiction, when transposed to the stage as sensation drama (as opposed to the pure melodrama of Barrie's characterization), very often rooted the cornerstone of its efforts to attract audiences to the theatre in a particularly dramatic sensation scene that would offer an awe-inspiring degree of visual stimulation.[35] Hume's novel was not without the ingredients to facilitate this sort of contrivance for a possible stage transposition. For instance, the final moments of the text that take place on the banks of the Yarra Yarra river had the makings of a spectacle to rival the climactic scene of one of the more fabled examples of this kind of entertainment, Boucicault's *The Colleen Bawn*. Yet, given that the stage adaptation of *Midas* came to life exclusively as a touring production calling at many of the leading provincial British playhouses, it is perhaps not surprising that something this elaborate was not attempted.

Interestingly, however, this is not to suggest that an evocation of the Southern hemisphere achieved through visual media and general playhouse effect mise-en-scène was not a critical factor in efforts to draw theatregoers to the dramatization. It is worth emphasizing that the novel's representation of life in the Antipodes had been a quality that some critical discussion had mentioned specifically.[36] In addition, the billing employed in the title page of the 1888 edition of Hume's novel announced that the book constituted 'a realistic and sensational story of Australian mining life'.[37] It would seem that it was the former generic classification in which the Chatterton company looked to root a significant proportion of the potential parallel or kindred visual stimulation quotient their production might offer. The prospect of an opportunity to gaze upon 'pictorial posters'[38] and recreations of those vistas of the Melbourne urban environment and the Victorian landscape that figured prominently in the novel represented one of the key selling points that the company believed would attract patrons to attend performances of the drama. The promotional notice publicizing the production in *The Era* promised scenic backdrops that would depict 'The Gold Mine at Ballarat, the Black Hill Gully, the Princess's Theatre, Melbourne, and the New Houses of Parliament, Bourke Street, Melbourne, Illuminated by Night, and the Post Office, Melbourne'.[39] Thus, the cross-media convergences that this particular hybrid cultural artefact precipitated for consumers who moved laterally between the book and the play pursuing a clockwise or counter-clockwise orbit had the potential to encompass 'readership' of visual, print, and performance media.

Conclusion

Considered solely as a book belonging to the late nineteenth-century stratum of print culture known as the 'shilling shocker', a work like *Madame Midas* most obviously figures as an article of disposable reading matter circulating in an ephemeral format, which was to be consumed for the evanescent pleasures it could yield and then discarded when these were exhausted. However, reconstructing the wider history of the consumption of this artefact, which pivoted on transmutations across media, it is clear that the life-cycle of this class of reading matter might not quite be so circumscribed. Moreover, in the case of a hybrid or 'bi-media' entity such as *Madame Midas*, it is clear that the associated stage adaptation represented a great deal more than an unfortunate by-product or a corruption of the book. Rather, the intended scenario was one of compound consumption and rereading. Readers of the cheap paperback would ideally be influenced to become theatregoers where they would have the opportunity to take in a performance of this tale in dramatic form. Similarly, the ideal outcome that this class of adaptation was intended to engineer was that attendees of the dramatization would be induced to acquire the volume that was the companion entity to the drama that had offered a pleasurable evening spent at the playhouse.

Hume's *Madame Midas* was a print culture commodity furnishing light reading matter primarily intended to offer amusement and an immersive reading encounter for its audience. Working with this premise, it has been my objective to illustrate how the experience of moving between media within this particular late nineteenth-century sphere of reading was driven by an impetus to heighten the gratification derived from the encounter with whichever iteration represented a consumer's initial medium of contact with this cultural property. I do not wish to suggest that the resulting lens brought to bear on the additional or subsequent encounter of a cross-media consumption orbit by all late-Victorian consumers of artefacts like *Madame Midas* would necessarily take the shape of the frame set forth here. However, it is my contention that the diagnosis and reconstruction offered does go some way toward illuminating the more likely strategies enlisted in navigating this kind of reading experience. I will conclude with an interesting case of cross-media circularity. We are currently witnessing something of a revival in the cultural prominence that Hume's early Melbourne-based novels achieved upon first publication, as readers and critics increasingly turn their attention to his work. It is intriguing to note that amongst this resurgence there featured a television film adaptation of *The Mystery of a Hansom Cab* broadcast on the Australian Broadcasting Corporation in 2012,[40] which suggests that the perceived impulse to 'read' anew that which has been previously read remains equally potent in the context of this kind of cultural matter.

Notes

1. J. Fowles, *The French Lieutenant's Woman* (London: Vintage, 1969), p. 46.
2. See for example: J. Sanders, *Adaptation and Appropriation* (London and New York: Routledge, 2006); G. Bluestone, *Novels into Films* (Baltimore: Johns Hopkins Press, 1957), C. Albrecht-Crane and D.R. Cutchins, eds., *Adaptation Studies: New Approaches* (Madison: Fairleigh Dickinson University Press, 2010); and L. Hutcheon, *A Theory of Adaptation*, 2nd ed. (London and New York, 2013).
3. N. Daly, 'Fiction, Theatre and Early Cinema' in D. Glover and S. McCracken, eds., *The Cambridge Companion to Popular Fiction* (Cambridge: Cambridge University Press, 2012) pp. 33–49 (p. 33).
4. A. Maunder, 'Sensation Fiction on Stage', in A. Mangham, ed., *The Cambridge Companion to Sensation Fiction* (Cambridge: Cambridge University Press, 2013) pp. 52–69.
5. Maunder, 'Sensation Fiction on Stage', p. 67.
6. E. Sinclair Bell, 'Appendix: The Publishing History of Fergus Hume's *The Mystery of a Hansom Cab*', in D. Craigie, G. Greene, and E. Allan Osborne, *Victorian Detective Fiction: A Catalogue of the Collection Made by Dorothy Glover and Graham Greene* (London: Bodley Head), pp. 123–26.
7. S. Knight, *Continent of Mystery: A Thematic History of Australian Crime Fiction* (Victoria: Melbourne University Press, 1997) offered one of the earliest examinations of Hume's writing. More recent scholarship on Hume's output (focusing particularly on *The Mystery of a Hansom Cab*) can be found in C. Pittard, *Purity and Contamination in Late Victorian Detective Fiction* (Aldershot: Ashgate, 2011) and C. Clarke, *Late Victorian Crime Fiction in the Shadows of Sherlock* (Basingstoke: Palgrave Macmillan, 2014). One of the few critical pieces on *Madame Midas* is the gender-based study offered in J. Kestner, *Sherlock's Sisters: The British Female Detective, 1864–1913* (Aldershot: Ashgate, 2003).
8. 'Madame Midas', *The Era*, 14 July 1888, 2599, p. 10.
9. See G. Law, 'On Wilkie Collins and Hugh Conway "Poor Fargus"', *The Wilkie Collins Journal* 3 (2000) for an excellent comparative discussion of the two authors.
10. 'An Australian Novel, of which 147,000 Copies have Been Sold in Six Weeks', *The Graphic*, 22 September 1888, 982, p. 322.
11. 'Letters to Some People', *Punch*, 14 June 1884, p. 280.
12. This term features in Mary Elizabeth Leighton and Lisa Surridge's discussion of nineteenth-century visual and serial literary culture. See M. Elizabeth Leighton and L. Surridge, 'The Plot Thickens: Toward a Narratological Analysis of Serial Fiction', *Victorian Studies* 51.1 (2008), 65–101 (p. 67).

13. Representative dramatic criticism of *The Hidden Hand* includes 'The Theatres', *The Saturday Review* 18 (19 November 1864), 631–32 (p. 631).
14. S. Murray, *The Adaptation Industry: The Cultural Economy of Literary Production* (London and New York: Routledge, 2011).
15. S. Murray and A. Weedon, 'Beyond Medium Specificity: Adaptations, Cross-Media Practices and Branded Entertainments', *Convergence: The International Journal of Research into New Media Technologies* 17.1 (2011), 3–5 (p. 3).
16. Title page of F. Hume, *Madame Midas* (London: Hansom Cab Publishing Company, 1888).
17. 'Madame Midas', *The Era*, 14 July 1888, 2599, p. 10.
18. Examples of these pieces include: 'The Author of Madame Midas', *The Illustrated London News*, 2581, 6 October 1888, p. 410; 'Literary Gossip', *The Athenaeum*, 3167, 7 July 1888, p. 36; and 'A Wonderful Book', *The Huddersfield Chronicle and West Yorkshire Advertiser*, 6645, 17 November 1888, p. 3.
19. I am indebted to Sheldon Goldfarb for this insight into the cross-media impact registered by Ainsworth. Additional discussion of this particular example can be found in H. Bleakley (1933) 'Jack Sheppard in Literature and Drama' in *Jack Sheppard* (Edinburgh: Hodge), pp. 92–102.
20. A.B. Walkley, 'The Novel and the Drama', *Novel Review* 121 (1892), 21–29 (p. 21).
21. Walkey, 'The Novel and the Drama', p. 24.
22. Walkey, 'The Novel and the Drama', p. 24.
23. M. Booth, *Theatre in the Victorian Age* (Cambridge: Cambridge University Press, 1991), p. 62.
24. 'Mr Balsir Chatterton's Company', *The Era*, 12 January 1889, 2625, p. 4.
25. Hutcheon, *A Theory of Adaptation*, p. 8. Hutcheon's italics connote that a conversancy with the adapted text figures in the frames of reference of the audience under discussion.
26. Hutcheon, *A Theory of Adaptation*, p. 128.
27. Hutcheon, *A Theory of Adaptation*, p. 21.
28. Hutcheon, *A Theory of Adaptation*, p. 4.
29. W. Davenport Adams, 'What is the Theatrical Public?', *The Theatre* 29 (1897), 198–202 (p. 199).
30. R. Pearson, '"Twin Sisters" and "Theatrical Thieves": Wilkie Collins and the Dramatic Adaptation of *The Moonstone*', in A. Mangham, ed., *Wilkie Collins: Interdisciplinary Essays* (Newcastle upon Tyne: Cambridge Scholars Publishing, 2007), pp. 208–21 includes an examination of the challenge of dramatizing literary works that turned upon a dramatic revelation of this variety.
31. Booth, *Theatre in the Victorian Age*, p. 151.

32. J.M. Barrie, 'What the Pit Says X. A Man's Shadow at the Haymarket', *Time* 10 (1889), 423–26 (p. 423).
33. 'New Novels', *The Graphic*, 29 September 1888, 983, p. 354.
34. 'New Leaves', *Fun*, 29 August 1888, 48, p. 96.
35. Additional discussion of these spectacles can be found in Maunder and also, M. Diamond, *Victorian Sensation or the Spectacular, the Shocking and the Scandalous in Nineteenth-Century Britain* (London: Anthem Press, 2003).
36. 'An Australian Novel, of which 147,000 copies have been sold in six weeks', p. 322.
37. Title page of Fergus Hume, *Madame Midas* (London: Hansom Cab Publishing Company, 1888).
38. 'Mr Balsir Chatterton's Company', p. 4.
39. 'Mr Balsir Chatterton's Company', p. 4.
40. *The Mystery of a Hansom Cab*, dir. Shawn Seet (Australia: Australian Broadcasting Corporation, Roadshow Entertainment, 2012) DVD.

CHAPTER 11

Reading Theatre Writing: T.H. Lacy and the Sensation Drama

Kate Mattacks

JOCELYN ... (*reads*) 'I had now arrived at that particular point of my walk, where four roads met. The road to Hampstead, the road to Finchley, the road to the West End, the road back to London. I had mechanically turned in the latter direction, and was strolling along the lonely high road.' (*speaks*) Now there's something coming. I'm sure! ... (reads) 'In one moment every drop of blood in my body was brought to a stop-----' (HARVEY *approaches* JOCELYN *stealthily, the latter continues to read*) 'by the touch of a hand lightly and suddenly on my shoulder, from behind me------' (HARVEY *places his hand on* JOCELYN's *shoulder, who, with comic start, springs up to his feet, upsetting some books, &c, in his surprise*)
Watts Phillips, (1864) *The Woman in Mauve*, 1.i.p. 9–10.

When Frank Jocelyn, the reluctant hero of *The Woman in Mauve*, is revealed to the audience reading directly from Wilkie Collins's *The Woman in White* (1860) the playwright Watts Phillips presents his audience with a cultural space where modes of reading and sensational representation could be debated alongside notions of legitimacy, identity and value. Jocelyn is found reading the popular novel in private, but Dr Harvey's

K. Mattacks (✉)
University of the West of England, Bristol, UK

© The Author(s) 2016
P.R. Rooney, A. Gasperini (eds.), *Media and Print Culture Consumption in Nineteenth-Century Britain*, New Directions in Book History, DOI 10.1057/978-1-137-58761-9_11

183

physical intervention functions to enervate both Jocelyn and the audience in a complex generic interplay between fictional and theatrical forms. Enervated by the act of reading a narrative, Jocelyn's character physically articulates the multiple somatic reactions to the appearance of Collins's ghostly Anne Catherick. The novel generates a mirrored, static response in Jocelyn, who is 'brought to a stop' by the narrative tension, creating the conditions by which he can read on with renewed focus. However, it is the actions of Dr Harvey which function to release that tension, partly for comic affect and also to allow the audience to see the immediacy of the drama as an alternative, paradoxically authentic mode of representing Collins's dramatic events. In staging a moment where the psychology of terror creates an increasingly autonomous physical form, Phillips articulates the nature of the sensational as a cultural form, a shifting set of influences and counter-responses which resonate across multiple mediums. As Deborah Vlock has provocatively argued, the Victorian reader was not a solitary figure but one who 'performed his or her reading in a highly public "space" drawing upon a set of consensual popular assumptions … novelists drew quite freely from the body of sociodramatic possibilities established by the theatre'.[1] Phillips's staging of the reading dynamic in the highly public space of first *The Prince of Wales Theatre* in Liverpool in 1864 and then at the *Haymarket* the following year, alludes to cultural practices of collaborative, cross-disciplinary reading.

Building on the work of Deborah Wynne and Andrew King, advances in periodical studies have developed notions of Victorian reading strategies founded on interplay between a magazine's narratives, serial fiction, cartoons, illustrations, poetry and journalism.[2] This multidisciplinary, multisensory mode is comparable with that of the nineteenth-century theatre experience. Mid-Victorian performance was typified by its integration of iconic statues or paintings as tableau at the end of each major Act drop, spoken and written words, political allusion, social realism and songs/lyrical poems which legitimated the performance before the monopoly of the patent theatres was broken by the 1847 Theatres Act. However, what is interesting is that despite this culturally embedded, cross-platform reading dynamic, there is a notable missing feature: the playtext itself. Whilst small comic pieces or charades were printed in the Christmas numbers of magazines such as M.E. Braddon's *Belgravia Annual, London Society* and *Punch*, these pieces were largely impractical in terms of performance.[3] There appears to be little evidence that Lacy's Acting Editions attracted a specific, private readership as they were only available by post directly from Lacy. Unavailable via lending libraries or reading groups, Lacy's List was successfully marketed towards readers who subsequently became performers. In a rare reference to Lacy's editions, the characters in Wilmot Harrison's *Special Performances* (1868) find the ideal farce for their amateur performance by perusing the list of Lacy's Acting Editions usefully listed by genre and size of cast needed.[4] Even in this evidence, the readers of the acting editions are actors playing socialites who become performers, indicating the inter-theatrical nature of Victorian culture. Scenes depicting private theatricals and public theatre experiences within narrative frameworks contain valuable evidence to aid reconstruction of the material practice of Victorian theatre. M.E. Braddon's *Strangers and Pilgrims* (1873), serialized in her Belgravia magazine from November 1872 to October 1873, describes a group of characters going to see a public performance of Charles Reade and Tom Taylor's *Masks and Faces* (1852) at the *Haymarket* theatre before they re-enact the play as a private theatrical. Here, the characters are encouraged to see the play before reading it for performative purposes only, suggesting the problematic status of the playtext, or what might usefully be termed the 'drama' of the period.

This chapter directly engages with the questions raised by this omission from wider cultural production and the very act of reading the extant Acting Editions published by T.H. Lacy as texts. I begin by outlining the act of reading theatre writing or the dramatic text, whilst the final strand of my argument focuses upon H.J. Byron's sensation dramas as a cultural space where dramatic and literary reading experiences are debated and converge. This work interrogates the issues raised by Watts Phillips's *The Woman in Mauve*: Did literary and dramatic reading experiences intersect or diverge? Did Victorians read plays? And more fundamentally, how and why should we read Victorian drama? Where does the drama fit into the symbiotic relationship between the theatre and the novel? Do we have the right terms to express ideas about what is effectively a written witness to the live medium? At this point, it is worth outlining working definitions of my areas of investigation, terms which in themselves reveal the inherent problems with existing hierarchies which privilege linguistic signs over the visual. As Mark Fortier explains, 'unlike drama, theatre is not words on a page. Theatre is performance ... theatre becomes a system of nonverbal signs, nonverbal language, nonverbal writing, yet dominated still by the predominance of language and letters as master-patterns for the workings of even the nonverbal.'[5] The world of mid-Victorian theatre can be at least partially discovered through the material objects, words and images that remain. These paradoxically show the conditions of performance, the intangible connections between practitioners and their art in a way that Jacky Bratton argues destabilizes literary dominance, one that arguably still persists in the field of nineteenth-century studies today. Rather, the theatre world engages in non-competitive strategies to foster collaboration and familial ties that negate the division between the drama and the stage, text and image.[6] Indeed, this creative interplay underpins the theatre's distrust of words in isolation and out of context. In a world where playtexts were initially only written in order to obtain a licence from the Lord Chamberlain's Office, words became the enemy within or at best were written with the recognition that the material conditions with which they would be performed could radically alter their meaning, decentring the playtext from the creative process. When the actress Peg Woffington in Charles Reade's *Masks and Faces* (1852) enters onstage reading from a play, she is quick to argue that the writer is indebted to the performer's skill in shaping dull, 'flat' words into successful, engaging theatre.[7] Images of reading novels within plays often provide a comic precursor to signify a character's inability to function socially, reconstructing them as a figure ripe for derision and ridicule. Richard Brinsley Sheridan's *The Rivals* (1775) introduces the audience to the class frictions created by Lydia Languish and Lucy the maid sharing a taste in lurid popular fiction. This idea reappears at the beginning of Watts Phillips's *The Woman in Mauve* as the comic landlady Mrs Beetles attempting to persuade Dr Harvey to read her penny magazines. Drawing the flimsy serials from her pocket, she illustrates the portability, predictability and disposability of a form containing the story '*The Death Rattle! A Romance of the Garotte*'.[8] Yet, this image of pulling a flimsy text from her pocket as she goes about her daily tasks is highly reminiscent of the fragile, single Acting Edition kept in the actor's pocket for reference.

Producing Theatre Writing: T.H. Lacy's Acting Editions

Examples of single Acting Editions published by T.H. Lacy which were used by practitioners show how the exigencies of practical use determined their physical, material form. The collection of playscripts owned by the mid-Victorian provincial actor Charles Harrington shows how the covers, all advertising material and endpapers were removed before the script was bound in light grade, brown cardboard.[9] This act of reframing the script facilitated the quick removal of the script from an actor's pocket lining during initial rehearsals before lines had been finalized. In direct contrast, T.H. Lacy also offered complete volumes, containing 12 plays, at 15 shillings each. By the 1860s, only 13 years into his publishing career, he was offering complete runs which were uniformly bound in half-leather octavo volumes. By the time he transferred his business assets to Samuel French in 1875, there were over 100 volumes available to the public. In addition, the *Amateur Theatre* anthology offered the chance to own 225 plays bound in half-morocco leather for the sum of £6. The weight and bulkier nature of these volumes suggests they were aimed at a very different market from the practising actor or stage manager. In addition, the cost of the uniformly bound volumes was significantly more than an aspiring theatre practitioner could easily afford. By way of comparison, Charles Dickens's journal *Household Words* cost 2d per issue. Discerning the intended readership of these superficially uniform volumes is problematic. Their outward uniformity belied the diverse typography, genres and authors contained within. Lacy's editorial process is equally divisive, although an analysis of his selections from all the possible plays submitted for licensing indicates his propensity for burlesques and farces rather than dramas. Lacy typically printed half of all performed burlesques and farces, but only 10 per cent of the dramas, which is revealing given the melodrama, nautical drama, gothic drama and domestic drama's closer proximity to the narrative form. The most transient and seasonal genre of pantomime was the least represented in Lacy's Acting Editions, a testimony to Tracy Davis's argument that the pantomime scripts had no residual value once the costumes were sold off.[10] As Lacy's dramatic texts were unavailable in journals or Mudie's Circulating Library, he ascribed multiple status values to the drama. In dislocating the printed dramatic text outside the reading culture of the masses, this exclusivity reduced the potential for piracy, retained the valuable performance rights, reconstructed the drama as a literary text in legal terms and turned it into an exclusive material object to be contained and displayed as a symbol of wealth. What is less clear is how dramatic texts could contribute to the Victorian reading experience, and how we might read them now.

In printing the playscripts, T.H. Lacy reassigned a literary status to his dramatic goods by virtue of its legal protection under Talfourd's Literary Copyright Act of 1842. Yet, the legibility and legitimacy of a dramatic text is still the subject of fierce debate amongst practitioners and cultural historians. Questions concerning narrative cohesion, intrusive stage practicalities and a disconnection from the expressive cues experienced in the live performative medium divide opinion as to whether the dramatic text is even viable as a text. The mid-Victorian theatre's use of bodily significance anticipates our own post-dramatic trends in physical theatre stemming from unscripted provocation, whilst the visual interplay and often counterplay between word and image indicates emerging modernist impulses towards internalized psychological narratives which resist physical utterances.[11] Despite some of the similarities between Victorian stage and our contemporary performance dynamics, our assessments of nineteenth-century theatre are often mediated through remaining narrative forms. Studies of the intersection between popular fiction and the theatre largely rest on how novels engage their readers through the theatrical tropes of gesture, display and melodramatic tactics or conversely of how theatre plundered novels for source material which resulted in litigious adaptations. Whilst we can partially reconstruct the cultural reading experiences that witnessed responses and counter-responses to shifting forms that alternated between the theatre and the journal format, the dramatic text has been decontextualized. Our reading relies upon a text which lacks the immediacy of the comparative theatrical moment and its integral performative sign system, a medium familiar to the Victorian reader and practitioner.

The dramatic text was a fluid, shifting form which was recorded and fixed at the points of licensing, promptscript and acting edition. The copy sent for licensing was normally devoid of any stage business (other than basic entrances, exits and tableau), providing just the spoken words for approval by the Lord Chamberlain's Office. Promptscripts are discernible by their additional stage directions, and notations indicating lighting, music and sound cues. Lacy's Acting Editions added full descriptions of entrances, exits, significant gestures, songs alongside costume descriptions, property lists, the cast for the première and often a copy of the original playbill. Whilst his editions were developed from promptscripts and the performances themselves, Lacy's dramatic texts resisted the notion of a fixed, stable form. For practitioners, the act of reading initiated the theatre event, and the 'read through' signalled both the end of the playwright's control over the work and the form of the dramatic text as it appeared in print. As the playwright H.J. Byron's novel *Paid in Full* (1865) explains, the process typically consisted of reconstructing scenes according to the practicalities of performance. Byron's fictional playwright witnesses the transformation of his farce from the original to a condensed, displaced version which adhered to the practicalities of moving scenery and retaining the star performer. The incidents of three scenes are condensed into one in order to allow the carpenters to construct the grand tableau flats/backdrops and the stage manager relocated and added scenes to allow the 'despotic' star actress to display her chief assets, here her shoulders, in a low-cut ballgown.[12] Lacy's Acting Editions had to offer multiple ways of reading and interpreting the drama and its characters in order to maximize the text's capital value and the subsequent performance rights. Providing provincial and touring theatre companies with material that allowed for artistic licence, smaller budgets, varying audience demographics was a key part of Lacy's business strategy. However, the drama's paradoxically adaptive yet familiar, marketable product has led to a critique of the drama as a medium lacking in narrative cohesion. Daniel Barrett contends that mid-Victorian drama was annexed from literature to its detriment, and that the plays contained in acting editions were not written for readers due to their focus on practicalities of transferring page to stage.[13] However, the Victorian readers were familiar with the visual strategies and practicalities inherent in the drama, and the material practice of the Victorian theatre is discernible from the texts. Readers could discern the emotions inscribed on the body through Lacy's stage directions and detailed proxemic descriptions. In reading the words 'red fire' the Victorian reader is no less affectively sensitized than when reading Jane Eyre's description of her enforced stay in the red room. The use of colour is equally legible, yet what the reader of the dramatic text lacks is a narrator, an internalized guide. The emotional cues created by sound and lighting need to be imagined in order to recreate an affective response. But in reading the cues and words of the characters, the reader of the drama can be paradoxically resensitized to the performance experience.

Despite George Bernard Shaw's contention that the level of detail in stage directions which included precise exit and entrance instructions made plays 'unreadable and unsaleable', Julie Stone Peters argues that this detail fulfilled a desire in the reader to see the secrets of the theatre, to see the forbidden world of the backstage.[14] Here a crucial interchange of senses occurs, as readers 'see', albeit imaginatively, when they read the dramatic text. In reading a drama, the tensions between concealment and revelation, stage and reality, performance and production, expressed and intangible embedded in Victorian theatre could be explored and potentially dispelled. Yet, an acknowledgement of what Dominic Johnson terms the dramatic 'scaffold of textual production and delivery'—upon which is constructed/hung the visual elements of lighting, set, movement, marketing tactics, allows only a partial dismantling of the hierarchy of textual and visual signs.[15] Insisting on the primacy of the visual within theatre creates not only the dialectic struggle between word and image which has plagued readings of mid-Victorian drama, but more importantly negates other sensory faculties—including sound and smell which inform the interplay between drama and performance. The actual performance venue and audience demographics created additional sensory dynamics. The most nostalgic sense, which is the sense of smell, could be invoked by purchasing Lacy's scented tableaux lights, scented coloured fire and scented magnesium tableaux lights. The act of reading also allowed the reader to see, and by extension 'hear', the words which might have been drowned by the noise of an audience, paradoxically reminding them of the etymological roots of the word 'audience', deriving from the Latin *audire*: to hear. The multisensory dynamics of performance are invoked by the stage business outlined in the material dramas of Lacy's Acting Editions. Here the object of the dramatic text suggests what Worthen terms the 'imprint' of performance, the dynamics of theatre from within a linguistic text.[16] The drama's references to the stage business of the theatre anticipate Marxist commodity theory where 'production produces not only the object, but also the manner of consumption'.[17] Here the word 'production' takes on the double meaning of theatrical output and manufacturing consumer goods, directly aligning the material and the less tangible performative practice. In rereading the drama we engage with an object and begin what W.T. Mitchell outlines as the process of restoring 'the dialogic power of these dead images, to breathe life into dead metaphors, particularly metaphors that inform its own discourse'.[18]

This approach to the products of consumer culture has now moved towards Thing theory, where objects of production become the subject of analytical focus. Rather than view objects as purely commodities, this approach argues for the material object's relationship with its cultural, creative context, allowing it to function as animate. The former object's new autonomy as mediator between cultural production and consumer is potentially useful for outlining Lacy's formation of an exclusive text which sought to paradoxically exist outside the cultural reading experience in literary terms at least. For Baudrillard, humans and objects are bound together in a 'collusion in which the objects take on a certain density, an emotional value—what might be called a "presence"'.[19] This sense of a tangible material object argues for another sense which explains the demand for Lacy's Acting Editions outside the business of performance practice, that of touch. The playscript creates a material object which contains the illusive and elusive performance modes temporarily within its covers, allowing the reader to contextualize the cultural anxieties surrounding the affective nature of theatre. The scripts of sensation drama allow a cultural space to emerge where ideas of theatricalized affect and narrative control were framed and debated. H.J. Byron's sensation dramas show that the dramatic form exploited the psychological urge to touch by producing material texts which could be held but resisted ideological containment. The act of holding a play in order to manage the emotional affect it creates falsely completes the desire for sensation and perception through haptic means.[20]

ACTS OF READING AND H.J. BRYON'S PERFORMANCE (IM)PRACTICALITIES

When looking at the works of the prolific playwright and novelist H.J. Byron, we see that the ideological practices involved in reading the material object of the novel were not immediately transferable to Acting Editions of popular dramas. In contrast to the regularized, specific rhythms of a narrative borne out of the serial format, the pace of sensation dramas increased with each successive act decreasing in length. H.J. Byron's oeuvre included theatre writing intended to precipitate stage production, trigger nostalgia and question the paradoxes of reading performance texts. Byron's parodies of the sensation drama based on familiar novels allowed theatre audiences to engage with a performative space in which modes of representation intersected to allow different reading practices to elicit variable responses. Complex intertextual references abound in Byron's work to form a vivid picture of the rapidly shifting adaptive cultural forms. His parody of generic categorization as a marketing strategy saw his play *1863; or, The Sensations of The Past Season. With a Shameful Revelation of Lady Somebody's Secret* listed as a 'comical conglomerative absurdity'.[21] Premiering at the *Theatre Royal, St James's*, this play depicts a playwright searching for inspiration, facilitating the use of the properties, costumes, and characters of the previous year in a parade of ghostly characters. The Haunted man, Old Hamlet, Banquo and the Corsican Brother appear to the Author, complete with signature costumes and concerted music. Scene 2 contains sequential appearances by Bel Domino, Leah and Manfred, before Byron's Author succumbs to the consumer demand for a popular sensation drama. The final scene is a miniature version of M.E. Braddon's *Lady Audley's Secret* (1862), but with a double twist. Lady Audley is played by the comic actor J.L. Toole and the character not only survives but escapes institutionalization. Here a subtextual critique of the demands placed on playwrights to produce adaptive responses to familiar narrative plots from infamous, financially successful novels. The act of reproduction allows the theatre to reuse properties, costumes, and scenery, signifying that this type of drama was about the dynamics of performance practice rather than narrative mimesis. The demands placed upon the theatre technicians, costume department, and musicians to reproduce recognizable iconic figures from the year's stage successes signify that this acting edition was aimed at professional theatres with a substantial budget and readers familiar with the original performances it references. The textual details underpinning Lacy's Acting Editions also function to paradoxically remind the subsequent reader that the performative medium is more adept at representing the textual nuances of gendered power and psychological impetus which remained extratextual to the original.

Byron's contribution to Lacy's 'Sensation Series' entitled *Rosebud of Stingingnettle Farm* (1862) was aimed at the domestic market for charity performances.[22] It was initially produced for a single event, the first Crystal Palace Dramatic Fete on Sunday 20 July. The cast list indicates that the original cast was an all-male cast, with Mr Worboys playing the character of Rose Turmutfield. Byron rewrote the play as *The Villanous [sic] Squire and the Village Rose* in order to stage it professionally for J.L. Toole's benefit at the *Adelphi* theatre on Wednesday 9 September 1863 and again in 1882. Byron's comic magazine *Fun* carried a brief advance notice of the new, revised version 'Mr Byron has cut a lot out of it—it ran to quite four pages of a "Lacy," I believe—and put a lot in, and turned it upside down'.[23] Despite the comic overtones with which Byron underplays his writing, the play itself was identified as a source for Horace Sedger's *Hidden Worth* at *The Prince of Wales's* theatre in November 1886.[24] The intertextual nature of the popular theatre saw Sedger rework Byron's farcical suicide scene where the Squire poisons, stabs, shoots and drowns himself almost simultaneously and transform it into an equally challenging murder scene. The brevity of Byron's drama and its catalogue listing according to how many characters are needed for its representation suggests that this playtext was potentially not as cohesive as a readerly text. However, this play also capitalized on the audience's affective memories of Mr Toole, allowing the transition between audience member and reader to develop. For now the reader was able to hold a tangible object which belied the passing of time and fixed a career grounded in dissimulating performance practice within the covers of a text.

In contrast, the collection of sensation dramas solely authored by Byron which were published by Lacy under the title *Sensation Dramas for the Back Drawing Room* (1864) was specifically aimed at a readership rather than theatre practitioners. The title suggests the anthology is written for the market in private theatricals, a subsidiary business for T.H. Lacy which gave the dramatic text a capital value alone with no subsequent performance rights. Lacy's catalogue indicates that the secondary value was in the sale of backdrops, make-up, lights and also his *Amateur's Guide*, a volume which had run to 7000 copies by 1870.[25] However, this volume was bound in half leather and listed as a single volume rather than a set of practical plays for a specific number of performers. The format of a single-authored volume of plays directs the text towards a readership more familiar with the literary model of non-collaborative creative outputs. Here Byron is the author, a contested term in performance culture, where the collaborative interplay of multiple voices created an adaptive, responsive theatrical text. Even the idea of a Dramatic Author's Society, founded in 1833 was, as Jane Moody asserts, arguably an elaborate 'cunning historiographic decoy, or at least a picturesque theatrical illusion'.[26] Byron's style of writing for pantomimes and burlesques was critically revered as a 'highly-trained faculty of stripping syllables of their original signification, and endowing composite words with a variety of hitherto unsuspected applications'.[27] This linguistic dexterity potentially aligned his drama with a more literary reading experience, as the possibility of rereading his words would reveal his multi-layered references. The volume contained 14 miniature dramas, ranging from parodies of well-known dramas to burlesque compilations of pantomimes and farces, all illustrated by William Brunton, a regular contributor for the *London Society* and *Belgravia Annual* Christmas numbers during the late 1860s and early 1870s.[28] Byron's fusion of genres provided the reader with vignettes of popular performances; *The Mendacious Mariner; or, Pretty Poll of Portsea and the Captain with His Whiskers* is a hybrid between Douglas Jerrold's domestic drama *Black Ey'd Susan* (1829) and Thomas Egerton Wilks's farce *The Captain is Not A-Miss* (1836). The cross-dressing Mary appears as the mysterious mariner in order to protect her husband, radically reversing the power dynamics of Jerrold's eponymous heroine as victim. Despite keeping to the standardized typographic style for professional stage business, Byron's stage directions are increasingly spectacular and ambitious in scope, suggesting a clear disparity between his drama and a possible domestic performance. Even with the backdrops available via Lacy's catalogue, a private theatrical would be unlikely to have the resources to realize the final stage directions: '(*the* CREW *cheer—land appears on the lee-bow—a rainbow spans the back of the scene—the enemy's vessel blows up, and* LIEUTENANT LEE SCUPPER *expires from the effect of a slow poison, as the curtain descends rapidly*)'.[29] *Green Grow the Rushes, Oh; or The Squireen, The Informer, and the Illicit Distiller* is directly dedicated to Boucicault and Falconer, highlighting Byron's intertextual sources for his parody of Boucicault's drama *The Colleen Bawn* (1860) and subsequent burlesque or farcical versions entitled *Eily O'Connor* (1860). Whilst Martin Meisel's argument that reading plays is recognition of the dual aspects of dramatic creative forces, those of organic creativity and the material conditions of practical scenic representation, Byron's sensation dramas work against this, resisting the possibilities of performance in the very descriptions of stage practice.[30] His mock stage direction for the Eily's entrance in Act 2 is particularly impractical: '*The red cloak of* EILY *is apparent on the rocky steps at the back of the stage; the stage is dark, and is only lit by the roguish, but characteristic, twinkle of* MILES'S *right eye*'.[31] The casting of his sensation dramas also reveals both the implausibility of actual performance representations and relocates the humorous witticisms into stage directions which lie outside the performative field. *The White Rose of the Plantation; or, Lubly Rosa, Sambo Don't Come* is a pastiche of dramas derived from *Uncle Tom's Cabin* (1852) and contains a description of the opening scene in which 'OVERSEERS *with whips are looking on; and in the back distance is distinctly observable, lending an enchantment to the view without interest. Two* OCTOROONS *and one* MACCAROON *are down in the front*'.[32] Again, Byron has displaced the word-play normally contained in pantomime speeches into an extra-theatrical moment which only a reader could enjoy. Here the tone verges on anti-theatrical, satirizing the paradoxical staged realism and authentic performance that Victorian theatre provided for its audience.

What emerges from Byron's volume of sensation dramas is a parodic discourse on the disparity between printed drama, performance possibilities for amateurs and the act of reading these texts. Reconstructing himself as an author, Byron created recognizable, inter-theatrical plays such as *Abandondino, The Bloodless* to appear in books rather than on stage. Appearing first in *Sensation Dramas for the Back Drawing Room* and later reprinted in H.S. Leigh's 1876 edited collection *Jeu d'Espirit*, *Abandondino* was an amalgamation of *Box and Cox* (1847) and the traditional *Bluebeard* pantomime.[33] Whilst Byron's ability to capitalize upon every publishing opportunity indicates a desire to attract a core readership in his magazines *Comic* and *Fun*, his contributions to Lacy's List allow the Acting Editions to function as an alternative cultural space where the complexities of reading theatre writing could be debated.[34] Byron's sensation dramas articulate the issues surrounding the nature of theatre writing which recorded the material practice of theatre from within a narrative form. Their status as legitimate texts is problematic and contested, but their existence after the performative moment has passed allows them to function as illusive, adaptive evidence. Lacy's Acting Editions offered a liminal cultural form where modes of representation for the live cues for expression, such as lighting, gesture, and sound, were openly questionable, anticipating W.B. Worthen's argument that 'texts cannot determine performance; they do not even determine the performance of reading'.[35] Lacy's control over the dissemination of his texts would have limited the demographic range of his readers, but what these playtexts did provide was a tangible place in which the management of the disruptive affective emotions engendered by Victorian theatre could be paradoxically expressed yet contained. What might be better termed as Lacy's readers-as-performers did encounter was the affective dynamics of reading outside the cultural reading practices of the theatre and the journal forms. The Acting Edition's form might have been at odds with both the regularized narrative form of serial fiction and the collaborative, shifting dynamics of performance practice, however the complex material conditions which shape theatre writing are discernible and legible even now.

NOTES

1. Deborah Vlock, *Dickens, Novel Reading and the Victorian Popular Theatre* (Cambridge: Cambridge University Press, 1998), p. 9.
2. See Deborah Wynne, *The Sensation Novel and The Victorian Family Magazine* (Basingstoke: Palgrave Macmillan, 2001). Andrew King, *The London Journal, 1845–83: Periodicals, Production and Gender* (Aldershot: Ashgate, 2004).
3. See T.R. Ellis, 'Burlesque Dramas in the Victorian Comic Magazines', *Victorian Periodicals Review* 1 (1982), pp. 138–43.

4. See Wilmot Harrison (1868) *Special Performances* (London: Thomas Hailes Lacy Acting Edition, Volume 80 c. 1868), 1.i. p. 11.
5. See Mark Fortier, *Theory/Theatre: An Introduction* (London: Routledge, 1997), p. 4.
6. Jacky Bratton, *New Readings in Theatre History* (Cambridge: Cambridge University Press, 2003), p. 129.
7. See Tom Taylor and Charles Reade (1852), *Masks and Faces* (New York: Samuel French, 1860). 1.i. p. 9. The play as published by Reade as the novel *Peg Woffington* in 1853.
8. See Watts Phillips (1864) *The Woman in Mauve* (London: Thomas Hailes Lacy Acting Edition, Vol. 76, c.1867), 1.i. p. 7. Reprinted with permission from *The Victorian Plays Project*, http://victorian.nuigalway.ie
9. This archive of over 40 playscripts, published by T.H. Lacy and his successor Samuel French, is now housed at the University of Worcester library.
10. See Tracy Davis, *The Economics of the British Stage 1800–1914* (Cambridge: Cambridge University Press, 2000), pp. 345–46.
11. See the key text on the shift towards non-traditional dramatic textual forms: Hans-Ties Lehmann, *Postdramatic Theatre*, translated by Karen Jürs-Munby (London: Routledge, 2006).
12. See a detailed review which includes long extracts from *Paid in Full* in *The Era*, Sunday 12 February, 1865, Issue 1377.
13. Daniel Barrett, 'Play Publication, Readers and the "Decline" of Victorian Drama', *Book History* 2 (1999), 173–87.
14. Stone Julie Peters, *Theatre of the Book 1480–1880: Print, Text, and Performance in Europe* (Oxford: Oxford University Press, 2000), p. 85.
15. See Dominic Johnson, *Theatre and the Visual* (Basingstoke: Palgrave Macmillan, 2012), p. 4.
16. W.B. Worthen, 'The Imprint of Performance', in W.B. Worthen and Peter Holland, eds., *Theorizing Practice: Redefining Theatre History* (Basingstoke: Palgrave Macmillan, 2003).
17. Katharina Boehm, ed., *Bodies and Things in Nineteenth-Century Literature and Culture* (Basingstoke: Palgrave Macmillan, 2012), p. 3.
18. W.T. Mitchell, *Iconology: Image, Text, Ideology* (Chicago and London: University of Chicago Press, 1986), pp. 158–59.
19. Jean Baudrillard (1968), *The System of Object*, translated by James Benedict (London: Verso, 1996), p. 14.
20. See Morton A. Heller and William Schiff, eds., *The Psychology of Touch* (New York: Psychology Press, 1991).
21. H.J. Byron, *1863; or The Sensations of the Past Season. With a Shameful Revelation of Lady Somebody's Secret*, Vol. 61 (London: Thomas Hailes Lacy, 1863).
22. The complete list of Lacy's '*Sensation Series*', published separately and not available in a uniform volume, was (1) F.C. Burnand, *The Blazing Burgee*

(1862); (2) Thomas Gibson Bowles, *The Port Admiral; or, The Mysterious Mariner* (1863); (3) Famars Hall, *Braganzio the Brigand; or, The Spirit and the Proof*. Also performed at a charity event by the First Hants Engineers on Bank Holiday Monday, 5 August 1872; (4) Anon, *The Tyrant! The Slave!! The Victim!!! and The Tar!!!!*; (5) John Smith [Anon], *The Domestic Hearthstone; or, The Virgin Maiden's Vengance*; (6) [Anon?], *The Pretty Jane*. This play is missing from the British Library collection; (7) John Smith [Anon], *Alice the Mystery; or the Parentless Maiden of the Cottage on the Cliff*; (8) H.J. Byron, *The Rosebud of Stingingnettle Farm* (1862). The British Library volume also contained F.C. Burnand *The Siege of Seringapatam; or, The Maiden of Mesopotamia* (1863).
23. See *Fun* (edited by H.J. Byron), Wednesday, 7 June 1882, Issue 891, p. 235.
24. Reviewed in *Fun* (formerly edited by H.J. Byron until 1884), Wednesday, 10 November 1886, Issue 1122, p. 192.
25. T.H. Lacy makes this claim on the frontispiece.
26. Jane Moody, 'Illusions of Authorship', in Tracy Davis and Ellen Donkin, eds., *Women and Playwriting in Nineteenth-Century Britain* (Cambridge: Cambridge University Press, 1999), pp. 99–124, 102–03.
27. [Anon] review of *Paid in Full* in *The Era*, Sunday, 12 February 1865, Issue 1377.
28. See *Belgravia Annual*, Christmas number for 1873, 'Told by a Comprador' by C.W. Hay and illustrated by William Brunton. He also illustrated J.C. Brough's 'Acting Charades' for *London Society* magazine for 1865–67.
29. See H.J. Byron, *Sensation Dramas for the Back Drawing Room* (London: Thomas Hailes Lacy, 1864), p. 50.
30. Martin Meisel, *How Plays Work: Reading and Performance* (Oxford: Oxford University Press, 2007), p. 11.
31. H.J. Byron, *Sensation Dramas for the Back Drawing Room* (London: Thomas Hailes Lacy, 1864), p. 30.
32. H.J. Byron, ibid., p. 95.
33. Reviewed in *Pall Mall Gazette*, Friday, 24 November 1876, Issue 3672, p. 10.
34. An advert in *Lloyd's Weekly Newspaper*, Sunday, 10 January 1864, Issue 1103, indicates that the *Comic* magazine is edited by H.J. Byron and carries his new 'Spectral Sensation Drama' entitled *The Bad Baron of Bavaria; or, The Limelight Ghost of the Cruel Corridor*. Each issue of the *Comic* cost 1 penny.
35. W.B. Worthen, 'The Imprint of Performance', in W.B. Worthen and Peter Holland, eds., *Theorizing Practice: Redefining Theatre History* (Basingstoke: Palgrave Macmillan, 2003), pp. 213–14.

Bibliography

Ablow, R. (2010) *The Feeling of Reading* (Ann Arbor: University of Michigan Press).
Adcock, J. (2011) 'Works of the Amateur Casual (ca. 1835–1927)', *Yesterday's Papers*, http://john-adcock.blogspot.ca/2011/02/works-of-amateur-casual-1832-1929.html
Albrecht-Crane, C., and D.R. Cutchins (eds.) (2010) *Adaptation Studies: New Approaches* (Madison: Fairleigh Dickinson University Press).
'Aliquis' (1887–1888) *Wellpark F. C. Literary Society M. S. Magazine*, 146.
'Aliquis' (1887–1888) *Wellpark F. C. Literary Society M. S. Magazine*, 7.
Altick, R.D. (1957) *The English Common Reader* (Chicago: University of Chicago Press).
——— (1978) *The Shows of London* (London, England and Cambridge, MA: The Belknap Press of Harvard University Press), quod.lib.umich.edu
——— (1983) *The English Common Reader: A Social History of the Mass Reading Public, 1800–1900*, Midway reprint (Chicago and London: University of Chicago Press).
'Amusements of the Moneyless' (1855) *Chambers's Journal of Popular Literature, Science and Arts*, 72, 401–05. *ProQuest British Periodicals*.
Anderson, P.J. (1991) *The Printed Image and the Transformation of Popular Culture 1790–1860* (Oxford: Clarendon Press).
'Answers to Correspondents' (1883) *Girl's Own Paper*, 181, 591.
'Answers to Correspondents' (1884) *Girl's Own Paper*, 259, 174.
'Answers to Correspondents' (1880) *Girl's Own Paper*, 19, 304.
'Answers to Correspondents' (1881) *Girl's Own Paper*, 69, 479.
'Answers to Correspondents' (1894) *Girl's Own Paper*, 732, 224.

'Answers to Search Questions (February)' (1890) *Atalanta*, 30, 396.
Anti-Caste (1889) January, 1.
Anti-Caste (1890) July–August.
Anti-Caste, List of Subscribers 1892 (1893), 8.
'An Appeal Concerning the Treatment of Coloured Races', MSS Brit Emp s. 20 E5/8, The Bodleian Library of Commonwealth and African Studies, University of Oxford.
Arata, S. (2004) 'On Not Paying Attention', *Victorian Studies*, 46.2, 193–205.
Armstrong, I. (2002) 'The Microscope: Mediations of the Sub-visible World', in R. Luckhurst and J. McDonagh, eds., *Transactions and Encounters: Science and Culture in the Nineteenth Century* (Manchester and New York: Manchester University Press).
——— (2008) *Victorian Glassworlds: Glass Culture and the Imagination 1830–1880* (Oxford and elsewhere: OUP).
Aspinall, A. (1946) 'The Circulation of Newspapers in the Early Nineteenth Century', *The Review of English Studies*, 22.85, 29–43.
'*Atalanta* Scholarship and Reading Union: Scholarship Competition Questions' (1889) *Atalanta*, 97, 493.
Athenaeum (1859) *Self-Help* by S. Smiles reviewed, 31 December, 883–85.
Athenaeum (1960) 'Our Weekly Gossip', 15 December, 832–33.
Augé, M. (1992) *Non-Lieux, introduction à une anthropologie de la surmodernité* (Paris: Le Seuil).
——— (1995) *Non-Places: Introduction to an Anthropology of Supermodernity* (London and New York: Verso).
'An Australian Novel, of Which 147,000 Copies have been Sold in Six Weeks' (1888) *The Graphic*, 982, 322.
'The Author of Madame Midas' (1888) *The Illustrated London News*, 2581.6, 410.
Bailey, S. (1860) 'Literary Adoption', *Athenaeum*, 1 December, 752.
Bailin, M. 'Victorian Readers', *Victorian Literature and Culture* (forthcoming).
Banham, C. (2006) '*Boys of England* and Edwin J. Brett, 1866–99', unpublished dissertation, University of Leeds.
——— and E. Stearns (2015) 'Introduction', in *The Skeleton Crew, or, Wildfire Ned* (Brighton: Victorian Secrets).
Barrett, D. (1999) 'Play Publication, Readers and the "Decline" of Victorian Drama', *Book History*, 2, 173–87.
Barrie, J.M. (1889) 'What the Pit Says X. A Man's Shadow at the Haymarket', *Time*, 10, 423–26.
Barry, W. (1909) 'New Books: Not Lancelot, but Galahad' [review of Arthur E. Waite, *The Hidden Church of the Holy Grail, its Legends and Symbolism*], *The Bookman*, 35.210, 271–73.
Baudrillard, J. (1968) *The System of Object*, translated by James Benedict (London: Verso, 1996).

Beck, P., and F. Hume (1888) *Madam Midas: A Drama in Five Acts*, unpublished Playscript.
Belfast News-Letter (1888), 5.
Bhattacharya, S. (2008) 'G.W.M. Reynolds: Rewritten in Nineteenth-century Bengal', in Anne Humpherys and Louis James, eds., *G.W.M. Reynolds: Nineteenth-Century Fiction, Politics, and the Press* (Aldenham: Ashgate).
Blair, K. (2014) '"Let the Nightingales Alone": Correspondence Columns, the Scottish Press, and the Making of the Working Class Poet', *Victorian Periodicals Review*, 47, 188–207.
Bleakley, H. (1933) 'Jack Sheppard in Literature and Drama', in *Jack Sheppard* (Edinburgh: Hodge), pp. 92–102.
Bleiler, E.F. (1975) 'Introduction to GWM Reynolds', in E.F. Bleiler, ed., *Wagner the Wehr-Wolf* (Dover Classics. New York: Dover; London: Constable).
Bluestone, G. (1957) *Novels into Films* (Baltimore: John Hopkins Press).
Boehm, K. (ed.) (2012) *Bodies and Things in Nineteenth-Century Literature and Culture* (Basingstoke: Palgrave Macmillan).
Bolton, H.P. (1987) *Dickens Dramatized* (Boston: G.K. Hall).
Bookseller (1868), 447.
Booth, M. (1991) *Theatre in the Victorian Age* (Cambridge: Cambridge University Press).
Bourgeois Richmond, V. (2013) King Arthur and His Knights for Edwardian Children, *Arthuriana*, 23.3, 55–78.
The Boy's Standard (1892), 580.
Braddon, M.E. (1882) *Mount Royal: A Novel*, 3 vols. (London: John and Robert Maxwell).
Bradley, M., and J. John (eds.) (2015) *Reading and the Victorians* (Farnham and Burlington: Ashgate).
Brake, L. (1986) 'Literary Criticism and the Victorian Periodicals', *The Yearbook of English Studies*, 16, 92–116.
Brantlinger, P. (1998) *The Reading Lesson* (Bloomington: Indiana University Press).
Bratton, J. (20 03) *New Readings in Theatre History* (Cambridge: Cambridge University Press).
Bressey, C. (2013) *Empire, Race and the Politics of Anti-Caste* (London: Bloomsbury Academic).
——— (2013) 'Four Women: Black Women Writing in London between 1880 and 1920', in F. Paisley and K. Reid, eds., *Critical Perspectives on Colonialism: Writing the Empire from Below* (Oxford, Routledge).
——— (2013) 'Geographies of Belonging: White Women and Black History', *Women's History Review*, 22.4, 541–58.
Briggs, A. (1955) 'Samuel Smiles and the Gospel of Work', in *Victorian People: A Reassessment of Persons and Themes, 1851–67* (Middlesex: Penguin).

——— (1958) 'A Centenary Introduction', in S. Smiles *Self-Help* (London: John Murray).
Brimmell, R.A. (1983) 'Old Bloods & Penny Dreadfuls Part 2', *Antiquarian Book Monthly Review*, 10.3, 80–83.
British Controversialist and Literary Magazine (1860) *Self-Help* by S. Smiles reviewed, 3, 44–49.
Burt, T. (1924) *An Autobiography* (London: T. Fisher Unwin).
Byron, H.J. (1863) *1863; or The Sensations of the Past Season. With a Shameful Revelation of Lady Somebody's Secret*, Vol. 61 (London: Thomas Hailes Lacy).
——— (1864) *Sensation Dramas for the Back Drawing Room* (London: Thomas Hailes Lacy).
Carter, I.R. (1976) 'The Mutual Improvement Movement in North-East Scotland in the Nineteenth Century', *Aberdeen University Review*, 46, 383–92.
Carver, S.J. (2008) 'The Wrongs and Crimes of the Poor: The Urban Underworld of The Mysteries of London in Context', in A. Humpherys and L. James, eds., *G.W.M. Reynolds: Nineteenth-Century Fiction, Politics, and the Press* (Aldenham: Ashgate).
Catalogue of Songs and Song Books, Sheets, Half-Sheets, Christmas Carols, Children's Books, &c. Printed and Published by J. Catnach (1832). Madden Papers, University of Cambridge Library, Cambridge, 1 September 2015.
Catherine Impey to Albion Tourgée, 16 June 1890, 4785, Albion W. Tourgée Papers, Chautauqua County Historical Society, Westfield, New York.
Catherine Impey to Frederick Chesson, 1 March 1888, Brit Emp. s. 18 C138/173, The Bodleian Library of Commonwealth and African Studies, University of Oxford.
Catherine Impey to Frederick Douglass, 15 February 1883, Frederick Douglass Papers, Library of Congress, Washington.
Caughey, A. (2013) 'Once and Future Arthurs: Arthurian Literature for Children', in Carolyne Larrington and Diane Purkiss, eds., *Magical Tales: Myth, Legend and Enchantment in Children's Books* (Oxford: Bodleian Library).
Cawelti, J.G. (1976) *Adventure, Mystery, and Romance: Formula Stories as Art and Popular Culture* (Chicago: University of Chicago Press).
Chartier, R. (1986) 'Les pratiques de l'écrit', *Histoire de la vie privée: Tome 3. De la Renaissance aux Lumières* (Paris: Seuil), pp. 113–61.
———, and trans. A. Goldhammer (1993) 'The Practical Impact of Writing', in *A History of Private Life: III. Passions of the Renaissance* (Cambridge, MA and London, England: Belknap Press of Harvard University Press).
——— (1994) *The Order of Books: Readers, Authors, and Libraries in Europe between the Fourteenth and Eighteenth Centuries*, translated by L. Cochrane (Stanford: Stanford University Press).
——— (1997) *On the Edge of the Cliff: History, Language, Practices*, translated by L. Cochrane (Baltimore: Johns Hopkins University Press).

Child, F.J. (1994) '"Ballad Poetry," *Johnson's Universal Cyclopedia*, 1900', *Journal of Folklore Research*, 31.1/3, 214–22.
The Christian Examiner (1860) *Self-Help* by S. Smiles reviewed, Vols. 69–70, 5th series, 147–48.
Clarke, C. (2014) *Late Victorian Crime Fiction in the Shadows of Sherlock* (Basingstoke: Palgrave Macmillan).
Clausen, C. (1993) 'How to Join the Middle Classes: With the Help of Dr. Smiles and Mrs. Beeton', *American Scholar*, 62.3, 403–18.
Colclough, S. (2007) *Consuming Texts: Readers and Reading Communities, 1675–1870* (Basingstoke: Palgrave).
Coleridge, C. (1 February–1 March 1892) 'Arthur as an English Ideal' [4 parts], 14–15.
Collins, W. (1999) *The Moonstone* (Oxford: Oxford University Press).
'Coloured Seamen and their Grievances' (25 August 1880) *Liverpool Mercury*, 5.
'Comic Valentines: Topical Ephemera 2' (2012) *The John Johnson Collection: Now and Then*, http://johnjohnsoncollectionnowandthen.wordpress.com/2012/02/13/comic-valentines/
'Constitution' (1883–84) 'Wellpark Free Church Young Men's Literary Society. Session 1883–84', Wellpark F. C. Literary Society M. S. Magazine.
'A Cornish Sister', 'A Visit to King Arthur's Castle', *Girl's Own Paper* 70 (30 April 1881), 496.
'A Country Lassie' 'Hop, Step and Jump', *Wellpark F. C. Literary Society M. S. Magazine*, (1887–88), 57–66.
Craik, G.L. (1831) *Pursuit of Knowledge under Difficulties* (London: C. Knight).
Crary, J. (1999) *Suspensions of Perception: Attention, Spectacle, and Popular Culture* (London and Cambridge, MA: MIT Press).
Crawford, J.C. (2014) '"The High State of Culture to Which this Part of the Country has Attained": Libraries, Reading, and Society in Paisley, 1760–1830', *Library & Information History*, 30, 172–94.
'A Critic' (1888) Wellpark F. C. Literary Society M. S. Magazine.
Cross, N. (1985) *The Common Writer: Life in Nineteenth-Century Grub Street* (Cambridge, England: Cambridge University Press).
Cruse, A. (1935) *The Victorians and their Books* (London: Allen & Unwin).
Curry, J.L. (1990) 'Children's Reading and the Arthurian Tales', in V.M. Lagorio and M. Leake Day, eds., *King Arthur Through the Ages* (New York and London: Garland).
'D. D.' (1883–84) Wellpark F. C. Literary Society M. S. Magazine.
Dallas, M.K. (1 October 1881) 'The Story of Excalibar', *Young Folks*, 565, 114.
Daly, N. (2012) 'Fiction, Theatre and Early Cinema', in D. Glover and S. McCracken, eds., *The Cambridge Companion to Popular Fiction* (Cambridge: Cambridge University Press), pp. 33–49.
Dames, N. (2007) *The Physiology of the Novel: Reading, Neural Science, and the Form of Victorian Fiction* (Oxford and New York: Oxford University Press).

Darnton, R. (1990) *The Kiss of Lamourette: Reflections in Cultural History* (New York: Norton).
Davenport Adams, W. (1897) 'What is the Theatrical Public?' *The Theatre*, 29, 198–202.
Davis, T. (2000) *The Economics of the British Stage 1800–1914* (Cambridge: Cambridge University Press).
De Certeau, M. (1985) 'Practices of Space', in M. Blonksy, ed., *On Signs* (Oxford: Basil Blackwell), pp. 122–45.
De Grey, U. (1 April 1893) 'Impressions of a Débutante', *Atalanta*, 67.
Delap, L., and M. Di Cenzo (2008) 'Transatlantic Print Culture: The Anglo-American Feminist Press and Emerging "Modernities"', in A. Ardis and P. Collier, eds., *Transatlantic Print Culture 1880–1940: Emerging Media, Emerging Modernisms* (Basingstoke: Palgrave Macmillan), pp. 48–65.
'Democrat' (1888) Wellpark F. C. Literary Society M. S. Magazine, 187–88.
'Demoralisation of Native Races by the Liquor Trade' (5 December 1887) *Liverpool Mercury*, 6.
The Devizes and Wiltshire Gazette (1859) *Self-Help* by S. Smiles reviewed, 29 December, 1–2.
Diamond, M. (2003) *Victorian Sensation or the Spectacular, the Shocking and the Scandalous in Nineteenth-Century Britain* (London: Anthem Press).
Dicks, G. (2015) *The John Dicks Press* (Lulu.com).
Dipple, E. (20 April 1851) *Bell's Life in London and Sporting Chronicle*, 1.
Donald, J. (1988) 'How English Is It? Popular Literature and National Culture', *New Formations*, 6, 31–47.
Doudney, S. (8 September 1883) 'A Long Lane with a Turning', *Girl's Own Paper* 193, 769–70.
Doughty, T. (2009) *'Girl's Own Paper'*, *Dictionary of Nineteenth-Century Journalism in Great Britain and Ireland*, Gen. eds. L. Brake and M. Demoor (London: Academic Press).
'Dugal Darroch' (1883–84) Wellpark F. C. Literary Society M. S. Magazine, 43–44.
'Editor's Address to Friends of Anti-Caste' (January 1893) *Anti-Caste*.
ELH 50 (Spring 1983), 155–73.
Ellis, T.R. (1982) 'Burlesque Dramas in the Victorian Comic Magazines', *Victorian Periodicals Review*, 1, 138–43.
1871 England Census, Class: *RG10*; Piece: *3796*; Folio: *8*; Page: *8*; GSU roll: *841901*.
'English Good Templary' (7 April 1885) *Liverpool Mercury*, 3.
The Era (Sunday, 12 February, 1865), 1377.
Erin Go Bragh & Tom Bowling c. 1863–1885 (London: H.P. Such) *Broadside Ballads Online* Edition—Bod11450, Harding B11 (1084), http://ballads.bodleian.ox.ac.uk/static/images/sheets/05000/01975.gif

Even-Zohar, I. (1990) 'The "Literary System"', *Poetics Today*, 11.1, 27–44.
Fahey, D. (1996) *Temperance and Racism: John Bull, Johnny Reb and the Good Templars* (Lexington: University Press of Kentucky).
Fielden, K. (1968) 'Samuel Smiles and Self-Help', *Victorian Studies*, 12.2, 155–76.
Fish, S. (1980) *Is There a Text in This Class?: The Authority of Interpretive Communities* (Cambridge, MA and London: Harvard University Press).
Flanders, J. (2012) *The Victorian City: Everyday Life in Dickens's London* (London: Atlantic).
Flint, K. (1993) *The Woman Reader, 1837–1914* (Cambridge: Cambridge University Press).
Fortier, M. (1997) *Theory/Theatre: An Introduction* (London: Routledge).
Fowles, J. (1969) *The French Lieutenant's Woman* (London: Vintage).
Fraser's Magazine (1860) *Self-Help* by S. Smiles reviewed, June, 778–86.
Fraternity (December 1893), 6–7.
'Free Thinking' (31 March 1892) *Liverpool Mercury*, 1.
Freeman, M. (Autumn 2001) 'Journeys into Poverty's Kingdom: Complete Participation and the British Vagrant, 1866–1914', *History Workshop Journal* 52, 99–121, http://www.jstor.org/stable/4289749, date accessed 12 January 2013.
'Front Matter' (1 November 2005) *Clinical Infectious Diseases*, 41.9, inside front cover, date accessed: 15 August 2013, http://www.jstor.org/stable/4463497
Fryer, P. (1986) *Staying Power: The History of Black People in Britain* (London: Pluto Press).
Fuller, D., and D. Rehberg Sedo (2013) *Reading Beyond the Book: The Social Practices of Contemporary Literary Culture* (New York: Routledge).
Fun (edited by H.J. Byron), Wednesday, 7 June 1882, 891, 235.
Fun (formerly edited by H.J. Byron until 1884), Wednesday, 10 November 1886, 1122, 192.
Fuwa, Y. (1984), 'The Globe Edition of Malory as Bowdlerised Text in the Victorian Age', *Studies in English Literature* (Japan), English Language No., 3–17.
'Gemini' (1887–1888) Wellpark F. C. Literary Society M. S. Magazine [unpaginated, p. 8].
Gissing, G. (1894) *In the Year of Jubilee* (London: The Hogarth Press, 1987).
'A Good Story-Book' (3 October 1885) *Young Folks' Paper* 774, 214–15.
Graebe, M. (2014) '"I'd Have You to Buy It and Learn it": Sabine Baring-Gould, his Fellow Collectors, and Street Literature', in D. Atkinson and S. Roud, eds., *Street Ballads in Nineteenth-Century Britain, Ireland and North America: The Interface between Print and Oral Tradition* (Farnham: Ashgate).
Greenwood, J. (1865) *The Adventures of Reuben Davidger* (London: S.O. Beeton).
——— (1869) *The Seven Curses of London* (London: Rivers).
——— (1873) '"Penny Awfuls"', *Saint Paul's Magazine*, 12, 161–68 (pp. 165–67).

―――― (1874) 'A Short Way to Newgate', in *The Wilds of London* (London: Chatto and Windus), pp. 158–72.
Grenby, M.O. (2000) *The Child Reader, 1700–1814* (Cambridge: Cambridge University Press).
Gunzenhauser, B. (ed.) (2010) *Reading in History: New Methodologies from the Anglo-American Tradition* (London: Pickering & Chatto).
Hall, D.D. (1996) *Cultures of Print: Essays in the History of the Book* (Amherst: University of Massachusetts Press).
Halsey, K. (2009) '"Folk Stylistics" and the History of Reading: A Discussion of Method', *Language and Literature*, 18, 231–46.
Hampshire Advertiser (3 September 1887).
Hanson, C.H. (1882) 'Preface' to *Stories of the Days of King Arthur*, ill. Gustave Doré (London: T. Nelson and Sons).
Harrison, W. (1868) *Special Performances* (London: Thomas Hailes Lacy Acting Edition, Vol. 80 c. 1868).
Hartley, J. (2001) *Reading Groups* (Oxford: Oxford University Press).
Hay, C.W. (1873) 'Told by a Comprador' Belgravia Annual, Christmas number.
Heller, M.A., and W. Schiff (eds.) (1991) *The Psychology of Touch* (New York: Psychology Press).
Hepburn, J. (2000) *A Book of Scattered Leaves* (Lewisburg: Bucknell University Press).
Hewitt, R. (2010) *Map of a Nation: A Biography of the Ordnance Survey* (London: Granta).
Hindley, C. (1871) *Curiosities of Street Literature Comprising 'Cocks,' or 'Catchpennies'* (London: Reeves and Turner).
―――― (1886) *The History of the Catnach Press, at Berwick-upon-Tweed, Alnwich and Newcastle-upon Tyne, in Northumberland, and Seven Dials, London* (London: Charles Hindley (The Younger)).
'Hints on Reading' (1 August 1858) *Monthly Packet* 92, 233–34 (234).
Hitchcock, P. (2001) 'Slumming', in M.C. Sánchez and L. Schlossberg, eds., *Passing: Identity and Interpretation in Sexuality, Race, and Religion*, Sexual Cultures series (New York and London: New York University Press), pp. 160–86.
Holton, S. (2005) 'Kinship and Friendship: Quaker Women's Networks and the Women's Movement', *Women's History Review*, 14, no. 3 & 4, 365–84.
Horrocks, C. (Spring 2003) 'The Personification of "Father Thames": Reconsidering the Role of the Victorian Periodical Press in the "Verbal and Visual Campaign" for Public Health Reform', *Victorian Periodicals Review*, 36.1, 3.
Hume, F. (1888) *Madame Midas* (London: Hansom Cab Publishing Company).
Humpherys, A. (1983) 'The Geometry of the Modern City: G. W. M. Reynolds and *The Mysteries of London*', *Browning Institute Studies*, 11, 70.

———, and L. James (2008) 'Dating Reynolds's Serial Publications', in A. Humpherys and L. James, eds., *G. W.M. Reynolds: Nineteenth-Century Fiction, Politics, and the Press* (Aldershot and Burlington, VT: Ashgate).
Hutcheon, L. (2013) *A Theory of Adaptation*, 2nd ed. (London and New York).
Impey, C. 'Templar Politics', *Village Album*, 29, Alfred Gillett Trust Archive, Street, Somerset.
'Independent Order of Good Templars' (11 April 1885) *Liverpool Mercury*, 6.
The International Survey of Adult Skills 2012: Adult Literacy, Numeracy and Problem Solving Skills in England (2013) Department for Business, Innovation and Skills, UK Government, https://www.gov.uk/government/uploads/system/uploads/attachment_data/file/246534/bis-13-1221-international-survey-of-adult-skills-2012.pdf
Iser, W. (1972) 'The Reading Process: A Phenomenological Approach', *New Literary History*, 3, 279–99.
J. M. B. (2 July 1892) 'The Legend of the Grail', *Girl's Own Paper* 653, 638–89.
'Jabez' (1883–84) Wellpark F. C. Literary Society M. S. Magazine, 21.
Jackson, F. Coppin (1913) *Reminiscences of School Life, and Hints on Teaching* (Philadelphia: A. M. E. Book Concern).
Jackson, L. 'Polytechnic Institution, Regent St', *The Victorian Dictionary*, date accessed: 12 June 2014, http://www.victorianlondon.org/index-2012.htm
Jackson, L. (2014) *Dirty Old London: The Victorian Fight Against Filth* (New Haven and London: Yale University Press).
'Jacobus' (1887–1888) Wellpark F. C. Literary Society M. S. Magazine, 178.
James, L. (1963) *Fiction for the Working Man* (London: Oxford University Press).
——— (2004; online ed. 2008) 'Reynolds, George William MacArthur (1814–1879)', *Oxford Dictionary of National Biography*, date accessed: 11 January 2015, http://www.oxforddnb.com/view/article/23414
——— (2006) 'G[eorge] W[illiam] M[acarthur] Reynolds (1814–79)', in *The Victorian Novel* (Malden, MA, Oxford, and Victoria: Blackwell).
——— foreword to GWM Reynolds (2013) *The Mysteries of London*, Vol. 1 (Kansas City: Valancourt Books).
Jaques, E.T. (1914) *Charles Dickens in Chancery; Being an Account of His Proceedings in Respect of the 'Christmas Carol', with Some Gossip in Relation to the Old Law Courts at Westminster* (London: Longmans, Green and Co.).
Jarvis, A. (1997) *Samuel Smiles and the Construction of Victorian Values* (Stroud, Glos: Sutton Publishing).
Jauss, H.R. (1970) 'Literary History as a Challenge to Literary Theory', translated by E. Benzinger, *New Literary History*, 2, 7–37.
——— (1982) *Toward an Aesthetic of Reception*, translated by Timothy Bahti (Minneapolis: University of Minnesota Press).
Jenkins, A., and J. John (eds.) (2002) *Rereading Victorian Fiction* (Basingstoke and New York: Palgrave).

John Dicks' Catalogue (1874) (London: John Dicks Press).
Johnson, S. (2009) *The Ghost Map* (London: Penguin).
Johnson, D. (2012) *Theatre and the Visual* (Basingstoke: Palgrave Macmillan).
Jones, D. (2012) '"As If the Waters Had but Newly Retired from the Face of the Earth": The Flood in Victorian Fiction', *Literature & Theology* 26.4, 1–20, doi: 10.1093/litthe/frs051, date accessed 8 November 2012.
Jordan, J.O., and Robert L. Patten (eds.) (1995) *Literature in the Marketplace: Nineteenth-Century British Publishing and Reading Practices*, Cambridge Studies in Nineteenth-Century Literature and Culture no. 5 (Cambridge, New York, and Melbourne: Cambridge University Press).
Joshi, P. (2002) *In Another Country: Colonialism, Culture, and the English Novel in India* (New York: Columbia University Press).
Keating, P.J. (1976) 'James Greenwood', in *Into Unknown England, 1866–1913: Selections from the Social Explorers* (Manchester: Manchester University Press), pp. 33–64.
Kellogg, J.L. (2003) 'Introduction', *Arthuriana*, Special issue: Essays on the Arthurian Tradition in Children's Literature, 13.2, 1–8.
Kestner, J. (2003) *Sherlock's Sisters: The British Female Detective, 1864–1913* (Aldershot: Ashgate).
Killeen, J. (2009) *Gothic Literature 1825–1914* (Cardiff: University of Wales Press).
King, A. (2004) *The London Journal, 1845–83: Periodicals, Production and Gender* (Aldershot: Ashgate).
——— (25 August 2013) 'John Dicks, Publisher, and "Dicks' English Library of StandardWorks"', *Greenwich English Prof*.Blogs.gre.ac.uk/andrewking/?p=453
Klancher, J. (1983) 'From "Crowd" To "Audience": The Making of an English Mass Readership in the Nineteenth Century' ELH 50.1 155–73.
Knatchbull-Hugessen, E. (1 July 1888) 'Papers on English Literature: 600–1400 A.D.', 91.
Kneale, J. (2001) 'The Place of Drink: Temperance and the Public, 1856–1914', *Social & Cultural Geography*, 2, 1, 43–59.
Knight, S. (1997) *Continent of Mystery: A Thematic History of Australian Crime Fiction* (Victoria: Melbourne University Press).
——— (2012) *The Mysteries of the Cities: Urban Crime Fiction in the Nineteenth Century* (Jefferson, NC and London: McFarland), pp. 7, 110.
Knowles, J. [as J.T.K.] (1862) 'Preface' to *The Story of King Arthur and His Knights of the Round Table* (London: Griffith and Farran).
Koven, S. (2004) 'Workhouse Nights: Homelessness, Homosexuality, and Cross-Class Masquerades', in *Slumming: Sexual and Social Politics in Victorian London* (Princeton, NJ and Oxford: Princeton University Press), pp. 25–93.
Koven, S. (2006) *Slumming: Sexual and Social Politics in Victorian London* (Princeton and Oxford: Princeton University Press).

Lamont, A. (June 1892) 'By the Gates of the Sea', *The Argosy*, 53, 524.
——— (August 1892) 'That Evensong of Long Ago', *The Argosy*, 54, 170.
Lanier, S. (1881) 'Introduction' to *The Boy's King Arthur: Being Sir Thomas Malory's History of King Arthur and his Knights of the Round Table, edited for boys with an Introduction by Sidney Lanier* (New York: Charles Schrivener's Sons).
Law, G. (2000) 'On Wilkie Collins and Hugh Conway "Poor Fargus"', *The Wilkie Collins Journal*, 3.
Ledger, S. (2007) *Dickens and the Popular Radical Imagination*, Cambridge Studies in Nineteenth-Century Literature and Culture (Cambridge and New York: Cambridge University Press).
Léger-St-Jean, M. *Price One Penny: A Database of Cheap Literature, 1837–1860*. http://www.priceonepenny.info/database/show_periodical.php?periodical_id=27
——— (2012) '"Long for the Penny Number and Weekly Woodcut": Stevenson on Reading and Writing Popular Fiction', *Journal of Stevenson Studies*, 9, 207–32.
Lehmann, H-T. (2006) *Postdramatic Theatre*, translated by Karen Jürs-Munby (London: Routledge).
Leighton, M.E., and L. Surridge (2008) 'The Plot Thickens: Toward a Narratological Analysis of Serial Fiction', *Victorian Studies*, 51.1, 65–101.
'Letters to Some People' (1884) *Punch*, 14 June, p. 280.
'Lexa' (1887–88) Wellpark F. C. Literary Society M. S. Magazine, 21.
'A Literary Bohemia' (April 1868) *The St. James's Magazine*, 1, 431–48. British Periodicals.
'Literary Gossip' (7 July 1888) *The Athenaeum*, 3167, 36.
Liverpool Mercury, 15 April 1884, 6.
Liverpool Mercury, 5 August 1886, 6; 11 August 1886, 6.
Liverpool Mercury, 28 April 1892.
Liverpool Mercury, 22 October 1894.
Lloyd's Weekly Newspaper (Sunday, 10 January 1864), 1103.
Long, E. (2003) *Book Clubs: Women and the Uses of Reading in Everyday Life* (London: University of Chicago Press).
Lumsden, C. (2014) 'Bristo Place Mutual Improvement Society: Victorian Self-help in Action', *The Baptist Quarterly*, 45, 356–68.
Lynch, A. (2004) 'Le Morte Darthur for Children: Malory's Third Tradition', in B.T. Lupack, ed., *Adapting the Arthurian Legends for Children: Essays on Arthurian Juvenilia* (Basingstoke: Palgrave Macmillan).
——— (2010) '"…if indeed I go": Arthur's Uncertain End in Malory and Tennyson', *Arthurian Literature*, 27, 19–32.
MacCallum, M.W. (1894) *Tennyson's Idylls of the King and Arthurian Story from the XVIth Century* (Glasgow: James Maclehose and Sons).
[Mackay, T.] (1888) 'Penny Dreadfuls', *Time*, 19.44, 218–25.

——— (1905) 'Preface' in S. Smiles *The Autobiography of Samuel Smiles* (New York: Dutton).
Macmillan's Magazine (1859) *Self-Help* by S. Smiles reviewed, 1 November, 402–06.
'Madame Midas' (1888) *The Era*, 14 July, 2599, p. 10.
Maidment, B. (2008) 'The Mysteries of Reading: Text and Illustration in the Fiction of G.W.M. Reynolds', in A. Humpherys and L. James, eds., *G.W.M. Reynolds: Nineteenth-Century Fiction, Politics, and the Press* (Aldenham: Ashgate), pp. 227–46.
Malory, Sir T. (2004) *Le Morte Darthur*, edited by Stephen H.A. Shepherd (New York and London: W. W. Norton).
Manby Smith, C. (1857) *The Little World of London; or, Pictures in Little of London Life* (London: Arthur Hall, Virtue and Co.).
Mancoff, D.N. (1995) *The Return of King Arthur: The Legend through Victorian Eyes* (London: Pavilion).
Manguel, A. (2010) *A Reader on Reading* (New Haven and London: Yale UP).
Maunder, A. (2013) 'Sensation Fiction on Stage', in A. Mangham, ed., *The Cambridge Companion to Sensation Fiction* (Cambridge: Cambridge University Press), pp. 52–69.
Maxwell, R. (1992) *The Mysteries of Paris and London*, Victorian Literature and Culture series (Charlottesville and London: University Press of Virginia).
Maxwell, R.C. Jr. (September 1977) 'G. M. Reynolds, Dickens, and the Mysteries of London', *Nineteenth-Century Fiction*, 32.2, 193.
Mayhew, H. (1861) *London Labour and the London Poor*, Vol. I (London: Griffin, Bohn, and Company).
McElroy, D.D. (1952) 'The Literary Clubs and Societies of Eighteenth Century Scotland, and Their Influence on the Literary Productions of the Period From 1700 to 1800', unpublished doctoral thesis, University of Edinburgh.
McGill, M. (2007) *American Literature and the Culture of Reprinting, 1834–1857* (Philadelphia: University of Pennsylvania Press).
McHenry, E. (2002) *Forgotten Readers: Recovering the Lost History of African-American Literary Societies* (Durham, NC: Duke University Press).
——— (2011) '"An Association of Kindred Spirits": Black Readers and their Reading Rooms', in S. Towheed, R. Crone, and K. Halsey, eds., *The History of Reading* (London and New York: Routledge), pp. 310–22.
Meisel, M. (2007) *How Plays Work: Reading and Performance* (Oxford: Oxford University Press).
'Mercury' (1888) Wellpark F. C. Literary Society M. S. Magazine.
Michel, J.-B., Shen, Y.K., Presser Aiden, A., Veres, A., Gray, M.K. et al. (2011) 'Quantitative Analysis of Culture Using Millions of Digitized Books', *Science*, 331, 176–82.
Mighall, R. (1999) *A Geography of Victorian Gothic Fiction: Mapping History's Nightmares* (Oxford: Oxford University Press).
'mij' (1883–84) Wellpark F. C. Literary Society M. S. Magazine.

Millington, E.J. 'King Arthur and his Knights, with the Legend of the Sancgrael', *Monthly Packet* 99 (1 March 1859)—159 (1 March 1864).
Miss Lucy Long & Travelling Tinker. c. 1845 (London: J. Sharp) *Broadside Ballads Online*, Edition—Bod12505, Harding B11(2442), http://ballads.bodleian.ox.ac.uk/static/images/sheets/05000/03343.gif
Mitch, D.F. (1992) *The Rise of Popular Literacy in Victorian England* (Philadelphia: University of Pennsylvania Press).
Mitchell, W.T. (1986) *Iconology: Image, Text, Ideology* (Chicago and London: University of Chicago Press).
Mitchell, S. (1994) 'Girls' Culture: At Work', in C. Nelson and L. Vallone, eds., *The Girl's Own: Cultural Histories of the Anglo-American Girl (1830–1915)* (Athens: University of Georgia Press), pp. 243–58.
'Mohamet and the Koran' (12 August 1892) *Lux*.
Moody, J. (1999) 'Illusions of Authorship', in T. Davis and E. Donkin, eds., *Women and Playwriting in Nineteenth-Century Britain* (Cambridge: Cambridge University Press), pp. 99–124.
'Moral Guide' (August 27 1892).
Morning Post (October 7 1887).
Moretti, F. (1998) *Atlas of the European Novel, 1800–1900* (London and New York: Verso).
Morris, R.J. (1981) 'Samuel Smiles and the Genesis of Self-Help: The Retreat to a Petit Bourgeois Utopia', *The Historical Journal*, 24.1, 89–109.
———— (1986) 'Introduction: Class, Power and Social Structure in British Nineteenth Century Towns', in R.J. Morris, ed., *Class, Power and Social Structure in British Nineteenth-century Towns* (Leicester: Leicester University Press), pp. 2–22.
———— (1990) 'Clubs, Societies and Associations', in F. M. L. Thompson, ed., *The Cambridge Social History of Britain 1750–1950* (Cambridge: Cambridge University Press).
Moruzi, K. (2009) *'The Monthly Packet'*, *Dictionary of Nineteenth-Century Journalism*.
———— (2010) '"Never Read Anything that Can at all Unsettle Your Religious Faith": Reading and Writing in the *Monthly Packet*', *Women's Writing*, 17.2, 288–304.
Moulder, P.E. (1913) 'The Morals of the Coming Generation', *Westminster Review*, 180.3, 299–301.
'Mr Balsir Chatterton's Company' (1889) *The Era*, 12 January, 2625, p. 4.
'M. S.' Farewell' (1883–84) Wellpark F. C. Literary Society M. S. Magazine, pp. 39–42.
———— 'And They Shall Spring Up as Among the Grass, as Willows by the Watercourses. Isa 44, 45' (1883–84) Wellpark F. C. Literary Society M. S. Magazine, pp. 39–42.

Mulock Craik, D. (1884) *An Unsentimental Journey Through Cornwall* (London: Macmillan and Co.).
Murphy, A. (2008) *Shakespeare for the People: Working-class Readers, 1800–1900* (Cambridge: Cambridge University Press).
Murray, H. (2002) *Come, Bright Improvement! The Literary Societies of Nineteenth-Century Ontario* (Toronto: University of Toronto Press).
Murray, S. (2011) *The Adaptation Industry: The Cultural Economy of Literary Production* (London and New York: Routledge).
——— and A. Weedon (2011) 'Beyond Medium Specificity: Adaptations, Cross-Media Practices and Branded Entertainments', *Convergence: The International Journal of Research into New Media Technologies*, 17.1, 3–5.
The Mystery of a Hansom Cab (2012) dir. Shawn Seet (Australia: Australian Broadcasting Corporation, Roadshow Entertainment) DVD.
Nash, W. (1990) *Language in Popular Fiction*, The Interface Series (London and New York: Routledge).
Nead, L. (2000) *Victorian Babylon: People, Streets and Images in Nineteenth-Century London* (New Haven and London: Yale University Press).
'New Leaves' (1888) *Fun*, 29 August, 48, p. 96.
'New Novels' (1888) *The Graphic*, 29 September, 983, p. 354.
'News of the Day' (March 2 1889) *Liverpool Daily Post*.
North American Review (1860) *Self-Help* by S. Smiles reviewed, 187, 562–63.
'Notices to Correspondents' (1 December 1862) *Monthly Packet* 144, 668.
'Notices to Correspondents' (1 May 1865) *Monthly Packet* 173, 559.
'Notices to Correspondents' (1 September 1884) *Monthly Packet* 45 (Second Series), 298.
O'Brien, E.L. (Summer 2001) "Every Man Who Is Hanged Leaves a Poem": Criminal Poets in Victorian Street Ballads by Ellen L. O'Brien in *Victorian Poetry*, 39, 2.
O'Connell, S. (1999) *The Popular Print in England: 1550–1850* (London: British Museum Press).
OECD (2016) 'Adult Literacy', *Innovation in education*. Organisation for EconomicCo-operation and Development, date accessed: 13 November 2015, http://www.oecd.org/edu/innovation-education/adultliteracy.htm
OECD and Statistics Canada (2000) *Literacy in the Information Age*, http://www.oecd.org/edu/skills-beyond-school/41529765.pdf
Okey, T. (1930) *A Basketful of Memories: An Autobiographical Sketch* (London: Dent).
'An Old Pupil' (1888) 'My Experience of Boarding Schools', Wellpark F. C. Literary Society M. S. Magazine, 53–66.
'Orion' (1883–84) Wellpark F. C. Literary Society M. S. Magazine, 43–44.
———. (1883–84) Wellpark F. C. Literary Society M. S. Magazine, [unpaginated preface].

Orsmond Payne, E. (26 November 1892) 'The Women of the "Idylls of the King"', *Girl's Own Paper* 674, 143–44.
[Anon.] review of *Paid in Full* (Sunday, 12 February 1865) *The Era*, 1377.
'P. T. Jr.' (Peter Thamson, Jr.) (1883–84) Wellpark F. C. Literary Society M. S. Magazine, 147.
Pall Mall Gazette (Friday, 24 November 1876), 3672, 10.
Pall Mall Gazette (26 February 1887).
Pall Mall Gazette (1 December 1888), 4.
Pall Mall Gazette (4 December 1888), 11.
Palmer, B., and A. Buckland (eds.) (2011) *A Return to the English Common Reader: Print Culture and the Novel 1850–1900* (Farnham and Burlington: Ashgate).
Parins, M. (1987) 'Introduction' to *Sir Thomas Malory: The Critical Heritage*, edited by Parins (London: Routledge).
Pearson, J. (1999) *Women's Reading in Britain, 1750–1835: A Dangerous Recreation* (Cambridge: Cambridge University Press).
Pearson, R. (2007) '"Twin Sisters" and "Theatrical Thieves": Wilkie Collins and the Dramatic Adaptation of *The Moonstone*', in A. Mangham, ed., *Wilkie Collins: Interdisciplinary Essays* (Newcastle upon Tyne: Cambridge Scholars Publishing), pp. 208–21.
––––––– (2015) *Victorian Writers and the Stage: The Plays of Dickens, Browning, Collins and Tennyson* (Basingstoke: Palgrave Macmillan).
Perkins, L.M. (February 2000) 'Coppin, Fanny Jackson', date accessed: 2 November 2015, http://www.anb.org/articles/09/09-00202.html, *American National Biography Online*.
Personal (1944) 'Georgiana R. Simpson', *The Journal of Negro History*, 29.2, 245–47.
Peterson, L.H. (2009) *Becoming a Woman of Letters: Victorian Myths of Authorship, Facts of the Market* (Princeton, NJ and Woodstock: Princeton University Press).
Peterson's Magazine (1860) 'Review of New Books', March, 251–52.
Phillips, W. (1864) *The Woman in Mauve* (London: Thomas Hailes Lacy Acting Edition, Vol. 76, c.1867).
Pittard, C. (2011) *Purity and Contamination in Late Victorian Detective Fiction* (Aldershot: Ashgate).
'The Press of the Seven Dials' (1856) *Chambers's Journal of Popular Literature, Science and Arts*, 130, 401–05. ProQuest British Periodicals.
Price, L. (2000) *The Anthology and the Rise of the Novel: From Richardson to George Eliot* (Cambridge: Cambridge University Press).
––––––– (2012) *How to Do Things with Books in Victorian Britain* (Princeton: Princeton University Press).
'Promises of Help in Distribution' (March 1889) *Anti-Caste*, 4.

'R. S.' (1883–84) Wellpark F. C. Literary Society M. S. Magazine.
Radcliff, C.J. (1986) 'Mutual Improvement Societies in the West Riding of Yorkshire, 1835–1900', *Journal of Educational Administration and History*, 18, 1–16.
Radcliffe, C. (1997) 'Mutual Improvement Societies and the Forging of Working-Class Political Consciousness in Nineteenth-Century England', *International Journal of Lifelong Education*, 16, 141–55.
Radway, J. (1984) *Reading the Romance: Women, Patriarchy, and Popular Literature* (Chapel Hill: University of North Carolina Press).
Ranking, B.M. (1870) *La Mort D'Arthur: The Old Prose Stories whence the "Idylls of the King" have been taken by Alfred Tennyson* (London: J. C. Hotten).
The Reasoner (1860) *Self-Help* by S. Smiles reviewed, 25 March, 101–02.
'Rev. Orishatukeh Faduman, Pastor at Troy, NC and Principal of Peabody Academy' (1909) *American Missionary*, 63, 2.
Rhys, E. (1886) *Malory's History of King Arthur and the Quest of the Holy Grail* (London: Walter Scott).
Rodgers, B. (2012) 'Competing Girlhoods: Competition, Community and Reader Contribution in *The Girl's Own Paper* and *The Girl's Realm*', *Victorian Periodicals Review*, 45.3, 277–300.
Rose, J. (1992) 'Rereading the English Common Reader: A Preface to a History of Audiences', *Journal of the History of Ideas*, 53.1, 47–70.
——— (2001) *The Intellectual Life of the British Working Classes* (New Haven, CT: Yale University Press).
Ryland, F. (October 1888) 'The Morte D'arthur', *The English Illustrated Magazine*, 61, 55–64.
Salmon, E. (1888) *Juvenile Literature As It Is* (London: Henry J. Drane).
Sanders, J. (2006) *Adaptation and Appropriation* (London and New York: Routledge).
'Sardanapalus' (1888) Wellpark F. C. Literary Society M. S. Magazine, 102.
Scott, C., and C. Howard (1891) *The life and reminiscences of E. L. Blanchard* (London: Hutchison & co.).
'Search Passages in English Literature' (1 June 1888) *Atalanta* 9, 532.
'Search Questions in English Literature' (1 February 1890) *Atalanta* 29, 334.
A Selection of Valentines from the John Johnson Collection of Printed Ephemera (2010) (Oxford: Bodleian Library, University of Oxford), http://www.bodleian.ox.ac.uk/__data/assets/pdf_file/0009/81387/season-for-love-leaflet.pdf
Shannon, M.L. (2014) 'Spoken Word and Printed Page: G. W. M. Reynolds and "The Charing-Cross Revolution", 1848', *19: Interdisciplinary Studies in the Long Nineteenth Century*, 18, 7.
——— (2015) *Dickens, Reynolds, and Mayhew on Wellington Street: The Print Culture of a Victorian Street* (Farnham and Burlington, VT: Ashgate).

Shepard, L. (1969) *John Pitts: Ballad Printer* (London: Private Libraries Association).
Shipton, H. (1 February 1895) 'A Romance of Chivalry', 528.
Sinclair Bell, E. (1966) 'Appendix: The Publishing History of Fergus Hume's *The Mystery of a Hansom Cab*', in D. Craigie, G. Greene, and E.A. Osborne, *Victorian Detective Fiction: A Catalogue of the Collection Made by Dorothy Glover and Graham Greene* (London: Bodley Head), pp. 123–26.
Sinnema, P. (2002) 'Introduction', in *S. Smiles Self-Help: With Illustrations of Character, Conduct, and Perseverance* (Oxford: University Press).
Skinner, T. Surr (1801) Splendid Misery (T. Hurst).
Smiles, A. (1956) *Samuel Smiles and His Surroundings* (London: Robert Hale).
Smiles, S. (1858) *Life of George Stephenson: Railway Engineer*, 5th ed. (London: Murray).
——— (1862) *Lives of the Engineers*, 1st Vol. (London: Murray).
——— (1905) *The Autobiography of Samuel Smiles* (New York: Dutton).
——— (2002) *Self-Help: With Illustrations of Character, Conduct, and Perseverance* (Oxford: Oxford University Press).
Smith, A. (1848) *The Struggles and Adventures of Christopher Tadpole at Home and Abroad* (London: Richard Bentley).
Southey, R. (1817) 'Preface' to Sir Thomas Malory, *The Byrth, Lyf, and Actes of Kyng Arthur; of his noble knyghtes of the rounde table, theyr merveyllous enquestes and adventures [...] With an Introduction and Notes by Robert Southey, Esq.*, [edited by William Upcott], 2 vols. (London: Longman, Hurst, Rees, Orme, and Brown).
Springhall, J. (1998) 'Penny Theatre Panic: Anxiety over Juvenile Working-class Leisure', in *Youth, Popular Culture and Moral Panics*, pp. 11–37.
——— (1998) *Youth, Popular Culture and Moral Panics: Penny Gaffs to Gangsta-Rap, 1830–1996* (New York: St. Martin's Press), pp. 42–43.
St. Clair, W. (2004) *The Reading Nation in the Romantic Period* (Cambridge: Cambridge University Press).
Stamper, J. (1960) *So Long Ago* (London: Hutchinson).
Steinbach, S.L. (2012) *Understanding the Victorians: Politics, Culture, and Society in Nineteenth-Century Britain* (London and New York: Routledge).
Stephens, M.D., and G.W. Roderick (1970) 'A Passing Fashion in Nineteenth Century English Adult Education: The Camborne Debating and Mutual Improvement Society', *Paedagogica Historica: International Journal of the History of Education*, 10, 171–80.
——— (1974) 'Nineteenth Century Education Finance: The Literary and Philosophical Societies', *Annals of Science*, 31, 335–49.
Stevens Powell, W. (1986) *Dictionary of North Carolina Biography*, Vol. 2 (Chapel Hill: University of North Caroline Press).
Stevenson, R.L. (1888) 'Popular Authors', *Scribner's Magazine*, 4.1, 122–28.

Stewart, S. (1993) *On Longing: Narratives of the Miniature, the Gigantic, the Souvenir, the Collection* (Durham and London: Duke University Press).
Stone Peters, J. (2000) *Theatre of the Book 1480—1880: Print, Text, and Performance in Europe* (Oxford: Oxford University Press).
'The Story of Music Hall; The Origins of Music Hall', *Victoria and Albert Museum*, http://www.vam.ac.uk/content/articles/t/the-story-of-music-halls/
Strachey, Sir E. (1868) 'Preface' to Sir Thomas Malory, *Morte Darthur. Sir Thomas Malory's Book of King Arthur and his Noble Knights of the Round Table. The Original Edition of Caxton Revised for Modern Use* (London: Macmillan and Co.).
Sturrock, J. (2006) 'Establishing Identity: Editorial Correspondence from the Early Years of *The Monthly Packet*', Victorian Periodicals Review, 39.3, 266–79.
Summers, M. (7 November 1942) 'John Dicks, Publisher', *Times Literary Supplement*, 552.
Sunderland Daily Echo and Shipping Gazette (28 September 1891).
Supplement to *Anti-Caste* (January 1890).
Supplement to *Anti-Caste* (January 1891), 4.
'survey, v.', 3, 4a, and 4b, in *Oxford English Dictionary*, date accessed: 15 August 2013, www.oed.com
'Syllabus 1883–84' (1883–84) Wellpark F. C. Literary Society M. S. Magazine, 147.
Tait's Edinburgh Magazine (1860) *Self-Help* by S. Smiles reviewed, 27, 552–55.
Taylor, T., and C. Reade (1852) *Masks and Faces* (New York: Samuel French, 1860).
'Ten Books' (1 June 1886) *Monthly Packet* 66, 594–95.
Tennyson A. to James Thomas Knowles, 10 December 1861 in (1987) *The Letters of Alfred Lord Tennyson*, edited by Cecil Y. Lang and Edgar F. Shannon, Jr., 3 vols. (Cambridge, MA: University of Harvard Press).
Tennyson, E. (1981) *Lady Tennyson's Journal*, edited by James O. Hoge (Charlottesville: University Press of Virginia).
'The Theatres' (1864) *The Saturday Review*, 19 November, 18, 631–32.
'Third Shelf. Notes and Queries' (1 November 1896) *Monthly Packet* 549, 589–90.

Thomas, T. (1996) Introduction to GWM Reynolds, *The Mysteries of London*, edited by T. Thomas (Keele: Keele University Press).
Thompson, E.P. (1963) *The Making of the English Working Class* (London: Victor Gollancz Ltd.).
[Anon.] (1 May 1871) 'Thoughts on Mr Tennyson's Poem of "The Holy Grail"', 65.
Tomkins, A. (2010) 'Greenwood, James William (bap. 1835, d. 1927)', *Oxford Dictionary of National Biography*, date accessed: 13 November 2015, http://www.oxforddnb.com/view/article/41224.

Towheed, S. (ed.) (2011) *The History of Reading. Volume 3: Methods, Strategies, and Tactics* (Basingstoke: Palgrave Macmillan).
——— and W.R. Owens (eds.) (2011) *The History of Reading. Volume 1: International Perspectives c. 1550–1990* (Basingstoke: Palgrave Macmillan), p. 2.
Travers, T. (1977) 'Samuel Smiles and the Origins of "Self-Help": Reform and the New Enlightenment', *Albion: A Quarterly Journal Concerned with British Studies*, 9.2, 161–87.
Trendafilov, V. (2015) 'The Origins of *Self-Help*: Samuel Smiles and the Formative Influences on an Ex-Seminal Work', *The Victorian*, 3.1.
Tyrrell, A. (1970) 'Class Consciousness in Early Victorian Britain: Samuel Smiles, Leeds Politics, and the Self-Help Creed', *Journal of British Studies*, 9.2, 102–25.
——— (1970) 'The Origins of a Victorian Bestseller—An Unacknowledged Debt', *Notes and Queries*, 17.9, 347–49.
——— (2000) 'Samuel Smiles and the Woman Question in Early Victorian Britain', *Journal of British Studies*, 39.2, 185–216.
UK Reading Experience Database (RED) http://www.open.ac.uk/Arts/reading/UK/
Venables Vernon, M. (1 March 1897) 'The Tale of Balin and Balan, from Sir Thomas Malory's *Morte D'Arthur*', *Atalanta*, 343–48.
Vincent, D. (1989) *Literacy and Popular Culture: England 1750–1914* (Cambridge: Cambridge University Press).
Visram, R. (2002) *Asians in Britain: 400 Years of History* (London: Pluto Press).
Vlock, D. (1998) *Dickens, Novel Reading and the Victorian Popular Theatre* (Cambridge: Cambridge University Press).
Walkley, A.B. (1892) 'The Novel and the Drama', *Novel Review*, 121, 21–29.
Warren, L. (2000) '"Women in Conference": Reading the Correspondence Columns in *Woman*, 1890–1910', in L. Brake, B. Bell, and D. Finkelstein, eds., *Nineteenth-Century Media and the Construction of Identities* (London: Palgrave), pp. 122–34.
Watson, L. (8 September 1894) 'A Modern Mistake' [Chapter 2], *Girl's Own Paper* 767, 778–79.
Webb, R.K. (1955) *The British Working-Class Reader, 1790–1848* (London: George Allen and Unwin).
Wellpark F. C. Literary Society M. S. Magazine (1883–84) 428697© CSG CIC Glasgow Museums and Libraries Collection: The Mitchell Library, Special Collections.
Wellpark Free Church Young Men's Literary Society. Session 1883–84 [1883] (Dennistoun, Glasgow: Robertson).
Westmoreland Gazette etc. (1865) 'Plagiari'.
'What Boys Read' (1886) *Fortnightly Review* NS 39, 248–59.
'What Girls Read' (1886) *Nineteenth Century* 20, 515–29.

White, R. (January–June 1897) 'Elves, Knights and the Great King' [6 parts], 551–56.
Wilson, C. (1995) *The Invisible World: Early Modern Philosophy and the Invention of the Microscope*, Studies in Intellectual History and the History of Philosophy (Princeton: Princeton University Press).
'A Wonderful Book' (17 November 1888) *The Huddersfield Chronicle and West Yorkshire Advertiser*, 6645, 3.
Worthen, W.B. (2003) 'The Imprint of Performance', in W.B. Worthen and P. Holland, eds., *Theorizing Practice: Redefining Theatre History* (Basingstoke: Palgrave Macmillan).
Wynne, D. (2001) *The Sensation Novel and The Victorian Family Magazine* (Basingstoke: Palgrave Macmillan).
Yonge, C.M. (1855) *The Heir of Redclyffe*, 2 vols. (Leipzig: Bernhard Tauchnitz).
[Yonge], 'Conversations on the Catechism: The Flesh', *Monthly Packet* 5 (1 May 1851), 328–43.
────── 'Cameos of English History: Arthur of Brittany' (1 May 1854), 41.
Zorrica, P. (1887–1888) 'The Sea Nymphs', Wellpark F. C. Literary Society M. S. Magazine, 193–96.

INDEX

A

Abandondino, The Bloodless, 194–5
Aborigines' Friend, 78
Aborigines' Protection Society (APS), 78
abridgement, 107n15
Arthurian legend, 40
Adams, William Henry Davenport [1828–91], 181n29
adaptation
  authorized,
  in context of postmodern cultural landscape, 174
  decontextualisation, 188
  experiences of, 9, 123, 166–8, 172–9, 188
  illegal,
  indications of discrete qualities, 176
  loose, 175
  shifting cultural forms, 191, 195
adaptation studies, 166, 174
Adelaide Gallery, 149

adultery, 44
  censorship of portrayal of, 44
adult literacy, 112
  Victorian England, 124n1
advertising
  democratic mixing in, 103
  Dicks' English Novels, 97, 99, 100, 103
  Dicks' Standard Plays, 97, 99–103, 107n14, 109n30
  illustrated, 11
  reprint series, 93–110
  societal influence of, 13
Africa, 75, 78, 82
  European colonization of, 75
African-American literature, 69n6
African-American readers, 82
  working-class, 82
African Methodist Episcopal Church, 79, 85
  Women's Home and Foreign Missionary Society, 85

Ainsworth, William Harrison [1805–82], 100, 119, 181n19
à Kempis, Thomas [c.1380–1471], 122
Alice, or the Mysteries, 103, 197n22
allegories, 38
Altick, Richard Daniel [1915–2008], 1, 13n1, 25, 54, 55, 58, 68n3, 71n24, 96, 97, 100, 149, 161n18
Amateur's Guide, 193
Amateur Theatre, 187
amphibious literary matter, 166
amusement, 12, 140, 179
  mid-Victorian forms of, 12
Amusements of the Moneyless, 140, 141
An Awful Tragedy, 64, 65
Anti-Caste
  black readers of, 80–8
  black Victorians and, 75–92
  distribution, 79, 80, 85, 90n16
  establishment of, 76–8, 89n1
  international readership, 76
  readership, 5, 76, 78–80, 88–9
  renamed *Fraternity*, 76
  subscribers, 78–82, 84, 85, 91n26
  transnational editorial aims of, 86
Antipodes, 178
  representation of life in, 178
anti-revolutionary propaganda, 135
anti-slavery campaigners, 78
Arabian Nights, The, 37
Areopagitica, 66
Armstrong, Isobel, 150, 152, 158, 161n21, 163n55
Arthurian legend
  abridgement and/or expurgation, 40, 44
  appeal to boys, 39
  censorship, 44
  female characters in, 36, 39
  magazine articles inspired by, 36, 38–42, 45–7
  rendered into modern English, 43
  artwork, 53, 55, 56, 59
Atalanta, 40, 49n28
Atalanta Scholarship and Reading Union, 40, 50n42
Athenaeum, 19, 29n26, 29n28
audience, 2–10, 12, 13, 20–2, 26, 35–8, 46, 67, 85, 86, 95, 99, 104, 115–17, 122, 132, 140, 147, 152–3, 165–8, 170–2, 179, 183–4, 186, 189–91, 193, 194
  etymological roots of word, 190
audience experiences
  cross-media, 174–8
  dramatized novels, 166, 175, 176
auditorium, 172, 173
  darkened, 173
Australia, 79
  Victorian depictions of, 178
Australian Broadcasting Corporation, 179
authorship, 45
  contested in performance culture, 193
autobiographical romancing, 121
autobiography, 16, 95, 98
  working-class, 16, 95, 98
Autobiography (Smiles), 17, 24, 29n30, 30n34, 30n45

B
Backdrops, 189, 193, 194
Baden-Powell, Sir Robert Stephenson Smyth [1857–1941], 36
bad reading, 18, 21
Bailey, Samuel [1791–1870], 19
Balsir Chatterton, Frederick [1834–86], 174
Band of Hope, 77
Banham, Christopher, 114, 126n10, 126n14

Barbara Allen, 138
Baring-Gould, Sabine [1834–1924], 142, 145n30
Barnaby Rudge, 100
Barrett, Daniel, 189, 196n13
Barrie, Sir James Matthew [1860–1937], 177, 182n32
Barry, Rev. William Francis [1849–1930], 47, 52n71
Baudrillard, Jean [1929–2007], 190, 196n19
Bay of Biscay, 133
Beck, Philip, 167, 171
Beeton, Isabella Mary [1836–65], 25
Beeton, Samuel Orchart [1830–77], 113
Belgravia Annual, 193, 197n28
bias, 121
   class, 121
bibliographical coding, 7
bi-media cultural commodities, 167, 170–4
biographies, 17, 19, 22, 25, 26, 30n46
   demonstrating success, 26
Birmingham, W., 136
Birt, T., 133, 135, 136
Black British readers, 5
Black British working-class, 83
Black Ey'd Susan, 193
Blackface Minstrelsy, 135, 136
Black Victorians
   Anti-Caste and, 75–92
   evidence of in cities, 88
   geographies of, 75–92
Black, William [1841–98], 65
Blanchard, Edward Litt Leman [1820–89], 114, 160n6
Bleiler, Everett Franklin [1920–2010], 147, 159n4
Bluebeard pantomime, 195
Bodleian Broadside Ballads collection, 135

Bohn's libraries, 96
book-buying, 117
   1840s London, 117
book distribution, 94
   revolutions in, 94
book-lending, 117
   1840s London, 117
Book of Household Management, 25
book of the moment status, 175
book reviews, 16, 21, 22
books, 1, 4, 11–13, 16–26, 33–9, 41, 42, 46, 53–7, 65, 66, 94, 97, 112, 117, 119, 123, 147–9, 165–72, 174–6, 178, 179
   humanizing influence of, 26
Bookseller, 97, 105n1, 159n1, 168, 175
Boucherette, Jesse [1825–1095], 25
Boucicault, Dionysius Lardner [1820/1822–90], 194
Bow Bells, 94, 97, 99, 100, 103, 109n34
Box and Cox, 195
boys, 6, 10, 11, 24, 33–52, 95, 111–13, 116–19, 122–3, 135, 138
   appeal of Arthurian legend to, 34
Boy's King Arthur: Being Sir Thomas Malory's History of King Arthur and his Knights of the Round Table, 34, 48n8
Boys of England, The, 38, 114, 116, 126n10
Boy's Own Magazine, 38
Boy's Own Volume, The, 113–14
Braddon, Mary Elizabeth [1835–1915], 49n24
Bradley, Matthew, 3, 13n5, 107n19
Bratton, Jacky, 186, 196n6
Bressey, Caroline, 5, 7, 75–92
Brett, Edwin John [1827–95], 114, 126n10

Briggs, Asa [1921–2016], 23, 28n11, 30n42, 30n43
Brindley, James [1716–72], 15, 21, 26, 27
  lack of reading ability, 15
British Empire, 75, 78, 86
  racial discrimination, 75
Britton, John [1771–1857], 18
Broadside Ballads Online, 135
Bronco Bill, 122
Brontë, Charlotte [1816–55], 38
Brotherton, Joseph [1783–1857], 22
Brunton, William, 193, 197n28
Buchanan, Robert Williams [1841–1901], 177
Buckland, Adelene, 3, 13n6, 13n7
Bulwer-Lytton, Edward George Earle [1803–73], 103, 126n11, 148
burlesques, 187, 193, 194
Burne-Jones, Edward Coley [1833–98], 38
Burns, Robert [1759–96], 65–6, 136
Burt, Thomas [1837–1922], 95
Buxom Young Tailor, The, 142
Byron, Henry James [1835–84], 40, 185, 191–4, 196n21, 197n29, 197n31, 197n32
  complex intertextual references in works of, 191
By the Gates of the Sea, 64

C
Called Back, 168
Campbell, Thomas [1777–1844], 65, 133
capitalism, 17
Captain is Not A-Miss, The, 193
Carlyle, Thomas [1795–1881], 66
Carnegie, Dale Harbison [1888–1955], 23
Carpenter, Kevin, 119, 128n35

Carrick Castle, Loch Goil. A Holiday Reminiscence, 60–1
cartoons, 149, 161n20
Carver, Stephen James, 160n10
Cassell's Family Paper, 115, 116, 118
casting, 13, 194
Catnach, James [1792–1841], 132, 133
Caulfield, Octavia (Mrs Jacob Christian), 84
Cawelti, John G., 120
Cellier, Alfred [1844–91], 174
censorship, 44, 51n52
  Arthurian legend, 44
Chadwick, Sir Edwin [1800–90], 151
Chambers Edinburgh Journal, 70n18, 104
Chamber's Journal, 139
Channing, William Ellery [1818–1901], 23, 30n41
character moulding, 24
characters, 4, 17, 21, 24, 36, 38, 39, 41, 43, 45, 63, 108n22, 120, 148, 152–6, 159, 162n37, 165, 168, 171, 172, 175, 177, 184, 185, 189, 191, 192
  resurrections of, 153
Charge of the Light Brigade, The, 37
Charles O'Malley, 103
Chartier, Roger, 27n3, 29n24, 125n3
cheap novels, 114
  format, 114
cheap reprints
  circulation, 94, 98
  readership, 5, 94, 104
Cherry, Andrew [1762–1812], 133
Chevy Chase, 138
Child, Francis James [1825–96], 142, 145n33
children, 29, 33, 36, 37, 40, 84, 86, 115, 118, 120, 121, 138, 140, 156

reading preferences, 37
Children in the Wood, 138
children's reading, 37, 120
  selective partiality, 118
cholera epidemic (1848), 151
Christian Evidence Society, 76, 82
Christian, Jacob, 82–9
Christian Leader, The, 65, 66
Church Music, 67
circularity, 179
  cross-media, 179
circulation, 9, 33–4, 38, 39, 78–9, 94, 98, 171, 174
  cheap reprints, 94, 98
Civil rights campaign, 81
Clare, John [1793–1864], 141
Clarke, Eliza, 79
class bias, 121
class friction, 186
Clementina Clemmins, 136
cliff-hangers, 123
  episodic, 123
climactic moments, 176
  revelation of book's in dramatization, 176
Cobb, Sylvanus [1823–87], 120
Colclough, Stephen [1969–2015], 3, 50n40, 68n1, 70n9, 73n55, 107n20
collaboration, 170
  theatre, 170
collaborative reading, 55, 184, 193, 195
Colleen Bawn, The, 177, 194
Collins, William Wilkie [1824–89], 98
Colman, George [1762–1836], 101
colonisation, 75
  Africa, 75
colour, 66, 76, 77, 82–4, 177, 189
  use of, 189
colour caste, 76
coloured seamen, 83

Comic, 195
comic opera, 65, 66
comic relief, 177
  high drama and, 177
comic songs, 66, 136
  marital violence in, 136
communal reading, 54, 67, 69n8
compound consumption, 179
consensus classification, 58
  social class, 58
consumers, 2, 5, 8–10, 35, 47, 167, 171–6, 178, 179, 190, 192
  marginalization of, 8–9
content migration, 170
Conversations on the Catechism, 41–2, 44, 50n45
Conway, Hugh. *See* Fargus, Frederick John
Cooper, Anna Julia Haywood [1858–1964], 81, 100
Cooper, Frederick Fox, 109n30
Coppin, Fanny Jackson [1837–1913], 79, 81, 85, 86, 91n24, 91n41
copyright, 96, 99–101, 103, 171
  securing, 171
Copyright Act (1842), 187
Corfe, Isabel, 6, 7, 9–11, 131–45
correspondence columns, 39, 70n18
  magazines, 39, 70n18
Couch, Rev. T.R., 79
Courtenay, Christabel, 37
cover illustration, 169
  Madam Midas, 169
Craik, Dinah Maria (Dinah Maria Mulock) [1826–87], 49n23, 49n26
crime, 122, 134, 137, 154, 155, 167
  street ballads heavily reliant on, 134
crime-related news, 122
criticism. *See* literary criticism
cross-disciplinary reading, 184
cross-media

audience experiences, 166, 167, 174–8
circularity, 179
consumption, 176, 179
navigating experiences of, 175, 179
Cruse, Amy [1870–1951], 12
Crystal Palace Dramatic Fete, 192
cultural experience, 9, 10, 88, 166
cultural form
  sensationalism as, 184, 191, 195
  shifting in adaptations, 184, 191
culture
  conception of what constitutes, 5
  Victorian audiences' consumption of, 4–7, 9, 165
Cunningham, Alison [1822–1913], 116
Curiosities of Street Literature, 143n1, 144n18

D
Daily Mail, 66
daily penny newspapers, 137
  comparison with street ballads, 137
Daly, Nicholas, 166, 180n3
Dark Days, 168
darkened auditorium, 173
Darnton, Robert Choate, 2, 13n2
Darwin, Charles Robert [1809–82], 16
Deadwood Dick, 122
Death of Nelson, The, 135
decontextualisation, 188
  adaptations, 188
De Grey, Una, 38, 49n28
Demon of the Sea, 136
de Troyes, Chrétien, 46
D. Green's 'Cheap Books', 96
Dickens, Charles John Huffam [1812–70], 95, 103, 105, 109n29, 123, 126n11, 147, 148

'Dicks' English Novels', 97, 99, 100, 103, 106n14
  advertising, 97, 99, 100, 103
Dicks, Guy, 98, 100, 105, 106n12
Dicks, John Thomas [1818–81], 5, 94–6, 98–101, 104, 105
  biographical details, 95
Dicks's Library of Standard Works, 99, 106n11
Dicks's Penny Shakespere, 97, 98
Dicks's reprint series, 94–9, 101, 104, 105, 106n8
  exports, 105
Dicks's Standard Plays
  advertising, 97, 99–102
  Othello, 97
discrimination, 8, 75, 86, 120, 156
  perceived lack of, 87
display, 10, 44, 53, 117, 120–2, 188, 189
  penny dreadfuls, 10, 121, 122
disposable reading matters, 178
dispossession, 119
  feelings of, 119
dissemination forms of newspapers, 139
distribution, 56, 79–81, 85, 94, 122, 139
  economics of,
Divine Providence Lodge (South Shields), 82
Doherty, Ruth, 5–7, 10, 11, 147–163
domestic drama, 187, 193
Doom of the Dancing Master, The, 103
Doudney, Sarah [1841–1926], 50n35
Douglass, Frederick Augustus Washington [1813–95], 81, 90n8
Dramatic Author's Society, 193
dramatic rights, 171
dramatic texts. *See* playscipts
dramatization
  conventions of, 171, 173, 175, 177

music demonstrating critical moments of novels, 173
revelation of climactic moments, 176
tonal recoding, 177
Dress Reform Society, 81
dying speeches, 39, 132, 134, 137
street ballads, 132, 134, 137

E
early years reading, 119, 172
East Ward Mechanics Institute, 20
Edited for Boys, 34
education, 17, 36, 59, 68n4, 112, 121, 124, 141
working-class, 19, 112
Education of the Working Classes (Lecture), 19
Edwards, Celestine [1858–94], 76, 79, 81, 82, 85, 86, 88
E. Hodges, Printer, 137
Eily O'Connor, 194
Eliot, George (Mary Ann Evans) [1819–80], 47
Eliot, Simon, 3
Eliot, Thomas Stearns [1888–1965], 38
Emerson, Ralph Waldo [1803–82], 23, 30n41
empire building, 104
Engelsing, Rolf, 16
English Common Reader, The, 1, 3, 13n1, 25
Englishness, 104
notion of, 104
engravings, 97, 113, 117, 123, 138
entertainment, 6–10, 66, 140, 141, 167, 177
mid-Victorian forms of, 6, 8, 167
episodic cliff-hangers, 123
epistolary exchanges (fictional), 43
Era, The, 171, 178, 180n8, 181n17

Erin Go Bragh, 135
Erin's children, 137
theme of, 137
Ernest Maltravers, 103
escapist reading, 112
class differences, 112
essay competitions, 36, 40
essays, 2–9, 11, 12, 36, 39, 40, 52n70, 53–6, 59, 62–5, 67, 77, 117, 119, 120, 148
Essays on the Formation of Opinions, 19
Estlin, Mary Anne [1820–1902], 79
Europe, 77
African colonisation, 75
Every Girl's Magazine, 40
Every Man a Winner, 23
evidence, 2, 7, 11, 13, 35–7, 47, 53–5, 70n10, 88, 95, 98, 112, 121, 132, 133, 135, 136, 138, 142, 147, 172, 184, 185, 195
black lives in Victorian cities, 88
executions, 131, 133, 134, 140
exports, 105
Dicks' Reprint Series, 105
expurgation, 44
Arthurian legend, 44

F
Faduma, Orishatukeh (William Stevens Powell), 81, 90n21
Faery Queen, 33
Fahey, David M., 90n6, 91n29
Fairchild, E.G., 83
fairy tales, 41
familial ties, 186
theatre, 186
Family Herald, 115
family networks, 79
farces, 185, 187–9, 193
Fargus, Frederick John [1847–85] (Hugh Conway), 168
female characters, 36, 39

Arthurian legend, 36
feminists, 78
Fenians, 137
  street ballads about, 137
Fenn, Amor, 40
Fenn, George Manville [1831–1909], 103
Fiction. *See also* novels
  varieties of light, 6
  window moment in, 158
  fictional epistolary exchanges, 43
Fish, Stanley Eugene, 59
Flint, Kate, 35–6, 49n16
folk stylistics, 7, 59–67, 68n2, 72n28
  methodology, 53, 67
For a Woman's Sake, 97
Fordyce, T., 136
foreign languages, 16, 18, 19
  learning in leisure time, 18
format, 97, 98, 109n31, 114, 121–3, 127n17, 135, 137, 152–3, 168, 170, 172–3, 178, 188, 191, 193
  cheap novels, 114
formulaic literature, 120
Fortey, W.S. (Printer and Publisher), 135, 137
Fortier, Mark, 185, 196n5
Fortune, Timothy Thomas [1856–1928], 78
Fowles, John Robert [1926–2005], 180n1
Frankenstein, 94
  sale of Dicks' reprint, 94
Fraser's Magazine, 15, 27n1, 29n25
Fraternity, 76, 80–2, 85, 87, 91n28
  Anti-Caste renamed, 76
French Lieutenant's Woman, The, 165, 180n1
French Revolution, The, 38
French, Samuel [1821–98], 187
From "Crowd" to "Audience": The Making of and English Mass Readership in the Nineteenth Century, 104
From Ritual to Romance, 47
Fun, 182n34, 195, 197n23
Fura, Yuri, 44

G
gallows literature, 132, 136–8, 143n1
Gamester, The, 98–9, 101
Garner, Katie, 5, 7, 33–52
Gender-specific style, 65
generic categorization, 191
Geoffrey of Monmouth [c.1100–c.1155], 46
Gilderoy was a Bonnie boy, 138
girls, 25, 33–52, 81, 108n21, 112, 136, 154
  expectations of in society, 43
Girl's Own Paper, The, 39, 40, 43, 45, 50n36
Gissing, George Robert [1857–1903], 12
good reading, 18, 21
gothic drama, 187
grammar, 18, 67
  correction by critics, 67
Grand Lodge of England, 83
Graphic, The, 177, 188n10
Greenwood, James [c.1683–1737], 10, 111, 113, 114, 116, 118, 122, 125n4, 126n13, 128n31
Grenby, Matthew, 36, 49n19
gruesome covers, 121
  penny dreadfuls, 121
Gunzenhauser, Bonnie, 7, 13n8

H
Hail to the Tyrol, 136
Hall, Donald, 21, 30n35
Halsey, Katie, 2, 60, 65, 68n2, 72n28

Hamlet, 101
handwriting, 67
hangings, 123, 132, 141, 158
high-profile, 134
Hansom Cab Publishing Company, 167–8
Hanson, Charles Henry, 34, 47, 48n9, 52n72
Hard Times, 100, 103
Harrington, Charles, 186
Harrison, Wilmot, 195n4
Haultain, Theodore Arnold [1857–1941], 3–4, 6
Hayward, William Stephens [1835–70], 117, 120
Hazlewood, Colin Henry [1823–75], 103, 109n34
H. Disley, Printer, 137
Heir of Redclyffe, The, 41, 42, 50n44
Hemyng, Samuel Bracebridge [1841–1901], 120, 127n17
Hersert de la Villermarqué, Vicomte Théodore Claude Henri [1815–95], 46
Hidden Hand, The, 170, 176, 181n13
Hidden Worth, 192
high drama, 177
comic relief and, 177
high-profile hangings, 134
Hindley, Charles, 132, 137, 143n3, 144n18
Hints on Self-Help: A Book for Young Women, 25
History of Reading, The, 2
History of Sir Thomas Thumb, The, 41
Hogarth House, 114
Holcraft, Thomas [1745–1809], 101
Holmes, Sarah, 134
horizon of expectations, 8, 59, 60
Household Words, 98, 187
How to do Things with Books in Victorian Britain, 12, 73n57

How to Read, 4, 15–31, 151–4
How to Win Friends and Influence People, 23
Hume, Fergusson Wright [1859–1932], 9, 167, 168, 174–7, 181n16
Humpherys, Anne, 5, 7, 93–110
Husband's Dream, 136
Hutcheon, Linda, 174, 181n25
hybrid texts, 170

I
identity, 67, 89, 153, 183
  notions of, 183
Idylls of the King, 37, 39, 40, 47
illegal adaptation,
illiteracy, 113, 119
  Victorian England, 113
illustrated periodicals, 115, 122
illustrated serials, 111
illustrations
  moral panic over, 122
  perceptions generated by, 118
image, 64, 80, 118, 121, 132, 149–52, 158, 168, 170, 185, 186, 188, 190
  dialectic struggle between word and, 190
immersive reading, 179
imperialism, 5, 75, 76
  influence of, 78
Impey, Catherine [1847–1923], 76–80, 82, 84, 85, 87, 89n5, 90n8
imprint, 190
  performance, 196n16, 197n35
"inappro-priate" educational ambition, 36
Independent Methodist Free Church (Macclesfield), 83–4
individual development, 18

through good reading, 18
industrial modernity, 16, 17, 24, 26, 27
  relationship with *Self-Help*, 16, 17, 24, 26, 27
Industrial Revolution, 16
  success of *Self-Help* linked to, 16
information, 24, 25, 39, 53–5, 57, 151, 153, 157, 158
  contained in *The Mysteries of London*, 151, 153, 157, 158
Ingaretha, 103
Institute for Colored Youth, 81
International Order of Good Templars (IOGT)
  segregated branches in United States, 85
  Toxteth Lodge, 85
International Right Worthy Grand Lodge, 84
interpretive community, 59
  historically-contingent, 59
intertextual references, 191
  in works of H.J. Byron, 191
In the Year of Jubilee, 12, 13n11
  plot summary, 12
intra-media experiences, 165
investigative journalism, 113
Irish Jem, the Ambassador, 134
Iron Chest, The, 101
Iser, Wolfgang [1926–2007], 59, 71n27
Italy, 24
  popularity of *Self-Help* in, 24

J
Jack Sheppard, 119, 172
Jack Wright, 122
Jacob Faithful, 103–4
Japan, 24
  popularity of *Self-Help* in, 24
Jauss, Hans Robert [1921–97], 8, 13n9, 59

Jerrold, Douglas William [1803–57], 193
Jeu d'Esprit, Abandondino, 195
John Dicks' English Classics, 94, 107n14, 110n37
John Dicks Press, 93, 94, 96, 105, 106n12
John, Juliet, 3, 13n5
Johnson, Dominic, 189–90, 196n15
journalism, 7, 113, 184
journals, 22, 77, 78, 80, 104, 121–2, 187, 188, 195
  increase in cheap, 104
juvenile fiction, 36, 115
juvenile readers, 36–40

K
Kellogg, Judith L., 36, 49n17
King, Andrew, 99, 184
King Lear, 98, 101
Kinship networks, 78, 90n12
K.J. Ford, Printer, 137
Klancher, Jon, 104
Knight, Stephen, 153, 160n7, 162n34, 180n7
Knowles, James Thomas [1831–1908], 33–8, 41, 48n5, 49n20
Koran, 24, 86

L
Lacy's Acting Edition of Plays
  control over dissemination, 195
  limited availability of, 195
  scope of, 194
  Sensational Series, 192, 196n22
Lacy, Thomas Hailes [1809–73], 6, 183–97
Lady Audley's Secret, 192
Lamentation for the four unfortunate Men at Manchester, 137
Lamont, Alexander, 62, 64, 70n14

Lanier, Sidney Clopton [1843–81], 34, 48n8
last dying speeches, 132, 134
sales of, 132
Last Rose of Summer, 133
Leckie, Barbara, 4, 7, 15–31
Leeds Mutual Improvement Society, 19
Legend of Sir Galahad, The, 41–3, 45, 51n47, 51n50
Léger-St-Jean, Marie, 6, 10, 11, 111–29
legitimacy, 77, 183, 187
  notions of, 183
Leigh, H.S., 195
letters, 16, 19, 24, 25, 30n46, 36, 39, 40, 77–9, 87, 100, 114, 141, 185
Lever, Charles James [1806–72]
licensing, 187, 188
  playscripts, 187
life writing, 7
literacy, 10, 18, 26, 94, 113, 119, 124n1, 125n3, 141
  level of, 18
Literary adoption, 19
Literary criticism
  correct forms of, 61
  correction of grammar, 67
  from literary society members, 7, 55
  penny dreadfuls, 98
  political and religious beliefs, 62, 63
  slang, 62, 63
  style and morality intermixing, 60, 62
  taste, 18, 61
  vulgarity, 62, 63
literary knowledge, 40
  emphasis on for self-improvement, 40
literary societies

  in context of socio-cultural environment, 56, 58
  criticism from members, 55
  North America, 54, 55
  Ontario, 54
  prevalence in nineteenth century, 65, 67
  Scotland, 54, 55
  literary status, 187
  playscripts, 187
literature, 6, 7, 9, 11, 18, 28n23, 40, 43, 54, 70n18, 94–7, 99, 101, 103–5, 109n29, 111, 113–16, 120, 123, 131–3, 135–41, 148, 165–8, 177, 189
Liverpool, 82–6, 88, 89, 136, 184
  seamen's accommodation, 83, 84, 86, 88
Liverpool Daily Post, 87
Liverpool Mercury, 83–5, 91n31
Lives of the Engineers, 26, 31n55
Livingstone, David [1813–73], 18
Lloyd, Edward [1815–90], 114
Lloyd's Penny Weekly Miscellany, 115
London
  dirty water of, 149
  microscopic survey of, 147–63
London Journal, 115, 120
London Labour and the London Poor, 116, 127n21, 143n2, 144n9, 145n25
London Pioneer, The, 115
London Society, 184, 193
London Water Companies, 149, 150
Long Lane with a Turning, A, 39, 50n35
loose adaptation, 175
Lord Chamberlain's Office, 127n18, 186, 188
Lucy Long, 136
Lux, 76, 82, 85, 88
Lyons, Albert Edwin, 23

M
Macbeth, 116
MacCallum, Mungo William [1854–1942], 34, 48n11
Mackenzie, Peter, 80
Mackenzie, W.F., 79
Madame Midas
 consumer experience of, 167, 172
 cover illustration, 169
 dramatic rights, 171
Madame Midas: The Gold Queen, 175–6
 plot of, 175–6
magazines
 boys and girls, 38
 correspondence columns, 39, 70n18
Malen, M.E.O., 103
Malins, Joseph [1844–1926], 77, 83
Malory, Sir Thomas [c.1415–71], 33–42, 44, 46, 47
Mancoff, Debra N., 34, 43, 48n12, 51n49
Mann, C.A.J., 65, 66, 79
Man's Shadow, A, 182n32
manuscript books, 55, 68
 by non-professional readers, 55
manuscript magazines, 5, 53–73
 communal aspect of, 56, 60
map production, 152
marginalia, 16
Mariner's Friend Lodge (London), 82
Mariner's Lodge (Glasgow), 82
marital violence, 136
 in comic songs, 136
Marryat, Captain Frederick [1792–1848], 68, 103
Marxist commodity theory, 190
Masks and Faces, 185, 186
Masse, Solomon, 82, 88
Massinger, Philip [1583–1640], 100, 101
mass literacy, 94

beginnings of, 94
mass market, 93
 emerging, 93
Mass Readership, 104
Master Timothy's Book-Case, 117
Mattacks, Kate, 6–9, 11, 183–97
Maunder, Andrew, 166, 180n4
Mayhew, Henry [1812–87], 116, 127n21, 132, 134–6, 138, 140–2, 143n2, 144n9, 145n25
McHenry, Elizabeth, 69n6, 90n11
Meade, L.T. (Elizabeth Thomasina Meade Smith) [1844–1914], 40
meaning, 8, 68, 119, 186, 190
 making of reading, 173
Mechanics Institutes, 20, 25
 perceived deficiencies in, 54
media
 convergence, 167–70
 nineteenth-century, 1–3, 5, 7, 8, 53–5, 58, 60, 68, 88, 94, 98, 104, 116, 121, 151, 158, 166, 170, 186
 shifts in, 172–3
medieval literature, 5
Meisel, Martin, 194, 197n30
Melbourne, 105, 167, 176, 178, 179
 Victorian depictions of, 167, 178
melodrama, 9, 95, 98, 101, 103, 167, 170, 173, 177, 187
 characteristics of, 9, 95
Mendacious Mariner; or, Pretty Poll of Portsea and the Captain with His Whiskers, The, 193
Merchant of Venice, The, 101
Merry Wives of Windsor, 101
Metropolitan Board of Works, 151
microscope, 149–54, 156
 potential of, 10
microscopic survey, 147–63
 purpose of, 153
Miller and His Men, The, 95

Millington, Ellen J., 46, 52n68
Mill, John Stuart [1806–73], 16
Mill on the Floss, The, 38
Milton, John [1608–74], 66
Missionary Travels, 18
Mitchell, Sally, 36, 50n33
Mitchell, W.T., 190, 196n18
modern english, 43
  Arthurian legend rendered into, 45
Modern Painters, 38
Monster soup, 149, 150, 154
Montgomerie Ranking, B., 35
Monthly Packet of Evening Readings for the Younger Members of the English Church, 38
Moody, Jane, 193, 197n26
Moore, Edward [1712–57], 98, 101, 103, 108n28
Moore, Thomas [1779–1852], 133, 135
Morality, 60, 62, 64
  conflation with style, 60
moral panic, 122
  over illustrations, 122
Morte d'Arthur, Le
  appeal to women, 38
  various editions of, 33, 34, 37, 44–6
Moruzi, Kristine, 44, 46, 51n59, 52n69
Mossell, Nathan T., 79
Mount Royal, 37, 49n24
Mudie, Charles Edward [1818–90], 3
Mudie's Circulating Library, 187
multi-media, 168
multisensory dynamics, 190
  performance, 190
Murray, Heather, 54, 69n7
Murray, Simone, 170, 181n14
music, 9, 43, 56, 59, 60, 67, 173, 189, 191
  demonstrating critical moments of dramatization, 173

mutual improvement societies, 5, 19, 53–5
  greatly understudied, 54
My Days have been so wondrous Free, 138
Mysteries of London, The
  drama of, 157
  information contained in, 157, 158
  methods of sale, 147
  as microscopic survey, 147–63
  narrative qualities, 152
  rhetoric devices in, 159
  summary of plot, 68
Mysteries of the Court of London, The, 93–4, 116–17
Mystery of a Hansom Cab, The, 167, 168, 179, 182n40
  television film adaptation, 179

N
Naoroji, Dadabhai [1827–1917], 86–7
narrative cohesion, 187–9
  playscripts, 187
national progress, 18
  through good reading, 18
nautical drama, 187
Negro Mission Committee, 77
Negro Race and Darwinism, The, 86
News, 44, 80–2, 85, 117, 122, 131, 138, 141
  street ballads as method of disseminating, 141
Newsagents' Publishing Company, 114
Newspapers
  correlation between street ballads and price of, 131, 141
  decline in price of, 139
  forms of dissemination, 139
newsvendors, 10, 112, 113, 117

New Way to Pay Old Debts, A, 100, 101
New York Age, 78
Nicholas Nickleby, 100
Night and Morning, 103
nineteenth century studies, 186
Nix, my Dolly, 136
nomenclature, 58
 no uniform system of social class, 58
non-competitive strategies, 186
 theatre, 186
nonverbal signs, 185
North America
 enthusiasm for *Self-Help* in, 23
 literary societies, 54, 55
Northern Star, 96
notations, 188
 promptscripts, 188
Novel and Drama, 172
Novels
 audience experiences of dramatized, 166, 167, 174
 cross-fertilization between Victorian theatre and dramatizations, 8
 less frequently cited in references, 66

O
occupations, 57, 58, 86
 types indulged in by literary society members, 57, 58
Okey, Thomas [1852–1935], 95
old Erin, 137
 theme of, 137
Oliver Twist, 100
One Summer's Night in Munich, 174
On Liberty, 16
Ontario, 54
 literary societies in, 54
On the Origin of Species, 16
Open University, 123

oral tradition, 141, 142
 roots of penny fiction in, 153
Ordnance Survey
 derivation of name, 151
 mapmaking, 10, 151, 152
Orr, Sarah, 81
oscillatory consumption, 175
Othello, 97
 Dicks's Standard Plays, 97
Owens, W.R. (Bob), 2

P
pacifists, 78
page, 17, 26, 36, 38, 39, 45, 46, 56, 60, 61, 63, 76, 88, 97, 99, 112–14, 117–23, 138, 148, 152, 155, 157, 168, 171, 172, 178, 185, 189, 192
 interconnection with stage, 168, 171
Paid in Full, 188, 197n27
Pall Mall Gazette, 91n42, 92n45, 95
Palmer, Beth, 3, 13n6
Pan-African Conference (London 1900), 81
pantomime scripts, 187
paper duty, 138
 abolition of, 138
Parins, Marylyn, 44, 51n57
Paris Sketchbook, 103
Parnell, Thomas [1679–1718], 138
Parzival, 47
pastiche, 194
patent theatres, 184
Peale, Norman Vincent [1898–1993], 23
Pearson, Jacqueline, 35, 49n15
Pearson, Thomas, 133
penny bloods, 112, 114, 115, 123, 124, 125n2
penny dreadfuls

INDEX   233

characteristics of, 111
criticism of, 114
displays of, 112, 113, 117, 120–2
gruesome covers, 121
ways of reading, 116, 117, 120, 121
window shopping reading, 111–29
penny fiction, 113, 115, 118, 120, 122
roots in oral tradition, 153
penny gaffs, 123, 140
Penny Illustrated Paper, 138
Percival, the Story of the Grail, 39
performance
   dynamics, 188
   imprint of, 190
   multisensory dynamics of, 190
   traversing between print and, 170
   typical mid-Victorian, 184
performance culture, 193
   author contested term in, 193
periodicals
   experimentation with in Victorian England, 115
   illustrated, 115, 122
   new mid-Victorian, 184
   Victorian, 78
periodical studies, 184
Permanent Aid Society, 83
personal change, 17
Peters, Julia Stone, 189, 196n14
phased reading, 173
Phillips, Watts [1825–74], 97, 107n16, 183–6, 196n8
Photo Bits, 122
Pickwick Papers, The, 103, 165
piecemeal reading, 173
Pirate of the Isles, 136
pirating, 136
   street ballads, 136
Pitts, John [1765–1844]
   plagiarisms, 114
   in *Self-Help*, 16–17, 19, 20

plaster-mould stereotyping, 133
playhouses. *See* theatres
Playing to Win, 103
playscripts
   fluidity, 188
   legitimacy of, 187
   licensing, 187, 188
   literary status assigned to, 187
   narrative cohesion, 187–8
   precipitating stage production, 191
   publishing and marketing, 187
   read through, 188
playtexts, 6, 9, 184–6, 192, 195
playwrights, 103, 183, 188, 191, 192
   control over work, 188
pleasure reading, 175
Pocock, Isaac [1782–1835], 95
poetry, 37, 47, 53, 55, 59, 61–2, 65, 66, 122, 184
Police Budget, 122
Police News, 122
political beliefs, 62, 63
   literary criticism, 39
political identity, 89
   developing women's, 88–9
Poor Dog Tray, 133
Poor Jack, 66
Popplestone, Charles Edward, 23
pornography, 122
Portsmouth branch (SRBM), 82, 88
postmodernism, 165, 174
Power of Positive Thinking, The, 23
Prest, Thomas Peckett [1810–59], 95
Price, Leah, 12, 30n36, 68, 73n57
Princess of Thule, A, 66
print culture, 2, 4–6, 10, 11, 16, 25, 93, 94, 141, 142, 167, 168, 178, 179
   inexpensive, 10
printers' catalogues, 133, 135
print(ing)
   advances in, 2

consumption of amidst wider media environment, 8–12
revolutions in, 94
traversing between performance and, 170
Prisoner of Zenda, The, 174–5
private reading, 60, 141
professional readers, 16–23
progressive radicals, 78
promptscripts, 188
provincial theatre companies, 189
psychological narratives, 188
psychological self-fashioning, 24
psychology of terror, 184
publication, 4–5, 16, 19–21, 42, 56, 76, 78, 79, 85, 93–5, 97–101, 114–17, 132, 133, 136–8, 148, 167, 171, 179
  announcement of imminent, 171
public hangings, 133, 141
public story-tellers, 117
publishers, 34, 93, 95, 105, 114, 115, 117, 123, 167, 170
publishing, 5, 94–7, 100, 101, 105, 122, 168, 187, 195
  new Victorian, 5, 97, 122, 187, 195
Punch, 168, 171, 184
Pye-Smith, Philip Henry [1839–1914], 18

Q
Quakers, 78, 81, 90n12
Quest of the Sangrael, 38, 46
quotations
  emphasis on reviews of *Self-Help*, 22
  purpose of, 66

R
racial discrimination, 6
  Anti-Caste first periodical countering, 75

racial prejudice, 76, 78, 80, 83–7, 89
  seamen, 83
racial segregation, 76
radicalism, 17
Ransom, J. Clinton, 23
Reade, Charles [1814–84], 185, 186, 196n7
readers
  responses, 25, 59
  self-reflective, 120
readership
  Anti-Caste, 78–80
  categorization of, 21
  cheap reprints, 5, 93–110
  Self-Help, 15–31
  solitary, 10, 184
reading
  aloud, 10, 25, 60, 116–18, 123, 155
  changes in material available for, 121
  collaborative, 55, 184, 195
  communal, 54, 67
  cross-disciplinary, 184
  discontinuous, 26, 27
  early years, 119
  evidence of, 11
  good and bad, 18, 21
  modes of, 19, 116, 177, 183
  multi-media, 168
  networks, 88, 89
  nineteenth-century practices, 1, 55, 67, 111, 116, 121, 165
  objectives of, 2, 11, 55, 179
  phased, 173
  piecemeal, 173
  for pleasure (*see* (pleasure reading))
  private, 60, 141, 184
  societies, 55, 67–8
  solitary, 10, 173, 184
  theatre writing, 183–97
  valued in *Self-Help*, 18–22

INDEX   235

variations in experiences of, 172, 174
Victorian compared to modern-day television, 39
Victorian consumption, 3–7
women, 35–6
working-class, 98, 105
reading ability, 6
socio-economic differences in, 6
Reading and the Victorians, 3
reading communities, 56, 67, 75, 80, 81, 88–9
importance to women, 75
Reading Experience Database (RED), 3, 7, 123
reading preferences, 37
children, 37
Reading Revolution, 16
read through, 41, 123, 188
playscripts, 188
references
purpose of, 81–2
types of work cited, 8, 9, 56, 66
Reid, Fred, 61
religious beliefs, 62, 63
literary criticism, 39
Remember the glories of Brian the Brave, 135
Renunciation, The, 62
reprint series, 5, 93–110
re-reading, 56, 179, 190, 193
Research Society for Victorian Periodicals (RSVP), 122–3
resurrections, 153–4
characters, 153
Return to the Common Reader: Print Culture and the Novel 1850–1900, The, 3
Reynolds, George William MacArthur [1814–79]
how to read, 151–4
legacy, 147

The Mysteries of London as microscopic survey, 147–63
prodigious output, 10, 147
Reynolds' Miscellany, 93–4, 115
Reynolds Weekly Newspaper, 94
Rhetoric devices, 153, 159
Mysteries of London, The, 153, 159
Rhys, Ernest Percival [1859–1946], 35, 48n14
Rivals, The, 186
R. March and Co, 135
Road to Ruin, The, 101
Robinson Crusoe, 37
romance, 6, 34–7, 39, 41, 42, 45, 117, 120
perceived as feminine, 35
Rookwood, 136
Rooney, Paul Raphael, 1–13, 165–82
Rosa Lambert, 104
Rosebud of Stingingnettle Farm, 192
Rose, Jonathan, 25, 31n51, 94, 98, 104n8, 105n3, 107n21, 147, 159n5
Ross, Charles Henry [1835–97], 99, 103, 108n22
Royal Literary Fund, 111, 126n12
Royal Polytechnic Institution, 149
Royalty Considered, 62, 64
Ruddigore, 66
Ruskin, John [1819–1900], 38
Ryland, Frederick, 34, 35, 37, 47
Rymer, James Malcolm [1814–84], 118, 120

S
Saint Paul's Magazine, 10, 111
Salisbury, Lord Robert Arthur Talbot Gascoyne-Cecil [1830–1903], 86, 87
racial prejudice of, 87
Salmon, Edward, 37, 49n21

sanitation, 151
  concerns about, 151
Scarborough Tragedy, The, 134
scenery, 121, 189, 192
scenic backdrops, 178
scented tableaux lights, 190
Scotland, 54, 55, 76
  literary societies in, 54, 55
Scott, Sir Walter [1771–1832], 18, 65, 66, 98, 141
scouting/guiding, 36
Scribner's, 111
Seaman's Mission (London), 79
seamen, 84, 86, 88
  racial prejudice, 83
Seamen's accommodation, 88
  Liverpool, 88
Seamen's Grievances meetings, 85
Search Questions in English Literature, 40
Sedger, Horace, 192
selective partiality, 118, 120
  children's reading, 120
self-advancement, 18
  dulled by bad reading, 18
Self-Help
  easy to read, 24
  emphasis on quotation in reviews, 22
  enthusiasm for in North America, 23
  fragmentary character of, 21
  how to read, 15–31
  international appeal of, 16, 21
  objectives of,
  plagiarism in, 16–17, 19
  readership, 16, 21, 23, 25
  readers' responses to, 21, 23
  reading valued in, 18–22
  relationship between industrial modernity and, 24
  reviews of, 15, 16, 20–2
  rich text for readership studies, 16
  structure of, 21
  style of, 19
  success linked to industrial modernity, 17
  translations, 16, 24
self-help genre, 16
self-identity, 18
  weakened by bad reading, 18
self-improvement, 19, 43
  emphasis on literary knowledge for, 19
Self-Made Reader, The, 25
self-reflective readers, 120
Self-Starter, The, 23
sensational drama, 183–97
  scripts, 186–7, 191
sensationalism, 184
  as cultural form, 184
sensational literature, 9, 97, 177
sensational representation, 183
Sensational Series, 192
  Lacy' s Acting Edition of Plays, 186–91
Sensation Dramas for the Back Drawing Room, 193, 195
Sensation Fiction on the Stage, 166
sensory dynamics, 190
Sentence of Death on Michael Barrett for the Clerkenwell Explosion, 137
seriality, 112, 123
  background to, 123
serials
  fiction, 113, 147–8, 184, 195
  illustrated, 111–29
Sessions, Frederic, 79, 85
sex, 36, 122
  depictions of, 122
sexual relations, 44
  censorship of portrayal of, 44
Shakespeare, 40, 65, 66, 95, 97, 98, 101, 103, 118, 119
  mid-Victorian working-class readers of, 95
Shakespeare's texts, 101

penny, 118
Shannon, Mary L., 153, 155, 161n32, 162n43
Shaw, George Bernard [1856–1950], 189
Shepard, Leslie [1917–2004], 137, 140, 144n19
Sheridan, Richard Brinsley Butler [1751–1916], 66, 186
shilling shockers, 168, 178
Shirley, 38
Short Way to Newgate, A, 114
silent spectatorship, 173
Simpson, Georgiana Rose [1866–1944], 81, 90n23
Sinnema, Peter, 17, 28n9
Skeleton Crew, or, Wildfire Ned, The, 114
Sketchy Bits, 122
slang, 18, 62, 63
  literary criticism, 62
Small, Alexander, 62
smell, 190
  stimulating sense of, 190
Smiles, Samuel [1812–1904], 4, 5, 15–31
Smith, Albert Richard [1816–60], 117
Smith, Charles Manby, 132, 140, 143n4, 145n24
Smith, John Frederick [1806–90], 120
social advancement, 24, 58
social class
  disagreement on classification, 58
  divisions, 151
  escapist reading, 112
  literary society use and, 58
  upward mobility, 22
social conditions, 3, 184, 185
socialists, 78
social media, 132
  street literature equated with, 132
societal influence, 13
  advertising, 13

Society for the Recognition of the Brotherhood of Man (SRBM), 76, 82, 88
  Portsmouth branch, 82, 88
  socio-cultural context, 7
  socio-economic differences, 6
  reading ability, 6
  solitary reading, 10
  somatic reaction, 184
  sorrowful lamentations, 132
  sales of, 132
Southern hemisphere, 178
  depiction of, 178
Southey, Robert [1774–1843], 33, 46, 48n1, 66
South Sea Bubble, The, 100
South Shields Divine Providence Lodge, 82
Special Performances, 185
spectatorship
  modes of, 177
  silent, 173
Splendid Misery, 103, 104n34
Springhall, John, 115, 126n16
stage
  adaptations, 166–8, 178, 179
  interconnection with page, 168, 171
  practice, 194
stage directions, 188, 189, 194
  increasingly spectacular, 194
Stamper, Joseph, 121, 122, 128n46
stamp tax, 138
  repeal of, 138
St Clair, William, 94, 105n2
Stead, William Thomas [1849–1912], 95
Stearns, Elizabeth, 114, 126n14
stereotyping, 96, 133
Sterling, John [1806–44], 18, 116
Stevenson, Robert Louis Balfour [1850–94], 6, 11, 111–29
  serialisation of autobiographical reminiscences, 111, 121

Stewart, Susan, 158, 162n54
Story of King Arthur and His Knights of the Round Table, The, 33
Strachey, Sir Edward [1812–1901], 34, 44–6, 48n10, 51n53
  censorship of Arthurian legend, 34
Strange Case of Dr Jekyll and Mr Hyde, 112
Strangers and Pilgrims, 185
Stranger's Nook, The, 64
Stranger, The, 101, 154
street ballads
  comparison with daily penny newspapers, 137
  correlation between price of newspapers, 138–9
  dying speeches, 132, 137
  early form of tabloid press, 131, 132
  Fenian, 137
  heavily reliant on crime, 134
  nineteenth-century England, 131–45
  pirating, 136
  printed format, 135
  range of experiences in, 141
  scope of, 9
  structure of,
street literature, 131–3, 135, 137, 141
  equated with social media, 132
Struggles and Adventures of Christopher Tadpole at Home and Abroad, The, 117, 127n24
style
  conflation with morality, 60
  gender-specific, 65
  stylistic concerns, 60, 61, 65, 67
stylistics, 60, 61, 64, 65, 67, 68, 148
subtitle, 176
  introduction of, 176
Successful Man in his Manifold Relations with Life, The, 23

Summers, Augustus Montague [1880–1948], 96–7, 103, 105, 106n13
Sunday Closing Bill, 84

T
tabloid press, 9, 131, 132
  street ballads early from of, 131, 132
Talfourd, Sir Thomas Noon [1795–1854], 187
taste, 15, 18, 26, 61, 62, 95, 139, 143, 186
  literary criticism, 61
Taylor, Tom [1817–80], 170, 185, 196n7
television, 123, 141, 166
  Victorian reading compared to modern-day, 39
Temperance and Racism, 82, 91n29
temperance movement, 76–7, 82, 84, 86, 89
  transatlantic, 82
Templar, 77, 82
Tennyson, Alfred [1809–92], 65
Thackeray, William Makepeace [1811–63], 103
Thames water, 149–50
theatre
  cross-fertilization between Victorian novels and, 8
  darkened auditorium, 173
  non-competitive strategies, 186
  nonverbal signs, 185
Theatres Act (1847), 184
Theatre, The, 174
theatre writing
  producing, 186–91
  reading, 183–97
The Gloaming of the Year, 64

The Lamentation and Last Farewell to the World of Michael Barrett, 137
There's a good Time coming, Boys, 135
Thing theory, 7, 190
Thomas, P.P., 96
Thomas, Trefor, 148, 156, 160n9
Thompson, Benjamin, 101
Thompson, Edward Palmer [1924–93], 57–8, 71n23
Time, 177
Tit-Bits, 66
Tobin, John [1770–1804], 101, 109n33
tonal recoding, 177
dramatization, 177
Toole, John Lawrence [1830–1906], 192–3
topical balladry, 141
topography, 10
illuminating representation of, 10
touring theatre companies, 189
Toussain L'Ouverture, François-Dominique [1743–1803], 81
Towheed, Shafquat, 2–3, 13n3
Toxteth Aid Society, 84
Toxteth Lodge, IOGT, 84, 85, 89
translations, 16, 24, 47, 81
Self-Help, 16, 24
Treasure Island, 112

U
Uncle Tom's Cabin, 194
Under the Earth, or, the Sons of Toil, 100
United States
racial discrimination, 75
segregated branches of International Order of Good Templars (IOGT) in, 82, 85
temperance movement, 77, 82, 86

Unknown Public, The, 98, 105
Unsentimental Journey Through Cornwall, An, 37
upward mobility, 22

V
Valancourt Press, 148
value, 18, 60, 61, 133, 134, 166, 183, 187, 189, 190, 193
notions of, 61, 183
Varney the Vampire, 95
vegetarians, 78
Verne, Jules Gabriel [1828–1905], 35
Vernon, Maud Venables, 40, 50n41
Victorians and their Books, The, 12
Viles, Rymer, & cie, 118
Villanous Squire and the Village Rose, The, 192
Vincent, David, 96
violence, 6, 36, 136
depictions of, 122
visual stimulation, 177, 178
visual-verbal convergences, 11
Vlock, Deborah, 184, 195n1
vulgarity, 62
literary criticism, 62

W
Walkley, Arthur Bingham [1855–1926], 172, 181n20
Waverly Novels, 98
Webb, R.K., 95, 96
Wedding Bells, 114
Weedon, Alexis, 170, 181n15
Weiss, Lauren, 4, 5, 7, 53–73
Wellpark Free Church Young Men's Literary Society
age range of membership, 57
demographic of membership, 55–6
female contributors to magazine, 56

folk stylistics of, 59–67
lack of records of meetings, 54, 55, 60
literary criticism in magazine, 58
manuscript magazines produced by, 53–73
membership, 55–6
nom-de-plume used by contributors to magazine, 59
objectives, 55
percentage of readers submitting contributions to magazine, 59
range of contributions to magazine, 58–9
readers and contributors to magazine, 56–9
social class of membership, 57–8
statistics on contributions to magazine, 54
use of magazines, 62, 63
Wesleyan Methodists, 82
Westminster Review, 139
Westmoreland Gazette, 19
Weston, Jessie Laidlay [1850–1928], 46–7
What is the Theatrical Public?, 174
White Rose of the Plantation; or, Lubly Rosa, Sambo Don't Come, The, 194
Wild Rover, 133
Wilds of London, The, 114
Wilks, Thomas Egerton [1812–54], 193
William of Malmesbury [c.1095–c.1143], 46
window moment, 158
window shopping reading, 117
penny dreadfuls, 111–29
Woffington, Margaret (Peg) [1720–60], 186
Wolfram von Eschenbach [c.1160/80–c.1220], 47
Woman in Mauve, The, 183, 185, 186
Woman in White, The, 183
women
appeal of *Le Morte d'Arthur* to, 38
developing political identity, 89
importance of reading communities to, 75, 88
inappropriate educational ambition, 36
reading, 58
response to concept of self-help, 21
women's activism, 88–9
Victorian, 88
Women's Home and Foreign Missionary Society, African Methodist Episcopal Church, 85
Woodbridge, John, 142
woodcut cover visuals, 10
word, 17, 20, 61, 101, 104, 116, 118–20, 123, 138, 147, 148, 158, 172, 175, 184–6, 188–90, 193, 194
dialectic struggle between image and, 190
work, 2, 4–9, 11–13, 15–21, 23, 26, 35, 37, 47, 53, 54, 56, 58–60, 62, 66, 67, 77, 79, 80, 83, 85, 88, 96, 98–100, 118, 119, 134, 137, 147, 148, 152, 153, 165, 167, 170, 171, 173, 175, 177–9, 184, 185, 188, 191, 194
types indulged in by literary society members, 58
working-class
African-American readers, 82
autobiographies, 95, 98
Black British, 83
education, 17, 19
intellectual, 98

readers, 16, 21, 79, 87, 95, 98, 99, 104, 105
readers of Shakespeare, 95
Worthen, W.B., 195, 196n16, 197n35
Wright, Thomas [1810–77], 45, 46
Wynne, Deborah, 184, 195n2

Y
Yeames, James, 77
Ye Banks and Braes o' Bonnie Doun, 136

Yonge, Charlotte Mary [1823–1901], 38, 41–6, 50n44, 51n61
Young Folks, 38
Young May Moon, The, 135
Young Men, 53–73
Youth, Popular Culture and Moral Panics, 115, 126n16

Z
Zorrica, Pedra, 58, 60

Printed in Great Britain
by Amazon